DAVID BETZ

Carnage and Connectivity

Landmarks in the Decline of
Conventional Military Power

HURST & COMPANY, LONDON

First published in the United Kingdom in 2015 by
C. Hurst & Co. (Publishers) Ltd.,
41 Great Russell Street, London, WC1B 3PL
© David Betz, 2015
All rights reserved.
Printed in India

The right of David Betz to be identified as the author of
this publication is asserted by him in accordance with the
Copyright, Designs and Patents Act, 1988.

A Cataloguing-in-Publication data record for this book is
available from the British Library.

ISBN: 9781849043229

This book is printed using paper from registered sustainable
and managed sources.

www.hurstpublishers.com

CONTENTS

CONTENTS

ACKNOWLEDGEMENTS

'A good teacher is a good learner', is what my mentor Harald Von Riekhoff, Professor of Political Science at Carleton University, taught me. It was a good lesson—the best of several which he taught me. I hope I have taken it to heart. I must, first, thank all my students from whom I learn constantly. Two in particular I feel it somewhat impertinent even to call students, Anthony Cormack and Tim Stevens. They have taught me so much for which I am grateful. Another student, the scholar and entrepreneur Adam Stahl, has done marvelously networking on my behalf, 10,000 per cent better than I would have. His colleague and co-editor William 'Wilf' Owen has also provided much useful food for thought. We disagree, I think, in a most productive manner. Frank Hoffman and Michael Noonan have provided much needed critical support over the years. I am glad to have such clever friends. Carl Prine has done much to entertain, distract, and inform. I would have finished a month earlier if not for them. The crew on my 'Kings of War' blog and the commenters there have been a massive help. Many of the ideas herein benefited from thinking out loud on the blog. Chris Ankersen has been a firm friend and sounding board of ideas good and bad, as has Michael Noonan of the Foreign Policy Research Institute where I have the pleasure of being a research fellow. Frank Hoffman has always been generous with his criticism and advice. Neville Bolt, with whom I teach the MA course 'Evolution of Insurgency' in the War Studies Department at King's College London, is a constant inspiration, as is John Mackinlay who invented the course before we took it over. Indeed, all my colleagues in the War Studies Department at King's College London, particularly Thomas Rid, Theo Farrell and Michael Rainsborough deserve much thanks for support and encouragement, and learned conversation. Intellectually, I owe enormous debt to Lawrence Freedman, Hew Strachan, Colin Gray and Christopher Coker—leading lights in this field with whom I have been lucky on occasion to rub shoulders. They each have made a great impression on my thinking as reflected throughout this work. I should also note my gratitude to my parents for the obvious reasons as well as for their habit of rescuing old books on war from charity shops and library discard shelves on the off chance that I will find them interesting. In this case one—a classic that I for some reason had not read before—proved to be so enormously. Finally, I must thank my publisher Michael Dwyer, whose patience has been enormous.

Parts of this book are based upon work I have done that has previously appeared elsewhere. I would like to thank Taylor & Francis for permission to use this material. Chapter 7 is based upon a chapter by me entitled 'Searching for El Dorado: The Legendary Golden Narrative of the Afghan War' in Beatrice De Graaf, Jens Ringsmose, and George Dimitriu (eds), *Strategic Narratives, Public Opinion, and War: Winning Domestic Support for the Afghan War* (Abingdon, Oxon: Routledge, 2015). Chapter 9 is based upon a chapter entitled 'Cyberspace and War' in *Cyberspace and the State: Toward a Strategy for Cyberpower* (Abingdon, Oxon: Routledge, 2011), which I co-wrote with Tim Stevens as an Adelphi book for the International Institute for Strategic Studies, and also 'Cyberpower in Strategic Affairs: Neither Unthinkable nor Blessed', *Journal of Strategic Studies*, Vol. 35, No. 5 (2012), pp. 689–711.

It seems to me that the best books are ones that tell a story—albeit a carefully constructed one informed by close study—but a story nonetheless with which the reader is invited to come along. Not all readers will or necessarily should agree with what I have written here, which is not really a very happy tale. I am, unfortunately, more pessimistic about the world now than I was when I started the book—less inclined to think that connectedness is inherently a good thing. The best that can be said is that if things seem irremediably and demoralizingly tumultuous now, history tells us that it is not the first time things have felt that way. It seems to me that for a generation at least the West has chased with huge energy and enthusiasm after a fantasy of war—cheap, decisive and congenial to its interests—that has serially failed to materialize. As a result, we face what is shaping up to be another bloody century from a position of fairly profound moral and intellectual disequilibrium. I suspect that things will get worse before they get better. If I am wrong I shall be glad to hear why.

For my wife Taisha and particularly my children, Charlie and Lily, in the hope that they will have the wisdom to fix the mess their forebears have left them.

ABBREVIATIONS

Co-operative Engagement Capability	CEC
Dominant Battlespace Knowledge	DBK
Earth Liberation Front	ELF
Follow-On Forces Attack	FOFA
Improvised Explosive Device	IED
International Institute for Strategic Studies	IISS
International Security Assistance Force	ISAF
Military Operations Other Than War	MOOTW
Network-Centric Warfare	NCW
Office of Net Assessment	ONA
Organisation for Economic Cooperation and Development	OECD
Revolution in Military Affairs	RMA
rocket-propelled grenades	RPGs
United Nations Operations in Somalia	UNOSOM
United Nations Protection Force	UNPROFOR

INTRODUCTION

This book began with a relatively straightforward observation of the 'landscape' of strategic affairs after the Cold War (that is to say, approximately in my adult lifetime). Despite the West's many strengths, its military endeavours in that period had proved successively more costly and the 'better peace' obtained by them less obviously better than the status quo ante, not to mention less durable. Global societal developments that were supposed to be bringing on a richer, more unified and less belligerent future, actually seemed to be driving things in the opposite direction by empowering movements passionately committed to the achievement (in my eyes, at any rate) of a poorer, more disunited and retrograde future of seemingly endless brushfire wars and global skirmishing. My sense was that at the heart of both the morally optimistic hope and the bitterer, more morally compromised reality was the burgeoning connectedness of human society. Given that scholars like Hannah Arendt in the 1950s, through Marshall Mcluhan in the 1960s, to Daniel Bell in the 1970s, and popular futurists like John Naisbitt in the 1980s, had long since identified this 'megatrend' that was 'transforming our lives', it was not a particularly oddball hunch on my part.[1] Nonetheless, it seemed worthwhile to explore in detail the simple question: what happens to war when you wire up the world as densely as we have done over the last twenty-five years or so?

It seemed to me that this question really had not been answered well. Indeed, quite a few of the answers provided turned out to be rather narrow and short-sighted, effective non sequiturs destined to be shown up by reality. In the 1990s huge attention was paid within strategic studies to the ways in which networking, literally a 'system of systems', was set to bring about a Revolution in Military Affairs (RMA) that would make wars faster, cheaper and inherently much less chancy for the most technologically advanced militaries of the world.[2] In the 2000s, of course, the struggle against insurgencies in Iraq and Afghanistan and more generally in the War on Terror revealed this to be something of a pipe dream as 'asymmetric' challengers proved to be the greater beneficiaries of the informationalisation of war.[3]

More recent analyses of conflict have argued that to varying degrees it has become a 'de-territorialised and globally connected' affair of transnational social movements engaged in discursive 'wars of ideas' which lack any permanent physical theatre but rather thrive on the ever-shifting network flows of globalisation.[4] Yet at the time of writing the two biggest stories in the security arena are the efforts of Islamic State to establish a territorially-defined caliphate and the on-going dismemberment of Ukraine at the hands of separatist forces in the east of the country backed by Russia. At the same time, the security of digital systems, or 'cyber security', has leapt to the top of the defence agendas of governments, industry and citizens.[5]

The point here is not simply the persistent pattern of getting things wrong, for, as I will explain, the reasons for this are quite complicated. Rather, the main point is that there is no single direction of developments but rather a multiplicity. While globalisation intensifies the long-range connectedness and fluidity of society, people also increasingly long for securer and more local identities. Similarly, while high-tech is becoming ascendant in the military thinking of the big powers, low-tech techniques and countermeasures proliferate amongst smaller ones. And, as the virtualisation of conflict seems to proceed apace so too does the demand for 'high-touch' tactics on the ground.[6] Unfortunately, much of the thinking around strategy is essentially reactive, uni-directional, and all-too-often akin to unconscious reflex action in the face of perceived threats, which themselves stem from the increasing connectedness of the world. Policy-makers and their advisors rarely seem to feel that they have got far enough ahead of events to achieve much sense of equilibrium; on the contrary, as the current *National Security Strategy of the United Kingdom* puts it, ours is an 'age of uncertainty'.[7]

This reflexivity is a problem. In 2006 the philosopher John Ralston Saul argued that globalisation, which he perceived above all through the prism of economics, was already in retreat and ultimately doomed. Whether this proves true or not of neo-liberal economics (Ralston Saul's bête noire), already in security terms as this book will show we are experiencing globalisation's rebel sting. His question, however, 'what comes next?' is surely one that will strike many readers as apposite. The future, he wrote, will:

be decided—a conscious act—or it will be left to various interest groups to decide for us, or simply to fate and circumstance. The soundness of the outcome will depend on the balance between these necessary mechanisms. The most dangerous disequilibrium will have favoured fate and circumstance over the other two. The most mediocre, interest groups. The soundest equilibrium would be led by conscious public decisions.[8]

The object of this book, in a nutshell, is to help bring about a sounder equilibrium in the discussion of strategic affairs. My intent is not only to inject some new ideas but also to distinguish in the existing literature where ideas that seem or are purported to be new actually are not new at all. There are many lessons of past strategic thinkers whose relevance to today's dilemmas is undiminished by time. It is a mistake to be ignorant of them. Thus, better equipped with perspective on how we got to the present and how it is different in some ways and not different in others from the past, readers will I hope be more able to navigate the coming turmoil.

No reader will have missed the accelerating pace of the wiring up of the world. In 2008, when it launched its 'Future of the Internet Economy' initiative, the Organisation for Economic Cooperation and Development asked 'can you remember life before the Internet?'[9] For many of its younger users, there was quite literally no life before the Internet. For those of us with memories that extend further back than the explosive growth of the World Wide Web in the middle of the 1990s, it is hard now to imagine how we lived without it. Always-on connectedness has become a part of daily life as vital to most people as electric light and power.

Without boring with statistics, a few are useful to illustrate the pace and the scope of change. At the end of 2012 it was estimated that there were 6.8 billion mobile phone subscriptions in the world. Many of those were in developed countries, where mobile penetration was reckoned at 128 per cent of the population. Even in developing countries, however, the rate was 89 per cent and the telecommunications sector is the most vibrant area of growth even in economies as war-blighted as Afghanistan's.[10] The 2012 CISCO Visual Networking Index predicts that by 2017 the gigabyte equivalent of all the movies ever made will cross over global IP networks every three minutes. Moreover, not just the flow of ideas but also transactional flows of people and goods are rising in volume and velocity like a flood.

Our lives are increasingly intertwined with those of distant others—economically, politically and culturally. Technology is knitting together societies, 'bringing the village to the world and the world to the village.'[11] There is a strong argument that this is all massively for the good: contemporary humans worldwide are generally wealthier, more productive, healthier, more peaceful, live longer and have more leisure time than ever before.[12] At the same time, there are real difficulties. For one thing, in an age of what Zygmunt Bauman has called 'liquid modernity' there is no longer an intellectual 'outside', nothing can occur to people completely 'over there' without bearing on 'how people in all other places live, hope, or expect to live.'[13]

It stands to reason that if this dense web of connectivity in which we are embedded is changing economics, politics and social life so variously and so profoundly, then it is also changing war in ways that are very unsettling to habits of mind that have grown deeply ingrained—not least in the way that it challenges the expectation of Western populations that they are insulated from war by distance and by solid frontiers. One can see how deeply embedded is the concept of a distinct 'over there' in Western ideas about war in the lyrics of the famous song 'Over There', suggesting that any change in this concept will indeed in turn change our ideas of war:

> Over there, over there,
> Send the word, send the word over there
>
> ...
>
> Send the word, send the word to beware.
> We'll be over, we're coming over,
> And we won't come back till it's over
> Over there.

And yet, in general with this topic there is a tendency to overemphasise the elements of discontinuous change and underemphasise those of continuity. The growth numbers above are staggering and yet we must observe that the purpose of all this traffic is ultimately to serve the need of humans to do what humans have always done: communicate, collaborate, consume and fight. To be sure they are doing these things differently to a greater or lesser degree, but they are not doing qualitatively new things. We must not lose sight of this ever-present dialogue in history between mutability and constancy—for all that it is a cliché drilled into first year undergraduates. We must not, in the enthusiasm to keep abreast of rapid developments in technology, forget that the best guide to navigating the turbulence of the present is always history.

The argument

The truth is that war itself has not changed. There is certainly a long-term trend toward war's diminishing usefulness as a tool of policy, to which connectivity is an important contributing factor among others, notably the enormous destructive power of modern weapons. This is not a surprise to anyone in the field, though there is voluminous controversy in the literature over the durability of the trend and the faith in human rationality that the theory requires. That is not the main focus of this book, although it does provide the main context.

But warfare—how we fight, to be precise—has changed enormously. Unfortunately, the story of that change is an unhappy one. Paradoxically and also rather quixotically, the major military powers in the West have serially tried and failed to use technology to disconnect from war's enduring nature. With great industry and ingenuity they have chased the fantasy of a type of war that is fast, easy and decisive, yet each time all they have managed to grasp is a slow, bitter and indecisive war. The advent of the information age loaned new vigour to this wild goose chase, impressing upon policy-makers and strategists a profound sense of urgency and obsessive fascination with speed, but did not actually start it.

Although it draws broadly upon history, this book picks up the story with the lopsided defeat of Iraq in the 1991 Gulf War, which tantalised a large fraction of the defence establishments of the world with the possibility that with the right sensors, communications and weapons the fog of war could be lifted. That is to say, that equipped with perfect knowledge of oneself and of the enemy one could shock the latter into a state of permanent surprise in which condition his existence as a conscious, living entity able to foil and counter efforts to subdue him could be disregarded, and his forces treated as passive targets that might as well be inanimate.[14] Of course, this never became a reality because enemies simply are not inanimate, and they are neither permanently paralysed by shock nor guaranteeably awed into mute compliance by manoeuvres no matter how swiftly performed. Faced with the proposition 'submit or be destroyed, choose one', humans are extremely inventive in finding a third option.

The messy conflicts of the 1990s might have shown that the hope of making war always a matter of administrative planning and mathematical certainty for the high-tech military powers was forlorn, but policy-makers and strategists attempted another disconnect in order to rescue policy from the dilemma that real war presented it. They contrived a form of war that largely replaced forces on the ground with force delivered by long-range weapons. The intent was to deal as economically as possible with the desire of governments to be seen by their own publics to be 'doing something' about highly-mediatised overseas conflicts by meddling in them just lightly enough to mollify their own voters from behind a thick layer of spectacular air power. This was a perfectly adequate, albeit cynical, strategy, until 11 September 2001 showed that even for the most powerful countries the frontiers beyond which no attack was possible had become blurred and permeable. Hatred and enmity combined with ingenuity and purposeful conviction can be a very powerful force in a radically connected world—enough to strike a body blow to the world's largest power on its home territory with an arsenal of box cutting knives and plane tickets.

The story of the expeditionary campaigns of the 'War on Terror' that followed is primarily one of painful readjustment to the reality that to fight 'wars amongst the people' one must actually be among them, and therefore that to use a way of war designed to avoid engaging the passion of the people is akin to being a heavyweight boxer with one hand tied behind the back and boot laces tied together. Even a scrawny flyweight in such a fight has the chance of doing real damage. It is not possible to look upon the wars in Iraq and Afghanistan and see success, no matter how artfully the media operations staffs of the contributing powers make the case. The costs have been too high, the results too meagre, and the desire of politicians to get their armies back as quickly as possible with the greatest amount of dignity intact is all too obvious. Unfortunately, as the wars of the War on Terror are wound down with very few of the initial victory conditions achieved it is not assured that the lessons learned will last.

In fact, more apparent is a final attempt to disconnect from the uncongenial reality that the policy of a decade's standing—based on a pattern of strategic choices of several decades' standing—is a failure. The means this time around are a combination of cyberattacks, ubiquitous surveillance, and 'high-value targeting' of enemies with drones, and the intent is to shift the war even further from public consciousness, where it can simmer quietly off the electoral agenda. It is likely that this new strategy will fail too since already the threat of al-Qaeda type terror spectaculars—which might plausibly have been contained by such measures—has hived off an even more virulent and even less tractable challenge in the form of Islamic State which looks to have ignited a war in the Middle East that resembles nothing so much as the Thirty Years War that ravaged Europe in the first half of the seventeenth century.[15]

Meanwhile, the 'postmodern system' more generally faces real challenges from revolutionary 'groupuscules' and movements that combine the networked advantages of flexibility, scalability and survivability that connectivity brings with potentially powerful means of disruption and coercion in support of the achievement of their own dreams of a better future.[16] As Anders Breivik demonstrated in July 2011 with his one-man attack on a youth camp of the Norwegian Labour Party in which he killed sixty-nine people, rarely before has so much of the world been as exposed to the creative energy of men bent on murdering their way to utopia.

It may be the case that connectivity is ultimately for the good of human society in the long term. In the meantime, however, the rationally pessimistic view is that there is a good future for carnage in the twenty-first century. The trade-off for the cessation of major war may be a more or less constant exhausting and indecisive global fracas—located not just safely 'over there' but everywhere.

Carnage

In choosing the word 'carnage' for my title I do not mean to suggest that the subject is something other than war. Indeed, as the reader may by now have recognized, the conceptual framework that forms the book's logical spine is the Clausewitzian trinity of chance, passion and reason. To recapitulate, the major armies of the world attempted: to replace chance in war with surety delivered by information systems; to make up for a deficiency of passion with an amalgam of long-range weapons and spin; and, finally, to compensate for failures of policy and strategic vision with a series of tactics based on avoiding contact with the enemy and ultimately avoidance of the actual underpinning points of contention. The first and second of these have been shown up as having failed and the last is, in my view, destined to disappoint. It seems to me that Clausewitz explains well why that is the case.

A few years ago one critic said, 'Like the aging Marxists with a Karl of their own the Clausewitzians today are more interested in exonerating their idol from the evil perpetrated in his name than in demonstrating what good he could bring to the current challenges facing the military.'[17] My intention has not been to prove Clausewitz right or to defend him against his legion of critics. There are others much better qualified for that upon whose work I have leaned quite heavily. I simply required an explanatory frame and found Clausewitz's to be more than sufficiently illuminating of the current confusion surrounding strategic affairs. The reader can judge whether the proof is in the pudding, so to speak.

I did, however, hope to trigger recognition in the reader of a parallel with Victor Davis Hanson's excellent book *Why the West has Won: Carnage and*

Culture from Salamis to Vietnam. Hanson explains that the West owes its preeminence in world affairs primarily to a superior way of war, amongst the main characteristics of which is a preference for decisive battle and eschewing fighting at a distance.[18] It seems to me that recent wars show quite well that 'the rest' have got the measure of the West, turning its preference for decisive battle into a millstone by relentlessly offering it no opportunity for one. In a startling reversal of roles it is now the West that stands metaphorically at longbow range, hoping that its opponents will submit to its will in the face of its occasional barbs fired from beyond the possibility of return in kind.

This book is intended to address some particular conundrums in the current conduct of war. It is not about the future of war, let alone the future of Western civilisation, at least not directly. I am mindful of the inherent trickiness of prediction, in particular academic prediction which, as we shall see further on, has a poor record in this field.[19] It is difficult enough to comprehend the present. Suffice to say that I think a self-confident civilisation would not fight in the way that ours does now.

Connectivity

If my point in talking about carnage is not to evade the term 'war', by contrast my choice of the term 'connectivity' is a most deliberate effort to avoid the word 'cyberspace', or simply to reduce the study to one of the effect of information technology. Admittedly, the latter term is extremely current and popular but it is also an active impediment to thinking about the broader challenges of war in the putative information age. There are two main points to consider in explaining why this is the case.

First, as noted above, the challenges confronting those attempting to comprehend war and warfare today are not simply about computers and computer networks. To be sure, there is now a 'virtual dimension' to war that is comprised of digital networks and multimedia technologies and that changes many things. But it is not truly separated from real space for all of its quality of intangibility. Twenty-first century reality is more complex—it is obviously a mixture of the tangible and the intangible, deeply and irrevocably intertwined. The network flows of virtual space supplement those of real space; they do not supplant them.[20] We see this all the time in our daily lives. Any analysis that proceeded from the opposite assumption would be fatally flawed. War must be understood holistically, grasping as much of its context as can be grasped, or not at all.

Second, none of the problems are actually totally new. Most of the issues discussed in this book have been a subject of concern one way or another for a century or more. The invention of the microchip, the Internet, mobile telephony, and the like has aggravated some of them, raising them to a greater salience than was the case before. Though even then it must be pointed out that some things which seem to be particularly worrisome now have been even more vexatious in the past. Interest, fear and honour, 'these Thucydidean coordinates', as the historian Michael Howard put it, define the problem of war.[21] In over twenty-five hundred years, technology has not altered that one bit.

Still, it cannot be denied that the pace of technological change has been very rapid of late. It is often said that Clausewitz's theory is too rooted in its time to explain today's very different world. It is true that in his day technology was relatively static. By and large, the pace of scientific discovery and developments in engineering was very slow across a spectrum of human activities, from agricultural and industrial enterprise to the techniques and implements of mass violence until quite recently. But ultimately I find such arguments unconvincing and agree with the academic strategist Colin Gray's maxim that 'nothing of real importance changes.'[22]

Power

It remains to say a few words about power. The commonplace understanding of power is as a capacity or attribute that an actor possesses and may exploit to achieve certain ends. In the field of politics and international relations this sort of power is usually reckoned in very simple terms such as the size of a country's army, the sorts of weapons it possesses, the size of its economy or cash reserves, or natural resource base and so on.

A slightly more complex notion holds that power may be viewed, as the philosopher Bertrand Russell put it, as 'the production of intended effects.'[23] In a similar vein, Max Weber defined power as the ability to impose one's will on another, whether a group or individual, against their resistance. Thus it may be said that A has power over B to the extent that A is able to get B to do something that he otherwise would not do.[24] Clausewitz would have had no difficulty with this definition; it is more or less exactly how he defined war and it is commonplace in the field of war studies.

There is, however, a further dimension of power—the power to shape people's perceptions, beliefs and ideals in ways that structure their responses to events in ways that are congenial to one's own ends. Michel Foucault famously declared:

We must cease once and for all to describe the effect of power in negative terms: it 'excludes', it 'represses', it 'censors', it 'abstracts', it 'masks', it 'conceals'. In fact, power produces; it produces reality; it produces domains of objects and rituals of truth.[25]

In my view, this dimension of power is one that must be more commonplace in the study of war than it currently is if we are to make sense of how to wage and to win wars in an increasingly densely connected world.[26] I modestly attempt to do some of that in this book, drawing on the work of several French philosophers, fully aware that I may annoy simultaneously scholars who work within postmodernism and have a quite different normative agenda than mine and those who think postmodern theory is nonsense. I have come to the view that postmodern theory in small dosage is a very good thing. Intuitively or no, our enemies grasp it better than we do—at any rate they grasp better that the mainspring of war is the manipulation of passion and they ruthlessly exploit the West's current conviction that passion is to be restrained, mistrusted and subordinated to strategies of war based more on material strength.[27]

All these dimensions of power are important to the present analysis. A basic problem nowadays is that the cost of the capacity to cause strategically meaningful, potentially extremely painful and damaging, effects is declining to the point where sub-state entities, potentially even very small groups or individuals, can produce significant carnage and massive disruption.[28] Particularly at risk are political communities based on an assumed 'positive desire for community' or, as the philosopher David Fisher put it, a 'shared interest in living together reflected, *inter alia*, in economic, cultural, religious, and social ties and underlain by common moral values'.[29] It is precisely this assumption that is being eroded by such actions. The slaughter of the editorial staff of the satirical French magazine *Charlie Hebdo* in Paris in January 2015 at the hands of French Muslim radicals incensed by the magazine's portrayal of Mohammed provided a dramatic case in point of the severity of the clash of identities and ideologies.

Another problem is that if we accept strategy as being the art of unleashing power to produce intended effects then we must acknowledge that the addition of so many new strategic actors combined with the radical connectedness of 'liquid modernity' makes this exceedingly difficult.[30] Finally, as war trickles back into the West along the network flows of globalisation, strategists, still primarily concerned with struggles between well-armed and organised states, will need to work much harder to comprehend that the long neglect of what Clausewitz called 'moral forces' in war is the key source of its strategic enfeeblement.[31]

1

ANTINOMIES OF WAR

Alice thought she might as well wait, as she had nothing else to do, and perhaps after all it might tell her something worth hearing. For some minutes it puffed away without speaking, but at last it unfolded its arms, took the hookah out of its mouth again, and said 'So you think you're changed, do you?'

The Caterpillar to Alice in Lewis Carroll's
Alice's Adventures in Wonderland (1865)

According to forensic examiners, Europe's oldest mummy—the five thousand-year-old Ötzi 'The Iceman', found frozen in the Italian Alps in 1991—was a warrior. His death came violently from a crushing blow to the head, but an arrow in the shoulder a few days before had also injured him. On his weapons and equipment scientists found traces of the blood of four other people: three whom he had injured or slain with his own arrows and knife and another, presumably a wounded comrade, whom he had carried on his back. Humans have probably always been warlike.

Given that this book is concerned in large part with information technology and war, a few basic points about what we can observe from Ötzi's time to our own are in order. The most pertinent is that war is about, for, and by people. In fact, everything that is important to know about war relates back to this fundamental point. After that, the next most important thing is that war is inherently chancy. This, of course, relates directly to the first point. Humans are massively ingenious animals and never more so than when their situation is kill-or-be-killed by another human. Thus we may say that there are, with the exception of the hydrogen bomb, so far, no permanently effective super weapons; something else, whether a technology or a technique, always comes along to counter it. Also, humans are not perfectly rational, which means that war has never been reducible to a straight mathematical calculation.

It seems likely Ötzi was a soldier and part of an organised war party engaged in some Copper Age act of politics by other means. It should be understood that the relationship of war and warfare is akin to that between politics and political order. The latter halves of these pairs are always changing while the former is constant. This mutability and constancy of war was explained in the early nineteenth century in a way that has not yet been superseded, and that provides the conceptual framework by which this book is organised.

War is, in the words of its greatest philosopher, the Prussian Carl von Clausewitz, 'chameleon-like in character', constantly changing as a whole in accordance with changes in the 'predominant tendencies' of which it is comprised. His 'remarkable trinity' of war is as follows:

I. Hatred and animosity (or 'passion'), which is primarily a characteristic of the people;
II. Probability and chance, the realm of which is primarily the province of the commander and his army; and,
III. The quality of reason (more precisely, political purpose), to which war is subordinate, and which is primarily the concern of the government.[1]

The relationship between these elements is not at all fixed, he said; on the contrary, the simile of the chameleon rests upon the essential mutability of these 'tendencies', their constant variance in strength and respective influence. He illustrated this with another visual metaphor, calling for 'a theory that maintains a balance between these three tendencies, like an object suspended between three magnets.'[2] The key thing is that these three 'interactive points of attraction' are not passive; instead they are actively 'pulling' on the pendulum, producing complex interactions with each other that are manifest in the unique character of any particular war.[3]

This much is true

War, therefore, has a number of important paradoxical permanent qualities. In the first place, there is the oft-observed contradiction between its essentially unchanging nature and its constantly shifting character.[4] This, in turn, is reflected in subsidiary antinomies. For one, while war is always simply 'an act of force' to compel one's enemy to fulfil one's will, the ways and means of actually exerting force constantly change as weapons technology and techniques change. For instance, the great battles of Agincourt (1415), Waterloo (1815), and the Somme (1916) differ enormously in various aspects of their physical conduct.[5] In the five hundred years that separate the first from the last of these wars, weapons became much more lethal at much longer ranges, and the scale of the combat geographically, temporally and in terms of manpower grew hugely. The effective range of the longbow with which dismounted English archers slew several thousand French armoured knights on one hot day at Agincourt on a strip of open land between two woods less than 1000 yards apart was just over 200 yards, with a rate of fire of about six arrows per minute. Compare this with the range and rate of fire of the machineguns, cannons and mortars that wiped out British and German infantry by the hundreds of thousands in the Somme battle, which raged for four and a half months over a front of 20 miles. But the purpose of the use of force in those instances, in the abstract, was no different: a clash of two thinking enemies each trying to render the other powerless through the physical destruction of their means and their psychological will to resist.

Indeed, war's reciprocal nature is another of its eternal verities. War, as Clausewitz put it, is a 'collision of two living forces' and not the action of a 'living force upon a lifeless mass'.[6] Which is to say that the conduct of war as a tool of policy is much more complex and fraught than the administrative planning, for example, of public health or transport policy, because of the inherent interdependence of choice that defines it.[7] What you imagine doing to your enemy—another thinking, reacting, human being—he can also imagine you doing, and he can prepare himself accordingly or act contrary to your expectation, thereby throwing you into confusion and imbalance. It is this basic observation that underlies one of the most famous admonitions of one of Clausewitz's most famous disciples, the late nineteenth century Prussian Chief of the General Staff Helmuth Von Moltke, who declared that:

> No plan of operation extends with certainty beyond the first encounter with the enemy's main strength. Only the layman sees in the course of a campaign a consistent execution of a preconceived and highly detailed original concept pursued consistently to the end.[8]

In a nutshell, war is intrinsically subject to what Clausewitz described as 'friction'[9] and this fact makes everything in it, even the simplest tasks in theory, very difficult to accomplish in practice. History's great commanders usually owe their fame to the possession of highly developed powers of imagination, the ability of getting 'inside the head' of their opposite number and anticipating their actions and movements, twinned with a profound deviousness that complicates efforts to do the same to them. Also, it must be said, luck is a key ingredient of command success.

The Second World War German General Erwin Rommel, for instance, was notoriously cunning, hence his *sobriquet*, 'The Desert Fox'. His 1937 book *Infantry Attacks* may be read as an extended essay on paralyzing and defeating one's opponent through speed and subterfuge; and while these were indeed aspects of his style as a field commander, it is also true that he was a willing gambler upon whom fortune, for the most part, smiled.[10] The ancient Chinese general Sun Tzu's aphorisms 'know yourself, know your enemies' and 'all war is deception' are frequently invoked in support of these elements comprising the acme of military skill.[11] But the theme is sufficiently basic to have impressed good commanders more or less everywhere throughout history. George Washington, in a letter to one of his officers written in 1777, put it pithily:

> The necessity of procuring good intelligence is apparent and need not be further urged. All that remains for me to add is, that you keep the whole matter as secret as possible. For upon Secrecy, success depends in most Enterprises of the kind, & for want of it, they are generally defeated, however, well planned.[12]

And yet there is no fixed rule that says war is conducted only by armies organised in like manner fighting against each other in a similar way. Quite the opposite, in fact.

The awkward dichotomy

A peculiar tendency in Western military thought is its preoccupation with 'conventional' as opposed to 'unconventional' war. The former is taken to consist of two more or less equally matched and similarly organised formations of men and machines manoeuvring in opposition to each other before clashing in 'decisive battle'; the latter to consist of mismatched forces with one side pursuing the hit-and-run tactics of the guerrilla—above all the avoidance of head on main force engagements—while the other conducts endless sweeps and pickets in an effort to pin him down. T.E. Lawrence ('of Arabia') artfully portrayed the difference between the two in a classic essay based on his role as mentor of the Arab Revolt against the Turks in the First World War entitled 'The Science of Guerrilla Warfare':

> Armies were like plants, immobile as a whole, firm-rooted, nourished through long stems to the head. We might be a vapour, blowing where we listed. Our kingdoms lay in each man's mind, and as we wanted nothing material to live on, so perhaps we

offered nothing material to the killing. It seemed a regular soldier might be helpless without a target. He would own the ground he sat on, and what he could poke his rifle at.[13]

More prosaically, we might say that the salient feature of unconventional wars is simply the gross disproportion between the weaker belligerent's political aims and their military means relative to those of the stronger belligerent. Given this profound asymmetry, unconventional warfare is (for one side, at least) about the avoidance of direct encounters, which would effectively be suicidal for it to undertake. That this behaviour is reckoned 'unconventional' and not simply military common sense is indicative of the degree to which Western military thought has for a long time tended to cluster around an ideal of a particularly symmetric form of war, despite its rarity since at least 1945.[14]

Some take the argument even further, in that not only are there two different ways of war but each of these ways is rooted in distinctively Western and Eastern cultures. Thus, people fight in the way they do not simply because it is expedient that they do so but because it is at some level an expression of who they are as a people or a 'civilisation'. Westerners seek direct battle, obliterating the enemy in a short, sharp, decisive show of force because these accord with cultural ideals such as freedom, individualism and 'civic militarism' that they esteem.[15] Whereas Easterners, as epitomised by Sun Tzu's admonition that 'winning without fighting' is the height of skill, prefer indirect methods because these accord with other cultural ideals such as tyranny, collectivism and despotic militarism.[16]

The point is obviously controversial; others find the cultural distinctiveness of ways of war to be rather more ambiguous, arguing to the contrary that while the '...rhetoric of war may be one of hostility and mutual abhorrence, the practice of war is often convergence.'[17] Be that as it may, one thing that is decidedly true is that most Western armed forces have for over a century regarded the practice of unconventional war (also known as, *inter alia*, 'low-intensity conflict', 'small war', 'irregular war', 'guerrilla war', 'revolutionary war', 'political war', as well as the awkward mouthful of an acronym 'MOOTW' for 'Military Operations Other than War'—itself a telling formulation) as a niche capability separate from proper 'high-intensity' and 'conventional' warfare.[18]

Thus have evolved in military doctrine, and to a large extent also in scholarship, two archetypes of war. First, orthodox conventional wars are thought to have well-defined beginnings and ends. They unfold in a regular sequence. One belligerent issues an ultimatum (or commits some outright provocation) against another. Then there is a declaration of war or, more commonly today, the invocation of a United Nations Security Council Resolution referencing chapter seven ('Action With Respect to Threats to the Peace, Breaches Of The Peace, and Acts of Aggression') of the United Nations Charter, which legalises the use of force.[19] Following said declarations there is armed combat consisting of one or several battles in the course of which one party is defeated and sues for peace. Finally, during a period of armistice a peace treaty is negotiated agreeing a new status quo between the parties to the conflict, detailing things such as any territorial concessions or reparations to be made, new rights or obligations of one side upon another, and so on. The Great Power wars of the eighteenth and nineteenth centuries, the world wars of the first half of the twentieth century, and a handful of wars in the latter half, conform generally to this pattern.[20]

The second archetype is that of the heterodox unconventional war. Such wars are hazy both at beginning and end. Generally, the distal causes of these wars are effectively irresolvable (for example, different ethnic or religious groups laying sole claim to the same territory), as a result of which they possess the character of a chronic ailment in which periods (sometimes decades long) of calm and relative comity between warring parties are punctuated by flare-ups of inter-communal violence (sometimes egregiously brutal or 'barbaric').[21] Such long-running confrontations do not feature declarations of war, nor are they typically brought to an end by treaty. Rarely do they involve decisive battles—and even then usually only because the weaker side has made a dreadful mistake; rather, they are attritional affairs that, more often than not, are fought by *ad hoc* irregulars instead of organised armies with strict military and political hierarchies, at least on one side and sometimes on both. The wars over Irish nationalism, for instance, which simmer on even today in attenuated form, can be traced back as far as the English invasions of the twelfth century (with added venom after the sixteenth century's Protestant Reformation, which added a religious dimension to the affair).[22] Chechen resistance to Russian rule has waxed, waned, and waxed again over two centuries.[23] The Israeli-Palestinian conflict, a comparative newcomer to world affairs if one dates its beginning to Israel's founding in 1948, looks just as durable and resistant to resolution.[24]

These archetypes are, of course, artificial: reality's conformance with them is notably patchy. They have heuristic value as 'rules of thumb' so long as they are not taken too far or regarded too reverently. It is quite true, for example, that Clausewitz's thinking, so dominated as it was by his own experience of the Napoleonic wars, was chiefly focused on inter-state war. He has, in consequence, been characterised by some critical readers as a sort of champion of high intensity conventionality in warfare. Most famously, the British strategist Basil Liddell-Hart bestowed on him the epithet 'Mahdi of mass and mutual massacre', laying primary blame on him for having constructed the intellectual foundation of the ghastly industrial slaughter of First World War trench warfare.[25] Later scholars consider this to be a purposeful misreading (or, indeed, potential non-reading) of *On War*.[26]

In actuality, Clausewitz was far from uninterested in, let alone unaware of, guerrilla warfare. In fact, we may read extensively in *On War* of the power of 'people's war', albeit as a strategy within a conventional military framework. He also lectured on small wars at the Prussian War College in 1810–11, reportedly inspired to do so by the work of his mentor, General Gerhard von Scharnhorst, who had also studied them.[27] Clausewitz neither exaggerated nor belittled its potential consequence as a form of war and his proscriptions on its proper conduct were eminently sound:

> A general uprising, as we see it, should be nebulous and elusive; its elusiveness should never materialise as a concrete body, otherwise the enemy can direct sufficient force at its core, crush it and take many prisoners. When that happens, the people will lose heart and, believing that the issue has been decided and further efforts would be useless, drop their weapons. On the other hand, there must be some concentration at certain points: the fog must thicken and form a dark and menacing cloud out of which a bolt of lightning may strike at any time.[28]

One may observe very similar passages in the writings of later nineteenth century revolutionaries, especially Karl Marx's intellectual partner Friedrich Engels, who wrote extensively on military affairs (frequently under Marx's name).[29] Above all, he enjoined potential revolutionaries:

> never play with insurrection unless you are fully prepared to face the consequences of your play. The forces opposed to you have all the advantage of organization, discipline and habitual authority; unless you bring strong odds against them, you are defeated and ruined.[30]

Neither did Clausewitz suggest that explaining 'people's war' was somehow beyond his theory. The point of his trinity of passion, chance and political purpose is its flexibility even when applied to wars that are unhinged from the state-on-state paradigm.

War and civilisation

There is a long tradition in scholarship of imputing apparent changes in war's character to fundamental changes in war's nature, thus requiring abandonment to a greater or lesser degree of the Clausewitzian model. The 'new wars' thesis represents something of an apotheosis of this line of reasoning, drawing as it does a firm bright line between not only the methods (ways and means) of warfare but also between the aims and purposes of war of today as compared to the past. That warfare has changed is undeniable, and the 'new wars' literature does much to explain these changes; but war in itself, war as an act of force to compel one's enemy to do one's will and war as a 'trinity' of passion, chance and reason has not changed. That is where the 'new wars' thesis goes wrong.

Mary Kaldor, the key exponent of the theory, claims the transition has been caused by factors for which the term 'globalisation' is a 'convenient catch-all'.[31] The variance is said to exist across a number of vectors: whereas old wars were primarily fought between states, new wars are fought largely within states; whereas old war belligerents sought decisive battles (the sooner to defeat their opponents and impose a peace better than the *status quo ante*), new war belligerents have a vested economic interest in the conflict's continuance, which inclines them to avoid decisive engagements; and, most importantly, whereas old wars were fought over 'ideas' (that is, politics), the new wars are about identity and honour. All these claims are contentious and have invited swingeing criticism from other scholars.[32]

They are also hardly new: in the early 1990s Martin Van Creveld wrote in *The Transformation of War* of the 'ghost' of major war haunting the corridors of general staff buildings the world over as a new paradigm of warfare dominated by non-state actors emerged;[33] and Robert Kaplan's mid-1990s book *The Coming Anarchy* ploughed similar terrain, describing what he had observed as a journalist in Africa as a 'premodern formlessness govern[ing] the battlefield, evoking the wars in medieval Europe'.[34] More generally, the characteristics ascribed to the contemporary 'new wars' might as easily be used to describe the wars of Europe from roughly the eighth through to the eighteenth century.[35] Which is not to say that they should be summarily dismissed. On the contrary, they touch upon various developments in world affairs that are unmistakably real. Internal conflicts and civil wars are indeed burgeoning as, arguably, is the level of war's barbarism.[36] The rise in the estimation of identity as a key driver of insecurity may be observed widely in both the social sciences and the humanities. In defiance of the vast criticism aimed at it, Samuel Huntington's 'clash of civilisations' thesis, which argued that 'civilisation identity' would be the primary source of conflict in the world of the twenty-first century, resonates more profoundly now than it did when it was written in the early 1990s.

Osama Bin Laden himself, perhaps not surprisingly, was a believer. When asked by television news channel Al Jazeera what he made of the 'so-called clash of civilisations', he replied 'there is no doubt about it.'[37] Among the many others now echoing this idea, consciously or unconsciously, the French novelist Amin Maalouf speaks of the emergence of 'global tribes' and warns that:

> in the age of globalisation and of the ever-accelerating intermingling of elements in which we are all caught up, a new concept of identity is needed, and needed urgently. ... If our contemporaries are not encouraged to accept their multiple affiliations and allegiances; if they cannot reconcile their need for identity with an open and unprejudiced tolerance of other cultures; if they feel they have to choose between denial of the self and denial of the other—then we shall be bringing into being legions of the lost and hordes of bloodthirsty madmen.[38]

To be sure, there is controversy, particularly over the degree to which 'civilisational' differences are clear enough to constitute the dividing lines across which conflicts are fought. Even critics, however, accept the premise that there exists a sharp division at the heart of many contemporary conflicts that is not neatly national. Dominique Moisi and Tzvetan Todorov characterise it as essentially a clash of passions rather than 'civilisations': in rapidly economically-growing Asia the dominant emotion is 'appetite' (or hope); in the developed, economically more static West, by contrast, there is a pervasive fear of absolute and relative decline; while in a third group of countries, predominantly but not exclusively Muslim, the overwhelming mood is resentment (or 'humiliation').[39]

In like vein, experts point to a divergence of old and new forms of terrorism and insurgency, both having evolved into de-territorialised 'network enterprises' or 'global insurgencies' operating in accordance with a nineteenth century concept of 'propaganda of the deed' rejuvenated for the internet era.[40] Moreover, scholars have explored the relationship between war and economic motives and commercial agendas, and have found recent wars, as Kaplan mused, not so much entirely new as reminiscent of the wars of the late mediaeval period when the modern pre-eminence of the nation state as the central organisational principle of society hardly pertained.[41]

Although an oversimplification of complex processes, it is common for students of international relations to point to the Peace of Westphalia (1648) as a historical watershed marking the beginnings of the state-centred, sovereignty-based international system.[42] According to the standard account, after the Peace, which brought to an end the Thirty Years War (perhaps the most brutal and horrific of Europe's many brutal and horrific wars), wars of religion and civil wars between kings and their just slightly less powerful vassals were displaced by wars among unitary states led by increasingly powerful kings ultimately wielding professional armies.[43] Henceforth, for as long as the 'Westphalian Age' lasted, wars would be fought, as Philip Windsor put it, 'over important but limited questions' such as dynastic marriages, territorial settlements, trade advantages and the like. In other words, 'they were fought over issues that war could actually decide rather than the imponderables it could not.'[44]

As late as the nineteenth century, attitudes to war and peace tended to reflect a starkly politically Realist (that is, anarchic and state-centric) understanding of the global politics of the time, as may be seen in another of Von Moltke's essays in which he argued '...not much weight should be attached to international agreements'. No third power would intervene in an armed conflict where one or other side had violated the laws of warfare because 'there is no earthly tribunal.'[45] In this context, states could use force to decisive effect—albeit, as Clausewitz warned, temporarily, for 'the defeated state often considers the outcome as a transitory evil, for which a remedy may still be found in political conditions at some later date.'[46]

Nowadays, by contrast, globalisation theorists have concluded that the 'Westphalian Age' reached its zenith in 1945 and has been in decline ever since, during which time the inviolability of state sovereignty has markedly diminished while states have grown progressively enmeshed not only in a complex range of social and economic interdependencies but also international law, most notably the United Nations Charter.[47] Contra Von Moltke, third powers do intervene in the conflicts of others, basing their right to do so on international agreements over human rights, the laws of war and governments' 'responsibility to protect'. According to this last ideal, sovereign states are no longer defined solely by their demarcated borders, within which they may brook no interference, but also by their obligation to protect (and not to harm) their citizens.[48] In case of the failure of a state in this duty the responsibility falls, it is argued, on the international community to intervene.[49]

Some scholars of international relations even go so far now as to compare the functional utility of states in twenty-first-century global politics to the Maginot Line fortifications built by France between the world wars to prevent German invasion—that is, as being hopelessly outmoded.[50] This seems an overstatement, for now, though there is a strong argument that the trend is towards the breaking down of the established system of nation states and power politics.[51] There is, however, an undoubted irony in the fact that the hope of regulating war by the *de jure* allocation of the decision to go to war (except in self-defence) solely to the United Nations Security Council has, paradoxically, resulted in its *de facto* deregulation. States avoid declarations of war, while actually going to war, so as not to fall foul of international law.

By no means does this mean that war has gone away, nor that states such as Britain, which is uncommonly militarily active relative to its size, have avoided conflict. In fact, since 1945 there has been only one year (1968) in which the British Army has not suffered a fatal combat casualty at least somewhere in the world. 'War persists,' writes the historian Hew Strachan in one of a series of essays on contemporary strategy and civil-military relations, 'but the state's involvement and interest in it are reduced.'[52]

It seems clear that there have been some significant changes in patterns of war since the mid-twentieth century. Whether these are new as in 'historically unparalleled' or merely 'new to us' as in not having been seen for generations, is a matter of debate.

Ball of confusion

Experts will differ, surely, on the categorisation of these changes as well as their range and extent. Nonetheless, one might propose that they include the following. First, we have seen a gradual 'privatisation' of war as the grip of states on the monopoly of violence weakens.[53] Though it threatens them, states have to an extent connived in the process of war's privatisation where it has been thought to benefit them in terms of new capabilities and efficiencies, by contracting with profit-making private security and military services firms.[54] Increasingly, non-state actors are seizing the initiative from states.

It is, however, the not-for-profit ones that provoke the most worry. The eminent historian Sir Michael Howard has written of loosely-knit extremist 'groupuscules', inspired by fanaticism, armed with modern weapons, and having set themselves the goal of overthrowing the world's existing political order. Added to this pressure on the state there was an even more Damoclean sword hanging over:

> the very essence of the Westphalian order: the sovereign state itself. This finds itself increasingly vulnerable to three kinds of erosion—from above, laterally, and from below.[55]

The 11 September 2001 attacks on the United States successfully goaded, critics of the 'Global War on Terror' have argued, America and some of its major allies into counterproductive and heavy-handed military reactions to what ought to have been regarded as a crime against the international community.[56] More generally, the attacks caused (or perhaps, more precisely, revealed) a profound disorientation of Western defence establishments. The sense of having lost the initiative, indeed of being structurally maladapted to the challenges of the twenty-first century, is palpably evident in most of the major armed forces of the world.

The basic apprehension is expressed in numerous forms and in relation to a number of key aspects of military organisation and practice. In one of his last speeches before retiring, US Secretary of Defence Robert Gates told cadets of the Military Academy at West Point that his biggest concern (among several) was the 'bureaucratic rigidity' particularly of the personnel system and that the consequences of failing to address it 'terrified' him.[57] The UK's Chief of Defence Staff, General Sir David Richards, described the challenge as being even more fundamental than that—greater even than the 'horse to tank' moment in the period between the world wars in which major armies adapted their organisation and fighting styles to take account of a suite of technological developments, notably mechanisation, radio communications and the aircraft:[58]

> This is not a change that happens once in a generation, it is less frequent than that. And in many ways this is more fundamental than that from horse to tank described by Liddell-Hart. While that occupied the minds of generals, the present shift is one that includes our entire society and therefore impacts our whole security infrastructure.[59]

Richards put his finger on the key aspect of the conundrum, that being that the main vector of change in strategic affairs is not primarily in military technology but in the technology underlying society more generally. Changes in information technology are causing, he said, the fading of 'old assumptions... old frontiers and old frontlines', which are no longer impregnable to 'global networks of competing cultures'. The resulting anxiety is particularly acute in what might be called the 'perceptual realm of conflict'.[60]

Again, this is a feeling shared on both sides of the Atlantic. Gates's predecessor as Secretary of Defence, Donald Rumsfeld, several times expressed incredulity at the way that he saw the United States being outperformed by its enemies in the 'war of ideas'. His public elucidation of the problem in 2006 was to the point:

> Our enemies have skilfully adapted to fighting wars in today's media age, but for the most part we, our country, our government, has not adapted... For the most part, the U.S. government still functions as a five and dime store in an eBay world... There's never been a war fought in this environment before.[61]

In 2007 the situation was no better when Gates professed it embarrassing that al-Qaeda was still beating America in the new environment. 'How has one man in a cave managed to out-communicate the world's greatest communication society?' he lamented.[62] We may see here, therefore, the second of the large changes in warfare: its 'mediatisation', the development of a 'virtual dimension' of conflict in parallel or intertwined with the physical dimension.[63]

Increasingly, for the major armed forces of the world engaging in 'wars of perception' is seen as a non-optional requirement of military campaigning.[64] Moreover, their non-state opponents feel the same way. In 2005, Ayman al-Zawahiri, then deputy head of al-Qaeda, wrote to the leader of al-Qaeda in Iraq, Abu Musab al-Zarqawi, urging him to refrain from further videotaped beheadings of prisoners, such as the American communications engineer Nick Berg whose gruesome and barbarous decapitation occurred in May 2004. Al-Zawahiri thought such stunts counter-productive to the global Islamist narrative effort. 'I say to you', he wrote, 'that we are in a media battle, and that more than half of this battle is taking place in the battlefield of the media.'[65]

The influential concept of 'wars amongst the people', coined by the British general Rupert Smith, is underpinned by the concept of mediatisation. Indeed, he sees the media as the essential medium that binds the Clausewitzian trinity in contemporary times:

> Those making the war amongst the people have also come to use the media to influence decisions, and above all the will of those people they seek to lead and co-opt. This is not so much the global village as the global theatre of war, with audience participation.[66]

In essence, the point is now widely pressed that while perception has always mattered in warfare it matters more now in the information age than it has in previous times. Thus we see such figures as H.R. McMaster, one of the most forward thinking and accomplished senior officers in the US Army today, write in the foreword to a recent text on influence and perception in modern warfare that:

> Although combat in Afghanistan and Iraq continue to require the defeat of the enemy on physical battlegrounds, US commanders have discovered that lasting success over terrorist and insurgent groups requires winning on the battle ground of perception ... Ideas are weapons in the information age...[67]

It is fair to question the validity of the perception that ideas matter more now than they have in the past. The sixteenth-century wars of religion in Europe were 'media wars as well as conflicts with swords and guns, conflicts in which pamphleteering, image-making, image-breaking and oral communications were all important'.[68] Any attempt to draw a line distinguishing today's putatively media-fuelled ideational conflicts, such as that now being waged by Islamic State in the Middle East, from wars of the past needs to be very tentative. Perhaps it is more accurate to say that as information technology allows more ideas to be disseminated more widely and quickly, and in more emotionally resonant multimedia forms, people's beliefs are potentially more malleable, more in play and open to remote manipulation.

For the most part, however, the gist of the debate over the future of war has in recent years focused upon a more proximate impasse, specifically whether or not the campaigning conditions of future wars will reflect the 'asymmetric' ones observed recently in Iraq and Afghanistan. On the one hand, 'crusaders' argue that they will and that failing to adapt our forces accordingly will doom us to defeat, wasted lives and money, and a less safe world in which the contagion of 'global insurgency' will thrive in failed and failing states. On the other hand, 'conservatives' argue that Iraq and Afghanistan are aberrations and that adapting our forces for counterinsurgency (COIN) is a craven bargain, trading a first class war-fighting army for a second rate COIN machine.

In actuality, the suppositions of both rest upon sound observations. For the crusaders: that those who wish to challenge the West's military power appear to have given up trying to do so head on. For the conservatives: that opponents adopt less dangerous 'asymmetric' techniques precisely because of our conventional predominance, which should not, therefore, be squandered.[69] The troubling conclusion of large parts of the defence community, which has wearied of the polarised debate, is that future wars will defy categorisation into either of these familiar archetypes. More likely, says the influential 'hybrid wars' model (largely driven by United States Marine Corps analyses stemming back to the 'Three Block War' concept of the early 1990s),[70] Western defence establishments may no longer assume that states will only fight 'conventionally' or that non-state actors will confine their efforts to the 'unconventional' end of the conflict spectrum:

> The future does not portend a suite of distinct challengers with alternative or different methods but their convergence into multi-modal or hybrid wars... Hybrid wars can be conducted by both states and a variety of non-state actors. Hybrid wars incorporate a range of different modes of warfare including conventional capabilities, irregular tactics and formations, terrorist acts including indiscriminate violence and coercion and criminal disorder.[71]

Regular armed forces have lost the monopoly of warfare. In fact, the distinction between regular and irregular has blurred nearly to meaninglessness while the 'game' of strategy has expanded to involve a greater diversity of players pursuing ever more esoteric objectives. Moreover, the targets of these new actors are rarely specifically military; more frequently their attempts to coerce are directed at the civilian population specifically and the non-military infrastructure of society more generally. The popularity of the concept of 'hybrid' wars is indicative of the struggle to reconcile war as we observe it in practice—which is waged in multiple modes and levels simultaneously by a range of national, sub-national and/or quasi-national actors—with the too neat categories and divisions that we have developed to explain it.[72]

In short, the state of war at the beginning of the twenty-first century is one of vexatious complexity and puzzlement to those whose task it is to fight them, plan for them, and harness them to the achievement of policy. All these tasks have turned out to be considerably more difficult and complex than anyone anticipated in the heady days of the Cold War's end, when some believed in a permanent triumph of liberal democracy and market capitalism, an 'end of history', as it were, and assumed that high-tech Western military forces would henceforth triumph easily and cheaply over less sophisticated enemies.[73]

2

THE CONTEXT OF CONTEMPORARY WAR

That which hath been is that which shall be; and that which hath been done is that which shall be done: and there is no new thing under the sun.

Ecclesiastes, 1:9

Wars can only be understood in context, which is to say in the light of the overarching preconceptions, ideals, and myths and delusions of their time. Our time is considered to be one of great flux, primarily as a result of advances in information technology, but also as a result of other causes. This confounds strategists charged with making sense of the workings of the world and considering how best to align the forcible means available to them with the ends desired by their political masters. It is said, for instance, that major war is obsolete—a thing of the past and no longer utile; but while this may be true now we must be aware that this has been said before for many of the same reasons and found to be untrue then. It is also said that the perceptual realm of conflict transcends that of the strictly material realm. Moreover, the emergence of a global consciousness as a result of connectivity is not without a significant dark side: to a degree it consolidates human society but it also fragments it, providing new vectors of conflict. At the same time, policymakers have become fixated by the apparent speed of events and convinced of the urgency of action to remediate or forestall threats before they are genuinely imminent (or even fully apparent). This complicates the deliberate making of strategy but also makes it very difficult to adopt a wait-and-see approach, which has historically often been a wise one. Overall, however, the sense of dislocation by events is heightened by exaggerating their unprecedented nature. Many things have changed and still are changing, but few of these changes are genuinely out of the blue. There is much that is happening now that can be understood better by a more careful consideration of the past.

For the major armies of the world, formed by the conventions of the industrial age, twenty-first century conflict seems almost unfathomably complex. The subtext of recent American and British doctrine is not difficult to discern. The *US Army Capstone Concept*, for example, which is meant to articulate how to think about future armed conflict, is subtitled 'Operating under conditions of uncertainty and complexity in an era of persistent conflict'.[1] The contemporaneous British *Future Character of Conflict* report summarised the future battlespace alliteratively as likely to be congested, cluttered, contested, connected and constrained—the only 'C' it missed out was confused.[2] And it is not only practitioners who are so afflicted; the academy is too:

> One of the central challenges confronting international relations today is that we do not really know what is a war and what is not. The consequences of our confusion would seem absurd, were they not so profoundly dangerous.[3]

There is every reason to believe that warfare is changing. Why else would practitioners and theorists alike be so at sea? The problem with theories in the 'new wars' tradition addressed in the last chapter is that they over-interpret these changes in war's character as a profound shift in war's fundamental essence. In parallel, there is a conflation of the Westphalian era with a putative Clausewitzian era that serves rhetorically to reinforce these claims. Ergo, they say: if the theory of post-Westphalianism is correct, then it is therefore time to overturn Clausewitz's idea of war as a rational instrument of policy. Not infrequently, for example, analysts on the popular edge of the future war debate, being currently occupied by the prophets of cyberpower and the effects of computer networks on warfare, implicitly or explicitly disparage Clausewitz, consigning his 'outdated' and 'ever more irrelevant' philosophy to the bin of history.[4]

Yet few take the same shot at similar luminaries such as Max Weber, another nineteenth-century German philosopher and political economist, although he defined the exercise of 'power' in almost exactly the same terms that Clausewitz defined war: as the collective action of a group of men aiming to realise their own will even against the resistance of another group.[5] In fact, quite the opposite is the case. The Spanish sociologist Manuel Castells, who perhaps better than any other at present has explained the social and economic relations of the emerging 'network society', concludes of Weber that '... the voice of the master resonates with force one hundred years later'.[6]

The 'Great Illusion' redux

The conceit of this book is to treat Clausewitz as similarly resonant and relevant to the present day, to seek not to unseat him but, rather, to see how his theories may still illuminate war despite changes in technology of which he could have had no apprehension. It is based upon a presumption that had Clausewitz written in the twentieth century then he would have read with great interest about such things as the growth of a factory proletariat, the urbanisation of the bourgeoisie, the consequent political adaptations of European regimes, and other developments of the Industrial Revolution, and adjusted his theory accordingly—no doubt observing the shift it caused in the basis of military power to one based in large part upon industrial capability.[7] Similarly, were he writing now, a time when the rapidity of technological change provides the leitmotif of much scholarship from anthropology through zoology, he would wonder about the sources and meaning of military power in the post-industrial information age.[8]

Lest this ambition seem impertinent, it bears noting that applying Clausewitz's theory in an era of rapid technological change, especially in computing and communications, is not all that difficult. Contrary to some scholars' claims, the 'remarkable trinity' is more than sufficiently malleable to encompass and to illuminate understanding of the wars of our time. Clausewitz himself was no dogmatist. Towards the end of *On War* he explained how every age has its 'own kind of war, its own limiting conditions, and its own peculiar preconceptions'. The events of every age, he said:

> Must be judged in the light of its own peculiarities. One cannot, therefore, understand and appreciate the commanders of the past until one has placed oneself in the situation of their times, not so much by painstaking study of all its details as by an accurate appreciation of its major determining features.[9]

On War remains acutely relevant; it should not be banished to the dusty back shelves of the library.[10]

A hundred years ago the English scholar Norman Angell wrote that major war had become unthinkable. His logic was twofold. First, war served no economic purpose in a world densely connected through commerce; and, second, human consciousness itself was changing in ways that were making violence a less natural-seeming way to resolve conflicts. He set out his case with great boldness and in a high moral tone that scorned those who still believed in war's glory, let alone utility:

> the believer in war justifies his dogmatism for the most part by an appeal to what he alleges is the one dominating fact of the situation—i.e., that human nature is

unchanging. [But] ... human nature is changing out of all recognition. Not only is man fighting less, but he is using all forms of physical compulsion less, and as a very natural result is losing those psychological attributes that go with the employment of physical force. And he is coming to employ physical force less because accumulated evidence is pushing him more and more to the conclusion that he can accomplish more easily that which he strives for by other means.[11]

Unfortunately, all this was spectacularly ill timed. Within five years Europe plunged the world headlong into what Philip Bobbitt has called 'The Long War' encompassing not just the world wars but also the subsequent Cold War and its myriad of proxy conflicts.[12] In the bloody twentieth century, fervour of all sorts (whether ideological, nationalistic, sectarian, ethnic or other) was pitched against reason—and reason lost out.

However irrational, in hindsight, it may have been, Germany twice attempted world domination by physical compulsion and, subsequent to Germany's defeat (primarily by the efforts of the mighty Red Army), the Soviet Union seemed to want to try something similar. Short of assenting to being conquered and tyrannised there was little else that the democratic powers could do but resist such attempts with physical force of their own, and cultivate the psychological attributes that go along with such a resolution. As a result, Angell became for much of the twentieth century a symbol of naïve optimism and his theses, though not without defenders, an object of Realist disparagement, perhaps most by those most wounded by his moralising barbs.[13]

In the early years of the twenty-first century, however, such thinking as Angell's is making a comeback, bolstered by both technological and social developments that appear to lend it greater credence. Interdependence is again purported to form a sort of bulwark against the outbreak of war, particularly among democracies, which do not go to war with each other—a phenomenon explained by the 'democratic peace' theory. The degree to which the potential for belligerency of non-democratic states, belligerency between democracies and non-democracies, and especially belligerency of new or unstable democracies is mitigated by economic interdependence is hotly contested:[14]

> Notwithstanding this, a key theme in explanations of, for instance, such vital matters of the day as the as yet still peaceful relationship between the United States and China (a classic 'rising power') is mutual dependence. China depends on the United States for access to its voracious consumers to whom it sells its goods, while the United States depends on China for access to its abstemious savers from whom it obtains credit. As one commentator acidly said of a putative Sino-American war, 'A conflict with Beijing might be lost on the empty shelves of Wal-Mart.'[15] Without this interdependency, it is argued, China's rise would indeed lead to confrontation,

though it must be said there are significant dissenters against this position who argue that even with the restraint of mutual economic dependence, the dreaded security dilemma is a still more powerful influence on the decision-making of states.[16] For the latter camp, then, conflict is inevitable.

More surprisingly, Angell's notion that human 'nature' is changing has received support from some scientists. The cognitive psychologist and neuroscientist Steven Pinker has recently argued that an 'expanding circle of empathy' and 'escalator of reason' have over time caused a diminishment of violence in human society:

> The forces of modernity—reason, science, humanism, individual rights—have not, of course, pushed steadily in one direction; nor will they ever bring about a utopia or end the frictions and hurts that come with being human. But on top of all the benefits that modernity has brought us in health, experience, and knowledge, we can add its role in the reduction of violence.[17]

The operative factor here is less the evolution of human nature (in the biological sense), on which point Pinker is conservative and cautious, than the expansion of empathy and reason, which has, in turn, broadened people's sense of social solidarity with others. Basically, he argues, our elastic sense of who is part of our social 'in group' (and, therefore, against whom we are loath to use violence) has grown while the sense of our social 'out group' (against whom we are more likely, possibly even eager, to use force) has shrunk.

Be this as it may, there is another factor of which Angell had no foresight in 1909 that adds enormous weight to his thesis: nuclear weapons ultimately—though it took the major powers two decades to fully realise it—elevated the costs of major war by many orders of magnitude and made it more futile than even the stalemated trench-fighting of the Great War.[18] Many scholars find this alone to be sufficient explanation for the post-1945 lull in major warfare.[19] The principle of Occam's Razor would tend to support such thinking. Why explain war's diminishing utility with a hard-to-measure and hard-to-explain thesis about changing human nature when good old human self-interest and survival instinct are sufficient?

There is a heavy bias within war and strategic studies towards time-tested 'tried and true' theories. One sees this, for instance, not just in the enduring popularity of Clausewitz but of even more timeless classics such as Thucydides' *History of the Peloponnesian War*. Though more than two thousand years old, still his well-worn maxims such as that war's cause is a composite of fear, honour and interest, and that the strong do what they will while the weak do what they must, are widely taught in officer academies and graduate schools.[20] We should be wary of too much conviction in eternal verities, though; it is one thing to have a historian's healthy regard for continuity—it is another thing to let that blind us to elements of change as they appear. Michael Howard put it best:

> Like the statesman, the soldier has to steer between the dangers of repeating the errors of the past because he is ignorant that they have been made, and of remaining bound by theories deduced from past history although changes in conditions have rendered these theories obsolete.[21]

Clearly, wars between states are on the wane. Richard Ned Lebow's recent study of ninety-four of them from the Franco-Spanish War of 1648–1659 to the Russo-Georgia War in 2008 found that all the state motives he considered—interest, security, standing and revenge—have lost traction as causes of war.[22] But this does not mean that war is going away, for the passions which drive us to compel others to do our will have themselves not disappeared.

Fragmentation vs consolidation

On the contrary, as Chantale Mouffe reminds us, wars have multiplied and manifested in ever smaller groups. Pinker's belief in the successes of Western humanism is misplaced:

> Western democrats view with astonishment the explosion of manifold ethnic, religious and nationalist conflicts that they thought belonged to a bygone age. Instead of the heralded 'New World Order', the victory of universal values, and the generalisation of 'post-conventional' identities, we are witnessing an explosion of particularisms and an increasing challenge to Western universalism.[23]

Like a chameleon, or more precisely a shape-shifter, war is working itself into new forms. States do not use force nearly so frequently as they once did to compel other states to do their will. Moreover, when they do act against other states such interventions are couched as being aimed not at the other state *per se*, but at the illegitimate regimes that run them and from whom the people need liberating. Alex Bellamy, reflecting mainly upon the lessons of a decade of wars in the Balkans, was among the first to raise disquiet about current strategic affairs. He noted that, in contrast to 'industrial-age warfare, "new wars" are characterised by uncertainty, ambivalent chains of command and ambiguous political objectives'.[24] The ongoing war in Ukraine between Russian-backed rebels and the Western-supported regime in Kiev perhaps epitomizes this air of ambiguity and deliberate obscuration of state involvement. The major expeditionary campaigns of the now over-a-decade-long War on Terror have also cemented this reality. War is less and less a matter of the state.

Afghanistan was invaded in order to punish the Taliban regime for harbouring al-Qaeda and refusing to give up its leader, Osama bin Laden, after the 11 September 2001 attacks. Then in 2003 Iraq was invaded to oust the regime of Saddam Hussein because he would not (arguably, could not) satisfy the United States and a handful of its allies of Iraq's compliance with the international regime of inspections of its weapons of mass destruction programme.[25] The trouble in both cases was that the resolution of the initiating problem merely forced the metastasising of another equally or more pernicious one. Jessica Stern's early description of al-Qaeda as a 'protean enemy' able to survive the destruction of its physical bases in one place only to reconstitute itself in another has proved durably accurate.[26] The emergence of al-Qaeda in Iraq subsequent to the American invasion in 2003, its near extirpation as a result of the later improvement of counterinsurgency operations (on which more in later chapters), and its rebirth in the form of Islamic State is another poignant example of the mutability and tenacious survivability of such networked movements.

More generally, it used to be that a main benefit of being victorious in war was that you got your army back more or less intact. Nowadays, it takes years to get your army back, even when you win, and then more likely than not only in an exhausted condition with its formations a shambles, tables of equipment and organisation an eclectic mess, chaotic personnel profiles, and often in a state of moral malaise after years of trying to put right societies deranged by mal-government, depredation and war.

At the beginning of the twentieth century, the British officer C.E. Callwell, the Victorian 'guru' of small wars, declared them to be 'protracted, thankless, and invertebrate'.[27] His main advice was to avoid them. Unfortunately, this has proved difficult for soldiers and statesmen in the twenty-first century in large part because they have been seized by the notion that the best that can be hoped for in the wars they fight is a form of risk management, where threats are mitigated but never eliminated.[28] 'Victory' in such wars, as Secretary Gates explained in a much-cited *Foreign Affairs* article, is more or less explicitly defined as beyond the scope of military operations as they are normally understood. The War on Terror was, in his words, 'in grim reality, a prolonged, worldwide irregular campaign' in which it would be impossible for the United States to 'kill or capture its way to victory'.[29] In effect, wars then have come to be used for their putatively prophylactic effect—violence is undertaken to stave off some conjectured outcome of doing nothing that would be even worse.[30]

Though the results of such interventionist thinking, or what one might call 'robust meddling', have been disconcerting—in stark contrast with the confident assertions made at its launch about its likely contribution to peace and security, few now see the post-9/11 invasion and occupation of Iraq as anything but at best a pyrrhic debacle—it does not always deserve the scorn poured on it. Both Madeleine Albright, then United States Ambassador to the United Nations, and Colin Powell, then Chairman of the Joint Chiefs of Staff, recorded in their memoirs an altercation at the White House in 1993 as the Bosnian War was heightening. 'What's the point of having this superb military that you're always talking about if we can't use it?' demanded Albright.[31]

In Powell's account he admits the question almost caused him an aneurysm: 'American GIs are not toy soldiers to be moved around on some global game board'.[32] The cautiousness and clarity of Powell's sentiments on the use of force, succinctly made in a 1993 *Foreign Affairs* article, are admirable: 'If force is used imprecisely or out of frustration rather than clear analysis, the situation can be made worse.'[33] Initially, the Bush administration echoed this ideal, as may be seen in the words of Condoleezza Rice (subsequently appointed Bush's National Security Advisor) during the 2000 election campaign:

> The president must remember that the military is a special instrument, and it is meant to be. It is not a civilian peace force. It is not a political referee. And it is most certainly not designed to build a civilian society.[34]

But the 11 September 2001 attacks caused a sea change in the Bush administration's attitude, suggesting that the point of Albright's question to Powell actually had a degree of non-partisan resonance; a much more militarily adventurous policy was the result. Undoubtedly, revenge and a desire to remedy wounded pride played a part in the new American willingness to wield military power against anyone so foolish as to place their face in the path of the 'clunking fist'. But underlying that was a belief that unless the deep causes of 'instability and aggression' were removed, aggression eventually would reappear.[35] 'We must take the battle to the enemy', the president told cadets at the West Point Military Academy, 'disrupt his plans, and confront the worst threats before they emerge. In the world we have entered, the only path to safety is the path of action.'[36]

Effectively, the administration adopted the view that American GIs were, in fact, assets to be moved around on a 'global game board' or, as a then much-lauded book by the American defence analyst Thomas Barnett, called it: 'The Pentagon's new map'. According to this 'new map', the world was divided into two zones. On the one hand, there was the 'functioning core' comprised of those parts of the world that had embraced globalisation—or, in Barnett's words, 'connectedness'; whereas on the other hand there was the 'non-integrating gap' comprised of those countries that had not, indeed which craved disconnection. Peaceful coexistence of the two was not reckoned desirable, or actually possible:

> the only truly global future worth creating involves nothing less than eliminating the Gap altogether. America can only increase its security when it extends connectivity or expands globalisation's reach, and by doing so, progressively reduces those trouble spots or off-grid locations where security problems and instability tend to concentrate.[37]

The War on Terror, it followed, was a zero-sum war of 'connectedness' against 'disconnectedness' and what the situation called for was a bifurcation of traditional military forces. In order to 'fight wars', that is to conduct conventional high intensity wars between states, one needed a 'Leviathan' force—effectively the traditional military; but in order to 'wage peace', that is to conduct military operations other than war, what was needed was a 'System Administrator' force. Whereas the Leviathan force would destroy regimes, the System Administrator force would 'build nations'. Whereas the Leviathan force's operations would be punitive, the System Administrator force's operations would be preventive. And whereas the Leviathan's force's aims would be 'event-focused'—finite, in other words; the System Administrator force's aims would be 'continuous'—infinite, in other words.[38]

If global connectivity promotes both consolidation and fragmentation—or causes a struggle between homogeneity and heterogeneity—in international affairs, then the hegemon essentially positioned itself as the defender of the former against the latter. The inevitable result of this was a plethora of small wars fought by an empire in all but name. As Robert Kaplan put it:

> by the turn of the twenty-first century the United States military had already appropriated the entire earth, and was ready to flood the most obscure areas of it with troops at a moment's notice.[39]

Ten years on, as noted earlier, this enterprise mostly seems to have gone spectacularly wrong and to the extent that such thinking influenced policy it proved to be substantially counterproductive. As it turned out, it takes relatively little military capability on the part of the peace-spoiler to force the System Administrator force back into the full combined-arms warfare mode of the Leviathan force, if only for its own protection. Moreover, the perpetual peace-waging of the System Administration force amounts more or less exactly to the 'protracted, thankless, and invertebrate' wars that Callwell warned about a century before.[40] More importantly, it mischaracterised the foe as some force of disconnectedness rather than as a highly connected entity in its own right that simply had a quite different view of globalisation's ideal end point.[41] Faced with al-Qaeda, an adversary that took the form of a global movement with little vertical hierarchy, hard-wired organisation, or need for territory, Bush's cabinet imagined it as something more familiar that could be destroyed with 'the weapons and ideas they already possessed.'[42]

I feel the need, the need for speed

Hindsight has always been the preferred fighting position of the know-it-all. It is terribly easy to point the finger at wrong decisions after the fact when the second and third order consequences have been observed and measured. It is equally easy to elide the fact that no American government, not even the most inert, could afford to ignore a movement that had demonstrated the desire and ability to attack it at its heart with such ferocity and malice. Notwithstanding these facts, policy-makers and their strategic advisors probably ought to have been more attentive to the changed context in which force was about to be applied.

Context has long been understood as all-important when it comes to strategy. In the words of historian Jeremy Black:

> [I]n its fundamentals war changes far less frequently and significantly than most people appreciate. This is not simply because it involves a constant—the willingness of organised groups to kill and, in particular, to risk death—but also because the material culture of war (the weaponry used and the associated supply systems) which tends to be the focus of attention, is less important than its social, cultural and political contexts and enablers. These contexts explain the purposes of military action, the nature of the relationship between the military and the rest of society, and the internal structures and ethos of the military.[43]

To be sure, there was a recognition after 9/11 that some things had changed. In 1993, Powell was writing in the shade of the West's peaceful triumph in the Cold War. 'The Soviet Union is gone', he observed. 'Replacing it is a world of promise and hope...'[44] 9/11, however, showed globalisation's sting. Gone was the world of promise and hope, replacing it was one in which 'grave and long term peril' had suddenly become starkly apparent.[45]

Arguably, the attack ought not to have been such a surprise. The official *9/11 Commission Report* described it as 'a shock, not a surprise', pointing out that there had been plenty of general warning that Islamic extremists were planning to kill Americans in large numbers, but that on the whole the information available was confused, often contradictory, and non-specific as to where and when a big attack might occur.[46] More scathingly, Michael Scheuer, the head of the CIA's Bin Laden unit from 1996 through 1999, wrote that American intelligence officers:

> knew a runaway train was coming at the United States, documented that fact, and then watched helplessly—or were banished for speaking out—as their senior leaders delayed action, downplayed intelligence, ignored repeated warnings, and generally behaved as what they so manifestly are, America's greatest generation—of moral cowards.[47]

But the attacks shattered whatever complacency there was, leaving behind a sense not just of rage, but also of profound urgency. Speaking in January 2002, just after the toppling of the Taliban and capture and destruction of some of al-Qaeda's bases in Afghanistan, President Bush illustrated the administration's new view of the state of strategic affairs. At the top of the list of fears was the nightmarish possible combination of terrorism and weapons of mass destruction:

> We have seen the depth of our enemies' hatred in videos where they laugh about the loss of innocent life. And the depth of their hatred is equalled by the madness of the destruction they design. We have found diagrams of American nuclear power plants and public water facilities, detailed instructions for making chemical weapons, surveillance maps of American cities, and thorough descriptions of landmarks in America and throughout the world. What we have found in Afghanistan confirms that, far from ending there, our war against terror is only beginning.[48]

The scholar and Reagan-era defence official Fred Charles Ikle, however, laid out the grimly simple new reality, which he called 'annihilation from within', in historical perspective:

> The fall of the Roman Empire did not empower ruthless cults or crazed anarchists to extirpate law and order in every province of the realm. But such an unprecedented reign of violence might become mankind's fate in this century. The ineluctable dissemination of technology and scientific discoveries will make nuclear and biological weapons accessible to merciless insurgent movements, small terrorist gangs, secretive anarchist groups, and genocidal doomsday cults.[49]

Ikle's influential earlier book, written at a time 'when American involvement in the war in Vietnam had become an agonising search for an exit', had shaped Colin Powell's thinking on how to end the Gulf War and was entitled *Every War Must End*. It was therefore ironic that he should be the one to elucidate this new threat because the War on Terror, for which it provides conceptual underpinning, is effectively a war that cannot end.[50] As traditionally understood, the term 'war' implies something finite. But the threat that 9/11 brought to the fore was not a finite one that might be appeased by political concessions on the one hand, or destroyed by military victories on the other. It was something more insidious and complex—the intersection of two historical forces.

The first of these was the generalised feeling of resentment within the Muslim world against the West, 'not only for its political and economic intrusion into the Middle East, but as what the Germans call the *Kulturtrager*, the bearers of a culture seen to be destroying their way of life and violating the tenets of their faith'.[51] In fact, one counter to the post-Cold War 'end of history' narrative was already old in the Middle East by the time of the Soviet Union's collapse. In the mid-1960s the Egyptian Islamist Sayyid Qutb wrote *Milestones*, a book which became something of a manifesto for political Islam, in which he explained that:

> Islam is not merely a belief, so that it is enough merely to preach it. Islam, which is a way of life, takes practical steps to organise a movement for freeing man. Other societies do not give it any opportunity to organise its followers according to its own method, and hence it is the duty of Islam to annihilate all such systems, as they are obstacles in the way of universal freedom.[52]

Qutb's life, work and eventual 'martyrdom' (he was arrested in 1954, suspected of having a part in an attempted assassination of the Egyptian dictator Gamal Abdel Nasser, and executed in prison in 1966) provided part of the foundation for al-Qaeda's ideology.[53] Until the tumbling of the Twin Towers, however, almost nobody in the West gave much credit to such talk. Fukuyama's *End of History*, for instance, acknowledged Islamic fundamentalism as a potential challenge to liberalism's triumph but characterised it as probably a forlorn one, rooted as it was in Islam's 'double failure to maintain the coherence of its traditional society and to successfully assimilate the techniques and values of the West'.[54]

He may, in the long-term, be correct about Islam's failings. It is hard, though, not to read the words of Osama bin Laden in homage to the 9/11 attackers as a direct rejoinder to the theory that history halted with the end of the Cold War simply because its victors in the West found their place in the sun congenial and wished that it remain forever so:

> [the bombers] undertook a brave and beautiful operation, unprecedented in the history of humanity, and struck down America's totems... they struck the American economy with full force, rubbed America's nose in the dirt, and dragged its arrogance through the mud... The most important consequence of the attacks on New

York and Washington was that it showed the truth about the fight between the crusaders and the Muslims. They revealed how much the crusaders resent us, once these attacks stripped the wolf of its sheep's clothing and showed us its horrifying face. The entire world awoke, Muslims realised how important the doctrine of loyalty to God and separation is, and solidarity among Muslims grew stronger, which is a giant step toward the unification of Muslims under the banner of mono-theism, in order to establish the rightly guided caliphate, please God. Finally, eve-ryone realised that America, that oppressive force, can be beaten, humiliated, brought low...[55]

These are grand claims for a man whose body now lies mouldering in a canvas sack at the bottom of the Indian Ocean having been hunted to his death by American military power. Nonetheless, their credence cannot be denied. The renewal of the 'rightly guided caliphate' seemed fantastically implausible until recently, but the turmoil of the 'Arab Spring', beginning with the self-immolation of the Tunisian fruit seller Mohammed Bouazizi in December 2010, has thus far resulted in the elevation of Islamism more than any other political force in the Middle East. Meanwhile, the War on Terror, initially inappropriately described by Bush as a 'crusade', has matured into a more cynical, weary, jaded, compromised and uncompromising thing. Bin Laden was a terrorist, undoubtedly, but also a master propagandist with a good deal of strategic foresight.

The other historical force at work was technology. As noted, the overt pre-occupation in Bush's speech was with the predicament caused by what Ikle called the 'curse of dual use technologies'. Molecular biology, genetic engineer-ing, and other life sciences, as well as nuclear technology, are all great civil achievements that could be used to build weapons of mass destruction, espe-cially with the connivance of a state.[56] But the underlying motif of the speech was a somewhat different but related point; at issue was a palpable sense of urgency—that somehow the speed and sheer interconnectedness of events in the world was now such that it was impossible, immoral even, for the admin-istration to simply wait on them. Instead, in the words of the president:

> time is not on our side. I will not wait on events while dangers gather. I will not stand by as peril draws closer and closer. The United States of America will not permit the world's most dangerous regimes to threaten us with the world's most destructive weapons.[57]

Thus American policy was hitched to a specific and very demanding tyrant—the need to continually not merely pre-empt enemies who might be on the verge of attack but to prevent their development of the means to pose an imminent threat in the first place.[58]

Myth behind us and myth before us

In 1829 the famously irascible Scottish philosopher Thomas Carlyle penned an essay titled with the biblical allusion 'The Signs of the Times'. The new shape of modern Europe was then becoming apparent in the wake of five great revolutions—scientific, industrial, American, French and romantic—which together had transformed the Western cultural and political landscape as well as its economic life and military prowess.[59] Carlyle was not happy with what he saw. In something of a presaging of those who now claim the irrelevance of the state and the decline of the West, he characterised the general mood of perturbation in society:

> Their cherished little haven is gone, and they will not be comforted! And therefore, day after day, in all manner of periodical or perennial publications, the most lugubrious predictions are sent forth. The King has virtually abdicated; the Church is a widow, without jointure; public principle is gone; private honesty is going; society, in short, is fast falling in pieces; and a time of unmixed evil is come on us.[60]

The single epithet Carlyle used to describe his time was, already, even before the middle of the nineteenth century when industrialisation really hit its stride, the 'Age of Machinery', in which, he said, 'our old modes of exertion are all discredited, and thrown aside.'[61]

Though acknowledging that mechanisation of labour made society vastly wealthier, overall, he deplored this new age because he perceived that the effects of machinery were not simply confined to industry; rather the 'mechanical genius of our time diffused itself into quite other provinces. Not the external and physical alone is now managed by machinery, but the internal and spiritual also.'[62] The lessons for our own day's apparent shift from industrial to informational society are manifold. For one thing, to the extent that one can blame the undoubted evils of imperialism, the world wars, and in the latter of those, the Holocaust, on the 'Age of Machinery' which Carlyle described, the process of the industrial revolution was, in hindsight, actually rather slow in unfolding.[63]

If Carlyle's perception that things were falling apart in 1829 seems just as applicable to 1929—the year of the Wall Street crash that precipitated the Great Depression—and seems likely (on current trajectory) to be as apposite in 2029, perhaps we ought simply to conclude that from the perspective of the present things have always seemed overwhelmingly tumultuous.

Conceivably, the pace of events in our time has accelerated. Indeed, this is the central idea of one of the most prominent works in the literature on discontinuous change in human society, which posits that technological change is accelerating exponentially rather than linearly and that we are nearing a point of explosive growth in knowledge and mastery of the world called 'The Singularity', beyond which prediction is impossible.[64] It cannot be denied that sheer number crunching power and ease of communications has increased enormously since the advent of the digital computer.

And yet it is already more than three quarters of a century since H.G. Wells declared the 'conquest of distance' by global communications and transport.[65] Half a century ago R.D. Laing was warning that 'we live in a moment of history where change is so speeded up that we begin to see the present only when it is already disappearing.'[66] A quarter century ago Zbigniew Brzezinski posited that the 'technological revolution fragments humanity and detaches it from its traditional moorings.'[67]

It may be that 'The Singularity' is near—but even so it has been a long time coming. There is a distinct tendency in discussions of digital media and society to emphasise its volatility and putatively unmooring effects. As one recent analysis put it:

> The information society is a society in constant flux and change. It moves at an ever quickening pace and causes the ties that bind us to the old, to the traditional, and to the known, to easily slip their moorings.[68]

As we have seen, there is something to such claims. Certainly, there is disorientation. But equally there is overstatement, caused by disconnection from the past and by market-driven fascination with the superficially new. Arguably, the accelerating pace of change is exaggerated—at any rate people have been talking of the information age in one way or another for a generation at least.

Inarguably, the belief that the challenges of the present are uniquely complex and unprecedented is untrue. In the same essay noted above, Carlyle declared that the beliefs of the present are always a product of two 'eternities', or stories that we tell ourselves, first about our past and second about our future. 'We were wise, indeed', he wrote, 'could we discern truly the signs of our own time; and by knowledge of its wants and advantages, wisely adjust our own position in it.'[69] Clausewitz's point about context was essentially the same, while Thucydides wrote long ago that the purpose of history was to inform 'those who want to understand clearly that which happened in the past, and which (human nature being what it is) will at some time or other and in much the same ways, be repeated in the future'.[70] We ought not to let slip traditional concepts merely because it is fashionable to assert new ones or, more commonly, to clothe old ones in more fashionable terms as though they were new.

It bears remarking too—without denying the reality of dangers that exist today—that strategic prognostication often takes on the quality of a jeremiad. Carlyle might have struggled more to find a publisher for 'The Signs of the Times' if his basic message was that there were structural reasons to be fearful of what was happening to society but the mixed consequences of mechanisation would be neither ineluctable, nor for the most part detectable, for another half century and more.

This, however, would have been essentially correct. At least until August 1914, the consequences of rapid technological, industrial, political and cultural change were hardly evil at all, for Europeans particularly. As the economist John Maynard Keynes remarked of the pre-First World War 'golden era', it was actually rather a high point of globalisation:

> The inhabitant of London could order by telephone, sipping his morning tea in bed, the various products of the whole earth, in such quantity as he might see fit, and reasonably expect their early delivery upon his doorstep; he could at the same moment and by the same means adventure his wealth in the natural resources and new enterprises of any quarter of the world, and share, without exertion or even trouble, in their prospective fruits and advantages; or he could decide to couple the security of his fortunes with the good faith of the townspeople of any substantial municipality in any continent that fancy or information might recommend. He could secure forthwith, if he wished it, cheap and comfortable means of transit to any country or climate without passport or other formality, could despatch his servant to the neighbouring office of a bank for such supply of the precious metals as might seem convenient, and could then proceed abroad to foreign quarters, without knowledge of their religion, language, or customs, bearing coined wealth upon his person, and would consider himself greatly aggrieved and much surprised at the least interference. But, most important of all, he regarded this state of affairs as normal, certain, and permanent, except in the direction of further improvement, and any deviation from it as aberrant, scandalous, and avoidable.[71]

Whether 9/11 represents as shattering a blow to connectedness as did the First World War remains to be seen. It is fair to say, though, that it was regarded as a distinctly alarming interference with a vastly more congenial reality. Whereas Carlyle looked about himself and saw machines everywhere replacing labour and in the process alienating mankind from other aspects of nature, nowadays computers are everywhere, enveloping us in a dense web of networks of flowing ideas, things and people.

This density of connectedness represents something of a paradox. It can be a force for good. Speaking of the way in which cyberspace was changing global society, the social and technology analyst Clay Shirky argued:

People want to do something to make the world a better place. They will help when they are invited to. Access to cheap, flexible tools removes many barriers to trying new things.[72]

In somewhat similar vein, speaking of the impact of massive increases in the mobility of people in the latter half of the twentieth century, as a result of political and cultural changes as well as new transport and communications technologies, Castles and Miller in their classic book *The Age of Migration* claimed:

> For the most part the growth of transnational society and politics is a beneficial process, because it can help overcome the violence and destructiveness that charac- terised the era of nationalism.[73]

But, equally, these same global structures conveying knowledge and people and goods, generally to everyone's betterment, can heighten insecurity and conflict to the extent that they also enable the propagation of violence and violent ideas.[74] This book is preoccupied with this 'dark side' of globaliza- tion—but, bearing in mind the paradoxical duality of connectedness, we would be wise to adopt a phlegmatic view of the 'unmixed evils' allegedly bearing down upon us. In actuality, the dark clouds have silver linings—a fact which good strategists ought always to recall.

Carlyle, on the other hand, was correct to draw attention to the way in which technological innovations in his time were not only changing industrial processes but also shifting society more generally to a mechanistic conception of itself. Ironically, as the philosopher most closely associated with the 'great man' theory of history, Carlyle seems to have been talking about the zeitgeist or animating 'spirit of the age'.[75] In our time, it seems it is the informational concept of society that is dominant. Perhaps nowhere is this made more explicit than in the writing of Kevin Kelly, the popular author and founding publisher of *Wired* magazine, who has described history essentially as the story of the evolution of the 'technium ... the greater, global, massively inter- connected system of technology vibrating around us' as well as 'culture, art, social institutions and intellectual creations of all types.'[76]

It is not that this schema is inherently better or more accurate than other ways of conceptualising the 'march of history'. Indeed, Marx and Engels used that particular phrase to describe the class struggle—the zeitgeist of their time, as they saw it. It was their all-purpose explanation for human progress.[77] It is, rather, that the choice of lens we use to interpret the past tells us a lot about the preoccupations of the present. Let us look at how that informational prism works when applied to war.

3

WAR WITHOUT CHANCE
SOMETHING BETTER THAN WAR

'We're Lima Lima Mike Foxtrot in Iraq', says sergeant Frank Cleveland, who's riding shotgun in the track where I've hitched a ride. 'What does that mean?' I ask from the backseat. 'We're lost like a motherfucker', he says.

A conversation near Baghdad in March 2003[1]

Around the time that the Cold War was winding down the major armed forces of the world were growing increasingly fascinated (or appalled—it depended a lot on where you sat) by the idea that information technology was 'lifting the fog of war'. To many, particularly in the West but not only there, the 1991 Gulf War appeared to confirm the possibility that the wars of the future might be won quickly, easily and cheaply with high-technology. It is not that evidence to the contrary of this theory was scant—actually, it was plentiful. Nonetheless, the dream was so powerful and attractive that a lot of practitioners who ought to have known better convinced themselves that friction, chance and sheer human emotion could be wiped away as problems in war by a strategy of gadgets. Funnily enough, among the first to recognise the fallacy for what it was and call attention to it was a French philosopher— traditionally not a quarter from which strong voices in mainstream strategic studies have emerged.

'The Gulf War did not take place', argued Jean Baudrillard in the last of a series of three provocative essays about the Gulf War of 1991. The first, entitled 'The Gulf War will not take place', was written in the lead-up to the war.

The second, 'The Gulf War: Is it really taking place?' was written actually during the sustained air campaign to wear down the Iraqi forces that had invaded and occupied neighbouring Kuwait—the war's *casus belli*. The last came in the aftermath of Operation Desert Storm's Blitzkrieg-like ground campaign that ended with a ceasefire and Iraqi capitulation on 27 February 1991 in a neat 100 hours.[2] The gist of his argument was not that nothing took place in the deserts of Kuwait and Iraq but that what took place was not a war. The disparity in military capability was so great that direct engagements rarely occurred and when they did the outcome was never in doubt. What happened instead was a 'hyperreal' event—a stage managed spectacle serving various political and strategic purposes. 'All those who understand nothing of this', he wrote, 'involuntarily reinforce this halo of bluff that surrounds us'.[3]

It is fair to say that scholars sharply divide over Baudrillard's thesis. On the one hand, there are those such as James Der Derian who find the interpretations of continental theorists highly persuasive and illuminating:

> As the realities of international politics increasingly are generated, mediated, and simulated by new digital means of reproduction; as the globalisation of new media further confuses actual and virtual forms; as there is not so much a distancing from some original, power-emitting, truth-bearing source as there is an implosion; as meaning is set adrift and then disappears into media black holes of insignificance, a little 'po-mo' [postmodernism] can go a long way.[4]

On the other hand, some scholars consider Baudrillard's thesis a worthless rhetorical flourish that makes no meaningful contribution to the study of strategy and military affairs. Daniel Pipes, among the more colourful of its critics, reckoned it to contain 'profound error and transcendent stupidity'.[5] For my part, to the extent that postmodernism represents a turn away from generality and towards specificity, away from universal explanations towards more contextualized ones, then I agree with Der Derian: the study of strategy, war and military theory could do with a modicum of it. The trick is probably to take it in small doses—too much equals befuddlement, but a little can be enlightening.

Precision fetishism

By and large, the strategic studies community has not much welcomed Baudrillard's dyspeptic and combative contribution to their field. And to be fair to them, the essays do take the form of a polemic bordering on diatribe, with assertion after assertion about the state of war offered without a single footnote, in a text littered with red flags and swingeing satire that is obviously designed to rankle:

> Block out the war. Just as Kuwait and Iraq were rebuilt before they were destroyed, so at every phase of this war things unfolded as though they were virtually completed. It is not for lack of brandishing the threat of a chemical war, a bloody war, a world war—everyone had their say—as though it were necessary to give ourselves a fright, to maintain everyone in a state of erection for fear of seeing the flaccid member of war fall down. This futile masturbation was the delight of all the TVs.[6]

The trouble is, though, that with twenty years more distance and several more wars to consider it is apparent that Baudrillard was considerably more right than he was wrong. In the following chapters we will look more closely at the mediatisation of war (its 'virtualisation' to use his term), which was his major theme. For the purposes of this chapter, however, we pick up on a secondary point, which ultimately has emerged to be even more convincing—or at any rate more easily subject to empirical testing:

> It all began with the leitmotif of precision, of surgical, mathematical and punctual efficacy, which is another way of not recognising the enemy as such, just as lobotomy is a way of not recognising madness as such. And then all that technical virtuosity finished up in the most ridiculous uncertainty. The isolation of the enemy by all kinds of electronic interference creates a sort of barricade behind which he becomes invisible.[7]

In a nutshell, Baudrillard measured, dissected and found wanting a view of warfare driven by the idea that information technology was 'transforming' the conduct of warfare. The major armies of the world had not at that time really dared to articulate this view, even to themselves.

The Gulf War did take place; indeed, it was in character a rather conventional war featuring all the normal attributes of such things including formal declarations of start and end to the hostilities. In almost all of its respects, it was not so much the first of the postmodern wars of the information age, which exercised the imagination of Baudrillard and his admirers subsequently; it was, rather, more the apotheosis of the modern wars of the industrial age that was just beginning to wane. Saddam Hussein chose to fight more or less exactly in the way that Western armies had been training, equipping and preparing themselves to fight ever since they discovered the 'modern system', the 'tightly interrelated complex of cover, concealment, dispersion, suppression, small-unit independent manoeuvre, and combined arms at the tactical level, and depth, reserves, and differential concentration at the operational level of war' that had unlocked the attritional stalemate of the First World War seventy years earlier.[8]

Having said that, the Gulf War also hinted at something more—a form of high-tech warfare in which such lopsided outcomes would be a permanent fixture of the emerging 'New World Order'. The popular press and hundreds if not thousands of factual television programmes greeted this development with bounteous relish:

> The world was awed and amazed when the first images shot by precision-guided munitions, or the aircraft that fired them, were broadcast during a post-strike military briefing the morning after the Gulf War began. No newspaper, no magazine article, no Discovery Channel special had given Americans a clue as to how effective surgical strikes using precision-guided missiles and bombs would be. Pictures of missiles striking parked aircraft, racing between buildings to obliterate a military target, or flying through the open window of an Iraqi government building alerted the population of the world to the revolution in warfare brought about by precision-guided munitions. The future had arrived.[9]

Some defence specialists were more wary. John Collins, then the senior specialist on national defence in the Congressional Research Service, and one of the most astute and experienced American strategists, advised that while the war's military conduct was impressive, 'postmortem specialists' attempting to draw lessons learned from the experience ought 'to proceed cautiously, because Desert Shield and Desert Storm unfolded under conditions that may prove to be exceptions rather than rules.'[10]

The pride in the American military's battlefield accomplishments (and relief that a bloody quagmire had been avoided) was palpable. 'By God, we've kicked the Vietnam syndrome once and for all!' noted the president in an apparently euphoric statement at the war's end.[11] At the same time, though, there was an apprehension that all was not well—that victory was somehow incomplete and unsatisfactory.[12]

Somewhat later James Webb, Assistant Secretary of Defense and then briefly Secretary of the Navy under the Reagan Administration, remarked pithily on the validity of the Vietnam comparison, noting that:

> We had one of the best-trained and best-equipped armies in American history in Vietnam. Our technology was just as good as it was in the Persian Gulf War. Not to denigrate what we accomplished against Hussein, but Hussein was no military strategist. If Ho Chi Minh had put sixty per cent of his army in one spot where there were not any trees, we would have blown them away in forty days too.[13]

At the time, however, it was the president who expressed a similar anxiety, recording in his diary on 28 February 1991 that he, in fact, was privately not at all euphoric. Instead, his mood was one of some disappointment:

It has not been a clean end—there is no Battleship Missouri surrender. This is what is missing to make this akin to WWII, to separate Kuwait from Korea and Vietnam.[14]

Notwithstanding these mixed feelings at the top about the strategic utility of force, the American military convinced itself that even if the Gulf War had not been what has since been called a Revolution in Military Affairs (RMA), it clearly pointed the way towards one. It became the key 'shaping event' of American defence policy throughout the 1990s, changing the 'whole course of American military thought'.[15]

Operating on the principle that Desert Storm was the model for future war, the military set about adapting its equipment, operational concepts and doctrines, and overall organisation to digitisation, the better to be able to take advantage of the new possibilities that advances in information and communications technology were presenting.[16]

The Gulf War was undoubtedly a strikingly lopsided combat, which few in military circles before the war had predicted. The lesson of the Iran-Iraq War of the 1980s, it was thought, was that the Iraqi Army was tough, professional, well-led, numerically strong and well-equipped—in contrast with the norm of Arab armies that had generally performed very poorly, particularly against Israel since its 1948 founding.[17] The Iraqi Republican Guard was reckoned to be significantly above par by that measure.[18] It was to be expected, therefore, that it would put up stiff resistance and that defeating it would entail substantial casualties in the assaulting force.[19] This proved not to be the case at all.

As it transpired, over the course of a six-week air campaign first the Iraqi air defence network was wrecked, making the country utterly vulnerable to attack from the air, then the army's command and control system was crippled thus removing its ability to act deliberately in accordance with political will and military logic, and after that ground targets of all sorts (tanks and artillery in revetments, aircraft in shelters, defensive fortifications, logistics nodes, and so on) across Iraq and throughout Kuwait were progressively and relentlessly pummelled by round-the-clock aerial attacks.

Finally, on 24 February 1991 American Marines, fighting dug-in Iraqi units, entered Kuwait via the Saudi Arabian border, while the main coalition force, composed chiefly of American and British mechanised forces, swung round in a 'left hook' from the east into southern Iraq in a massive envelopment operation that would have done Genghis Khan proud. The Iraqi army collapsed almost immediately; thousands of Iraqi troops surrendered, in some cases attempting to do so to overflying aircraft, and many more fled back to

Iraq, hounded by coalition air attacks, ultimately along the luridly named 'Highway of Death' between the Kuwaiti capital and the Iraqi border. The Republican Guard fought back against the onslaught rather more than the regular army did but to no particular avail. In one famous and well-documented engagement in the open desert along a map reference line known as '73 Easting' the US 2nd Armored Cavalry Regiment simply blew through the Iraqi Tawakalna Division in a swift battle that destroyed 113 Iraqi armoured vehicles and caused about 600 casualties. The Americans lost one armoured Bradley Fighting Vehicle and one soldier, killed by Iraqi fire.

Such were the outcomes of ground combat more or less throughout the 100 hours of the ground campaign.[20] The swiftness and apparent ease of the victory was radically different from the American experience in the limited wars of the Cold War, most notably Vietnam but also Korea. Only 293 Americans died in the Gulf War (just half of those, 148, in combat), compared to the 58,000 who had died in Vietnam, while total allied casualties (wounded and killed from all causes) amounted to 1116.[21] The precise total of Iraqi casualties is unknown and a matter of some debate but was many, many times larger. That strikingly imbalanced loss rate was the key thing: fewer than one fatality per 3000 soldiers was less than the Israelis achieved in the 1967 Six Day War (heretofore the benchmark of modern military routs) and less than a twentieth of the loss rate of the German *Wehrmacht* in the 1939 and 1940 invasions of Poland and France respectively (traditionally the touchstones of excellence in manoeuvre warfare).[22] It therefore seemed to signify something potentially very important.

It transpired, however, that the tactical impressiveness of the war's conduct belied a deeper, more ambiguous, more worrisome reality which Baudrillard perceived:

> Electronic war no longer has any political objective strictly speaking: it functions as a preventative electroshock against any future conflict. Just as in modern communication there is no longer any interlocutor, so in this electronic war there is no longer any enemy, there is only a refractory element which must be neutralized and consensualised. This is what the Americans seek to do, these missionary people bearing electroshocks which will shepherd everybody towards democracy.[23]

The mindset of the American military at that time, though, could hardly have been more different. A passage in the memoirs of General Tommy Franks, who as US Central Command (CENTCOM) commander would go on to lead the post-9/11 invasions of Afghanistan and Iraq, is illustrative of the mindset of the time. Then a brigadier, in 1992 Franks was appointed by

Army Chief of Staff General George Sullivan to be the director of a 'futures laboratory' based in the headquarters of the army's Training and Doctrine Command in Fort Leavenworth, Kansas, which was tasked with developing the underpinning concepts of a digitised army dubbed Force XXI. Franks described the prevailing assumption:

> Future operational doctrine would no longer be three-dimensional, with victory going to the side that marshalled the largest fighting force with the greatest number of tanks, ships, and aircraft. Now there would be a fourth dimension: time. In the twenty-first century, operational success—what the military calls 'effect'—would be found in both space and time: putting the most effective force, at the right place, at the right time. In this new way of thinking, the historical strategic imperatives of objective, mass, and economy of force would acquire new meaning. Suddenly, the time worn banner 'Revolution in Military Affairs,' trotted out by strategic thinkers every few years to trumpet some small advance, was no longer mere hyperbole. It would become the new reality of war.[24]

Unfortunately, that 'new reality of war' that the American defence establishment hared after with all the considerable energy of which it was capable, dragging along in its wake most of its major allies, proved mostly illusory.[25] The story of the realisation of the chimerical qualities of this form of war is not pleasant but is instructive in the telling. Equally vital, however, is the partial extent to which tactically—as a means of generating combat power—the vision came true. Not all such talk of being able to do more with less was moonshine.

The bounty of data, beauteous and baffling

Proponents of the 'new reality' of war and the derivative operational concepts that flowed directly or indirectly from it often dichotomise Sun Tzu and Clausewitz—consciously or unconsciously—and tend to favour the former. One of the most memorable maxims of the former emphasises clarity of vision and presents its achievement as the ideal of military practice: 'Know the enemy and know yourself, then in a hundred battles you will never be in peril.'[26] It is indubitably wise advice. As noted above, much attention after the Gulf War was focused upon the remarkable precision of some of the weaponry applied by the coalition against Iraqi targets. Gun-camera footage of missiles and bombs zeroing in with deadly accuracy on individual tanks, bunker ventilation shafts, the windows of specific government offices, and the like, were visually highly impressive.

A main contribution of information technology to the success of the campaign, however, was rather more prosaic and un-telegenic. To appreciate this, however, one needs first to appreciate something of the peculiar nature of desert warfare. A German general, captured by the British during the North African campaign of the Second World War, once memorably described war in the desert as a 'tactician's paradise and the quartermaster's nightmare'.[27] Tactically, the key advantages of the terrain are the lack of cover and the consequent difficulty of concealment—which favours the side with the most effective long-range weapons and detection systems—and the lack of major physical obstacles to advance through—which benefits a highly mechanised force designed for fast moving operations. Equally attractively for American forces, the desert, being mostly devoid of population, allows combat operations to take place with relatively little distraction from civilians embroiled in the fighting.

Logistically, though, the picture is quite different. The arid climate is extremely hard on men, who require huge external sustainment efforts to maintain their health and fighting order, while equipment requires constant maintenance efforts that go well beyond the routine in order to keep up with the accelerated wear and tear caused by ubiquitous grit. Even more challengingly, as with war on sea, the featurelessness of the desert makes it difficult to know one's own position with exactitude, making it extremely hard for an army to perform coordinated manoeuvres.

The specialist skill of the British Army's famed Long Range Desert Group and Special Air Service in North Africa during the Second World War was not really its fighting power, which, being based on little more than the light weapons (machine guns and mortars) that could be carried by a patrol of a handful of jeeps and light trucks, was small. Rather it was its ability to go into the trackless Libyan-Egyptian desert, survive there over long periods, and emerge from it more or less where it intended to after journeys of many hundreds of miles to attack Italian and German supply lines and rear installations as a bolt 'out of the blue', as it were.

When the Gulf War started, the NAVSTAR Global Positioning System (GPS), which allows the electronic pinpointing of one's position to within a few metres, was a new and not widely known technology, and was only partially implemented with sixteen of twenty-four satellites deployed. Moreover, there were relatively few GPS receivers available (ultimately, 4490 commercial and 842 military hand units were supplied). This was enough, however, to transform a large general-purpose force into a specialist desert manoeuvre force essentially overnight, at least in so far as its ability to navigate relatively accurately was concerned.

The results were highly gratifying—it is doubtful that the 'left hook' envelopment could have been conducted without this navigation aid, which allowed the rapid and reliably accurate prepositioning of vital logistics bases along the army's desert march routes. Captured Iraqi officers explained that one reason they were so effectively dislocated was that, knowing all too well how difficult it was for a regular army to navigate in the desert, they had not anticipated or prepared for attacks from that direction until coalition forces started appearing in their rear areas moving fast and smashing up their logistic bases and defensive fortifications. Post-war analyses also highlighted numerous unintended benefits of the system:

> Although not specifically designed to prevent fire from friendly forces, high technology navigational systems, such as the Global Positioning System (GPS), helped reduce the risks of inadvertently firing on friendly ground forces. The small, lightweight GPS receiver provided units with exact coordinates and locations on the ground. This information, together with knowledge of the coordinates and locations of adjacent units, helped control manoeuvre forces. In addition, GPS was instrumental in navigating across long distances and helped ensure that units advanced and manoeuvred to designated checkpoints on time, and successfully converged on objectives without mingling with other manoeuvre forces.[28]

In relatively short order after the war commanders such as Franks, who was involved in the adaptation of what was then a civilian GPS-based technology for tracking commercial deliveries into a military system called 'Blue Force Tracker', began to build upon these capabilities and to dream of achieving in warfare 'the kind of Olympian perspective that Homer had given his gods.'[29]

Hyperbole aside, this is a potentially achievable goal with respect to knowledge of oneself and enormously beneficial to operations. Where things got sticky was when soldiers began to wonder how much better it might be if that knowledge of oneself could be coupled with equally or nearly as precise knowledge of the enemy's position and movements and, furthermore, have that knowledge shared amongst all allied units in real time. To be fair, there was clearly some attempt to curb such enthusiasm in the literature on information age warfare that began to proliferate:

> Recent advances in technology offer an opportunity to reduce fog and friction. However, despite all of the advances that have and likely will be made significant residual fog and friction will persist. The nature of this residual uncertainty is, as yet, unclear and its implications are not fully understood. Nevertheless, there is an historic opportunity to reconsider how best to deal with the fog and friction that

will persist, and this is likely to have profound implications for military operations and organisations.[30]

Nonetheless, descriptors such as 'residual' and 'profound' certainly imply a rather sharp diminishment of the scale and significance of chance in warfare. Admiral Bill Owens put the case for the revolution most emphatically:

> the computer revolution, if correctly applied, presents us with a unique opportunity to transform the US military into a lethal, effective, and efficient armed force that will serve the United States in the twenty first century. This is the American Revolution in Military Affairs. This new revolution challenges the hoary dictums about the fog and friction of war, and all the tactics, operational concepts, and doctrine pertaining to them.[31]

The vision was a highly attractive one—not least to policy-makers as it was predicated explicitly on the principle of cost efficiency. In Owens' view, the United States was an 'exhausted superpower' that was fatally overstretched by its extensive global commitments. This was not a new opinion—the historian Paul Kennedy, somewhat prematurely, had called the mismatch of its wealth and military spending America's 'grand strategical dilemma' even before the Cold War's end—but it was a resonant one that fitted well with the desire of governments to obtain a post-Cold War peace dividend.[32]

The RMA was supposed to make wars not just easier but also the burden of Western military pre-eminence less onerous. Since Kennedy's thesis was that economic overstretch caused the downfall of previous great powers, this was obviously a boon. The collapse of the Soviet Union served as an object example of the consequences of failure. The overwhelming preoccupation, however, was not with economy but with speed—especially the speed of decision-making. In this respect, there was a high degree of concordance between military thinking and political thinking, which, as we saw in the previous chapter, had also become obsessed with this quality.

Chance!

Overall, the tendency of the early RMA literature was to stress the potential of information technology to bring an almost mathematical 'near perfect clarity and accuracy' to military decision-making.[33] Thus it ran counter to what surely is one of the most vital of all Clausewitz's dicta—that 'mathematical factors' never find a firm basis in military calculation:

> War is the realm of chance. No other human activity gives it greater scope: no other has such incessant and varied dealings with this intruder. Chance makes everything more uncertain and interferes with the whole course of events.[34]

In war, knowledge of the situation is always imperfect. 'The only situation a commander can know fully is his own; his opponent's he can know only from unreliable intelligence.'[35] If the RMA enthusiasts were right, then Clausewitz had to be wrong.

The other 'revolution in military affairs'

As it happens, the United States was not the first country to latch on to the idea that information technology was revolutionising the conduct of warfare. Ironically, although it was the West that had the vibrant microelectronics, computing and communications industries upon which the revolution depended, it was in the Soviet Union (in the late 1970s and early 1980s) that the theorisation of a potential discontinuity in military affairs caused by these technologies first occurred. At that time, analysts in the Soviet General Staff were beginning to regard with alarm NATO's development of a new operational concept for the defence of Western Europe called 'Follow-On Forces Attack' (FOFA).

The basic problem for NATO (North Atlantic Treaty Organisation) then was its underdeveloped conventional strength relative to that of the much more numerous Warsaw Pact forces, which meant, as General Bernard Rogers (then Supreme Allied Commander Europe) wrote in a *NATO Review* article, '...if war broke out today, it would only be a matter of days before I would have to turn to our political authorities and request the initial release of nuclear weapons.'[36] The assumption of Western military leaders was that while they might be able to withstand an initial attack across the inter-German border by Warsaw Pact conventional forces, they would fairly soon be overwhelmed by successive reinforcing (that is, 'Follow-On') echelons exploiting weaknesses in their badly battered defensive line. The goal of FOFA was simply to forestall the necessity of escalating to nuclear weapons by attacking 'with conventional weapons those enemy forces which stretch from just behind the troops in contact to as far into the enemy's rear as our target acquisition and conventional weapons systems will permit' in order to 'reduce to a manageable proportion the number of Warsaw Pact forces arriving at our General Defensive Position.'[37]

It was not just that this seemed a credible threat to Soviet strategy, which was based on being able to bring to bear its considerable reserve material superiority over NATO's forces; it was also that the USSR, with its underdeveloped and unimaginative consumer electronics industry, was poorly placed to match the new Western military capabilities.[38] No one perceived this more clearly or more anxiously than the experts of the Soviet General Staff.

Such thinking was slower to catch on in the West, possibly because it lacked the Soviet Union's emphasis on military science (as in the scientific study of the principles of war, not just the science of weapons systems). In Britain, a few figures, notably Brigadier Richard Simpkin, speculated boldly on the future of war. The dominant theme in his thinking, as one would guess from the title of his mid-1980s book *Race to the Swift*, was speed. Though his thoughts were dominated by the scenario of a massive all-arms superpower confrontation on the North German Plain in which NATO forces would be on the defensive, Simpkin's vision of the future battlefield was highly imaginative and presaged some of the arguments of later theorists. It would be covered, he thought, by a 'universal net' able to call down an 'instant anvil of fire' wherever required, facing an attacker at every step 'with a threat he cannot identify because it does not concentrate or move. In Sun Tzu's phraseology it is "shapeless."'[39]

Firepower, however, as he acknowledged, was not the vital thing. More fundamentally:

all this is really about not firepower but information. For it is really the acquisition, processing, and dissemination of information that lies at the root of speed and accuracy with which fire can now be applied.[40]

Perhaps, however, Simpkin's keenest observation came with his realisation that the greatest impact of connectivity (which he referred to simply with the word 'electronics') on warfare would come from a 'field wholly devoid of direct physical effect—the media.'[41] After playing with this conclusion for a page and a half, however, he concluded that the implications were beyond him except to say that:

My instinct is that the management of a body politic accustomed to being saturated with information poses a problem in the political conduct of war just as difficult and just as important as the exercise of command on the military side.[42]

It was an astutely prescient observation, but was also characteristic of a tendency in the literature on future war of edging up to the really vexing problems of war's informationalisation only to then back away in order to concentrate on subsidiary, albeit valid, questions of command and control and the application of firepower.[43]

In the American Defense Department, specifically in the Office of Net Assessment (ONA) headed by Andrew Marshall, it was rather towards the end of the Cold War that people began to speculate on the larger implications of technological change, especially information technology, and slowly to introduce these ideas into doctrine and planning. Initially through reading Soviet military analyses of what they called a 'Military-Technical Revolution', and later as a robustly independent concept, the Americans developed the notion of the aforementioned 'Revolution in Military Affairs'. Interestingly, a main reason for the name change was the thought that the Soviet concept was too narrowly technical in orientation.

No doubt aware of how thoroughly dominated by technological optimism American strategic culture was at the time, and to some extent still is, the ONA's definition of the RMA stressed the importance of doctrinal development and organisational adaptation over technological innovation *per se*.[44] Therefore, in their view, an RMA was:

> what occurs when the application of new technologies into a significant number of military systems combines with innovative operational concepts and organisational adaptation in a way that fundamentally alters the character and conduct of conflict... by producing a dramatic increase—often an order of magnitude or greater—in the combat potential and military effectiveness of armed forces.[45]

In practice, however, the problem proved to be that once the RMA as an abstract concept became 'general property', as Colin Gray put it, within the culturally highly technophile American defence establishment (as opposed to the rather more intellectually multifaceted ONA), it was invoked in support of grand hopes of a 'new golden age of enhanced effectiveness' resting upon a deceptively narrow ledge of technological superiority.[46] Again, Owens introduced one of the key ideas:

> the 'system of systems' at the heart of the Revolution in Military Affairs promises a new capacity for the US commander—knowing the results of his military operations almost immediately, which is central to building a military that can adapt to a highly complex situation faster and better than an opponent can. With this information the US forces can operate within an opponent's decision and action cycles—outthinking and outmanoeuvring the enemy commander. If we are able to make the right choices faster than an opponent can and we can move more agilely, we will be able to win in any kind of military confrontation.[47]

In hindsight, this would turn out to be one of the more egregiously hubristic statements of military futurism in recent memory. In actuality, the blind faith in military technology that it evinced would prove to be the most self-defeating habit of mind since the cult of the offensive wrong-footed the generals of the First World War.

The messy wars of the 1990s, from Somalia to Yugoslavia, might have dented confidence in the likelihood of the uniquely advantageous conditions of the 1991 Gulf War reappearing. They might also have suggested how difficult it would prove for Western forces to play the role of the more agile fighter in contests with vastly less encumbered opponents than themselves in years to come. Perhaps more importantly, they might have demonstrated the near impossibility of operating within the decision-cycle of any opponent without a high degree of political clarity about the purpose of the use of force in the first place—more or less precisely the issue that Baudrillard pointed out and Simpkin had also raised and then dodged.

The British general, Sir Rupert Smith, who commanded the United Nations Protection Force (UNPROFOR) in Yugoslavia at a crucial stage in the Bosnian conflict, raised just this point with sobering clarity and directness:

> The starting point to understanding all operations in the Balkans in the 1990s, including the NATO bombings of 1995 and 1999, was that they were without strategies. At best, events were coordinated at theatre level, but on the whole, especially with regard to the international interventions they were reflexive... [O]n the whole the forces deployed and employed, whether UN or NATO, were used in response to events on the ground rather than with a view to attaining a strategic objective.[48]

Generally, though, this lesson was not learned. In 1992–93 the United States essentially stumbled into war when Operation Restore Hope, under the rubric of the first United Nations Operations in Somalia (UNOSOM I) mission, which was intended to provide security for humanitarian operations, expanded into UNOSOM II, which aimed at the forcible disarmament of Somali militias. Blinded by their beliefs about how wars ought to be fought and 'flawed thinking about peacekeeping', the American-led manhunt for the biggest of the warlords, Mohammed Farah Aideed, leader of the Somali National Alliance, culminated on 3 October 1993 in a vicious battle in the streets of Mogadishu in which two American helicopters were shot down, eighteen American soldiers were killed, seventy-eight wounded, and one pilot was captured.[49]

The 'Black Hawk Down' incident illustrated a number of significant things. For one, it demonstrated the self-defeating potential of strategic rudderlessness and cultural ignorance combined with awesome military power. Without intention, or indeed realisation, the American Army Rangers who suffered the greatest losses on the day had seemingly acquired a sort of infamy with the regular residents of Mogadishu. Mark Bowden recounted the feelings of one

Somali man in his minute-by-minute story of the incident (later made into a popular film):

> These soldiers, Ali knew, were different from the ones who had come to feed Somalis. These were Rangers. They were cruel men who wore body armour and strapped their weapons to their chests and when they came at night they painted their faces to look fierce.[50]

In itself, the cultivation of a reputation for martial expertise and ferocity is hardly a bad thing for a military unit—in fact, it is a good thing, even in a peacekeeping role in a scenario not intended as an active theatre of war, provided that it is paired with a sense of purposeful discretion. The motto of the First Marine Division, 'No better friend, no worse enemy', used by General James Mattis in a message to his troops before the invasion of Iraq in 2003 is a good example of this ideal.[51]

The trouble was that rather than cowing Somali militiamen and dissuading them from violence, the Rangers' reputation was a spur to action. It made more people want to fight them than might have wanted to otherwise:

> Now, as the armada of American helicopters roared overhead he was reminded of the shock, pain, and terror. The sight filled him and his friends with rage. It was one thing for the world to intervene to feed the starving, and even for the UN to help Somalia form a peaceful government. But this business of sending Rangers swooping down into their city killing and kidnapping their leaders, this was too much.[52]

Even worse, this aggressiveness was combined with an underestimation of the enemy's ingenuity and adaptability. Blackhawk helicopters flew with seeming impunity over Mogadishu because it was reckoned that the Somalis, lacking an effective weapon against attack from the air, notably a shoulder-fired surface-to-air missile such as the American Stinger, which had famously bedeviled Soviet air operations against the Afghan mujahedeen, could not touch them. There were plenty of rocket-propelled grenades (RPGs) available; but RPGs, it was thought, could not usefully be directed at targets above. Not only were they unguided and short-range weapons, the act of firing one vertically would injure or kill the shooter whose legs would be exposed to the weapon's powerful backblast.

The Somalis, however, with the advice, it is said, of Islamist fighters from other Muslim countries, came up with effective methods of shooting from the ground:

> They dug deep holes in the dirt streets. The shooter would lie prone with the back of the tube pointed down into the hole. Sometimes he would cut down a small tree

and lean it into the hole, then cover himself with a green robe so he could be under the tree waiting for one to fly over.[53]

As it was, the main lesson taken by the Americans was different from those set out above: it was the point, admittedly pertinent, that Mogadishu revealed that the coordination of air and ground assets was still a long way from the aspired-to common real-time situational awareness. The ground convoy of the 10th Mountain Division infantry sent in to extract the Rangers from the city suffered heavier casualties than it might have if communications lags between aircraft observing the events in small detail from above and the Humvee drivers in the alleys below had been smaller. Overhead observers could have steered the convoy out of the ambush zone instead of, inadvertently, steering the soldiers back into it.

Bowden described the experience of an air force combat controller who had ridden with the 'lost convoy':

> Schilling felt disbelief and some guilt. He had steered the convoy the wrong way for at least part of this calamity. Stunned by the confusion, he struggled to convince himself this was all really happening. Over and over he muttered, 'We're going to keep driving around until we are all fucking dead.'[54]

Tactically, perhaps the fog of war had been lifted, in some senses, but the enemy, it seemed, just moved into the places where it was as thick as ever. As one American general put it, 'To be quite honest, we are groping in the fog between traditional peacekeeping and peace enforcement.'[55]

Similar lessons were apparent in the bitter civil wars that followed the dissolution of Yugoslavia. Again, Rupert Smith's observations were incisive:

> In sum, the trend of our recent military operations is that the more the operation is intended to win the will of the people, the more the opponent adopts the method of the guerrilla and the more complex the circumstances, the longer it will take to reach the condition in which a strategic decision can be made and a solution found. And while it is being found the condition has to be maintained, and since in part at least it has been arrived at by force it must be maintained by force for want of the strategic decision.[56]

The problem that Smith illustrated so well is that the theatre commander in such conflicts finds himself in the crux of the scissors. Tactically, opponents quickly learn how to drop below the threshold of the regular force's weapons systems while strategically it is impossible for the commander to make progress if political forces persistently fail to set goals directly related to the confrontation in question.[57]

Smith was not alone: other commanders confronted with the reality of 'waging modern war' recognised its increasingly typical strategic ambiguity.

In the words of the American general Wesley Clark, who commanded NATO forces during the Kosovo War in 1999, launched in order to forestall the ethnic cleansing of predominantly ethnically Albanian Kosovo by the Serbian forces of rump-Yugoslavia ruled by Slobodan Milosevic:

> Though NATO had succeeded in its first armed conflict, it didn't feel like a victory. There were no parades except by the joyful Albanians returning to Kosovo. The military and the diplomats within NATO were simply relieved that the operation was concluded, and they were absorbed in the next mission, working on the ground inside Kosovo.[58]

Moreover, these were by no means specifically American or British problems, nor even problems of the West generally. Russia's first intervention into its breakaway Caucasian province Chechnya featured in late December 1994 and early January 1995 an ambush on regular troops by Chechen irregulars in the capital Grozny that dwarfed the Rangers' debacle in Mogadishu in scale, ferocity and degree of calamity. Most of the mechanised rifle brigade—with tanks and armoured personnel carriers—that had been sent in to occupy the capital's central square and major public buildings as a show of force to quell the rebellion was effectively cut off while deployed in an extended column and very nearly totally wiped out. Estimates of casualties suffered in the battle by the Russian force vary somewhat but there were probably not less than 1000 dead and 3000 wounded, in addition to dozens of tanks and more than 100 armoured personnel carriers destroyed.[59] It is true that the Russian army in 1994 was in a shambolic state of extreme debasement—badly led, ill-equipped, underpaid (or not paid at all) and composed largely of undisciplined and undertrained conscripts.[60] Moreover, the Chechens, by contrast, were highly motivated and, though lightly armed, tactically very astute and boldly led.[61]

But the root cause of the debacle was the same deeper and more complex mixture of tactical hubris and strategic vacuity that had hurt the US in Mogadishu. In late November 1994, the Russian Minister of Defence Pavel Grachev, abjuring responsibility for a much smaller but similarly disastrous previous intervention by covert Russian troops, argued that 'If the army had fought, we would have needed one parachute regiment to decide the whole affair in two hours.'[62]

The over-promoted and corrupt Grachev had no idea what he was talking about. This was perhaps not surprising: he owed his position to his personal loyalty to President Boris Yeltsin rather than to his military accomplishments.[63] And as for strategic vacuity: the key failing was political—it was hoped by Yeltsin's political advisors that a 'small, victorious war' in Chechnya would go down well with the electorate in the 1996 presidential elections, allowing the president to position himself as a tough ruler amidst a field of bellicose and nationalistic challengers.[64]

4

OVERESTIMATE YOURSELF, UNDERESTIMATE YOUR ENEMY, NEVER KNOW VICTORY

Technology is so much fun but we can drown in our technology. The fog of information can drive out knowledge.

Daniel J. Boorstin (1914–2004), Director of the Smithsonian Institution's National Museum of History and Technology

In the 1990s and into the early 2000s the principle 'knowledge is power' was firmly impressed on the consciousness of military leaders and their political masters alike. It is a reasonable supposition but it came to be understood narrowly, as primarily a matter of efficiently mechanically aligning weapons with targets. Then, on this rather limited concept was anchored a much more ambitious strategic hope that the fundamentally chaotic nature of war could be largely if not completely compensated for by technology. In truth, this was not an idea confined only to military strategic circles: economists and business leaders were to be found declaring such things as the 'end of boom and bust' and the era of 'great moderation'. At first, the swift campaigns in Afghanistan and Iraq seemed to confirm the theory. The curious thing about it, though, was how blind it was to the idea of the enemy as a living, thinking opponent rather than merely a target to be serviced by long-range weapons—an enemy, that is, who would not mutely comply with demands when presented with furious manoeuvres, no matter how swiftly they were performed.

In Chechnya in 1994–96, the Russians badly underestimated their enemy, overestimated their own abilities, and had no clear idea of why they were fighting in the first place. Nobody understood this better than the

Chechens, one of whom, armed with just an assault rifle, anti-tank grenades, and a martyr's conviction, declared on the eve of the Grozny battle:

> It's better for us in the dark and in the city. Here, they're our guests and we're the hosts. They have come in, but they won't leave. They're not fighting for anything, but we're fighting for our homeland—we're not afraid to die. They have planes and tanks and all we've got is Allah and the RPG. But we know what we're fighting for.[1]

This was a vital ingredient of their success. As bad as December 1994 and January 1995 were for the Russian Army, things actually got worse. In August 1996 the Chechens accomplished a historical rarity for an irregular force—recapturing their capital city from a superior Russian force of dug-in regular troops.[2]

Much better led, trained and equipped armies were also caught out by the irregular challenger, though none nearly as comprehensively as the Russian military. Describing Israel's operation in the 'Lebanese morass' at the end of the 1990s, Martin Van Creveld captured the tepid indecisiveness that was becoming a general phenomenon of modern wars:

> [I]n Lebanon the IDF is facing an opponent who, although numerically weak and falling well short of a regular army, consists of uniformed troops rather than unarmed civilians—many of them women and children, as was usually the case in the Occupied Territories. Therefore, if fighting them is scarcely glorious, at any rate it is not demeaning, and morale, though not great, has not declined to the point where it constitutes an insuperable problem. Judging by its own past performance as well as that of other armies, the IDF will almost certainly be unable to win. Then again barring a crisis of confidence inside Israel there is no reason why it should lose.[3]

He turned out to be quite correct about the conditions of Israeli withdrawal. Between 1995 and 1999, 120 Israeli soldiers were killed by Hezbollah attacks in Israel's 'security zone' in Southern Lebanon, which did not generate much security. There was a crisis of confidence in Israel as a result, which is why Ehud Barak's 1999 campaign promise to unilaterally withdraw from Lebanon within a year helped him to win the elections and become Prime Minister.[4]

In search of proper war

The thing was, though, that it was possible then to interpret these conflicts differently. One possibility was to re-categorise them as Military Operations Other Than War (MOOTW) or, more candidly, 'operations that are not meant primarily to kill people and break things—unless they have to.'[5] In which case, while not 'out of sight out of mind' *per se*, whatever lessons might have been derived from them were a priori of second order significance in comparison to real war.

It was a Canadian officer (ironically, since the Canadian Forces had self-identified for decades with peacekeeping operations), the departing commander of a UN contingent in Cyprus, who supplied the killer quotation illustrating such thinking. Asked by his commander, a British brigadier, how he had found the peacekeeping role, he replied, 'All right, but it will be good to get back to *proper soldiering*.'[6]

To be fair, though, the views of the various military services and their leaders are not so easy to caricature. General Sullivan, who, as noted in Chapter Three, was enthusiastic about the potential of the RMA, was also wary of the misleading oversimplification of MOOTW:

> As useful, convenient, and important as these categories are, however, their simplicity can be seductive. Categorizing 'war' as separate from all other uses of military force may mislead the strategist, causing him to believe that the conditions required for success in the employment of military force when one is conducting 'war' differ from use of military force in operations 'other than war'.[7]

It became clear, however, that Sullivan was largely speaking in this respect to his own service—the army.[8]

The other services, particularly the air force, focused on aspects of these wars that were more congenial to the RMA theory. For example, the American Air Force officer John Warden wrote in his retrospective on the meaning of the Gulf War for war in the twenty-first century that a 'new kind of war had its birth in Mesopotamia', a 'hyperwar' in which air power had become dominant.[9] The 1999 Kosovo War was particularly useful to this line of argument because Serbia was ultimately forced to capitulate and to withdraw its forces from Kosovo as a result of an aerial bombing campaign that involved no use of ground troops by NATO at all. Indeed, even the bombing aircraft stayed above an altitude of 10,000 feet, beyond the range of the most common air defence systems.

Wars, it seemed, could successfully be prosecuted from a safe distance, at least on the part of one belligerent. Lieutenant General Michael Short, who ran the bombing campaign, boldly pointed out the route which 'victory' had followed: 'NATO got every one of the terms it had stipulated in Rambouillet and beyond Rambouillet, and I credit this as a victory for air power'. Meanwhile, historians such as John Keegan, who probably ought to have been more cautious, agreed:

I didn't want to change my beliefs, but there was too much evidence accumulating to stick to the article of faith. It now does look as if air power has prevailed in the Balkans, and that the time has come to redefine how victory in war may be won.[10]

By no means was everyone so convinced. On the fringes of the American defence establishment some argued that developments in information technology portended a future quite different from one in which opponents could be disarmed and bent to one's will safely from above the clouds.[11]

The idea of 'fourth generation warfare' enjoyed a measure of popularity in the United States Marine Corps.[12] It was initially associated with William Lind, a military analyst who was an influential figure in the 1980s-era adoption by the US of 'manoeuvre warfare' concepts, and was later championed by Marine Colonel Thomas X. Hammes. The theory was not regarded highly by historians who disagreed with its generational characterisation of warfare's development through the ages, from the line-and-column tactics epitomised by the Napoleonic wars, through industrialisation seen first in the American Civil War, followed by combined arms developed towards the end of the First World War, and then on to today's *ad hoc* warriors combining regular and irregular characteristics.[13] Critics rightly pointed out that the first three nominal generations would be more accurately described as tendencies in thinking about regular battle, while the 'fourth generation' is really a tactic of avoiding symmetric regular engagements that has been part of the art of war since time immemorial.

Notwithstanding these flaws, the historical conception of fourth generation warfare was at least preferable to that of the RMA. Moreover, some of the ideas it expressed even before the Cold War's end about the direction of future warfare have been quite accurate. In particular, the proposition that actors with a 'non-national or transnational base', using terrorism, high technology and 'sophisticated psychological warfare, especially through manipulation of the media', to attack their enemy's 'culture' from within and without would constitute a major future threat, from the perspective of nearly a quarter century later is actually pretty close to the mark, as we shall see.[14]

In fact, the Marine Corps—admittedly the smallest of all American military services—was considerably more switched on than others in the 1990s to the perils of asymmetry, the drawbacks of technology, and the unhappy possibility that what happened to the Russian Army in Chechnya was not a *sui generis* oddity but probably a harbinger of a more general pattern.[15] As Marine Commandant Charles Krulak explained, the coming challenge to Western armies was to learn how to fight what he called the 'three block war'—a blend of humanitarian assistance, peacekeeping and high-intensity combats all happening at once in close proximity to each other. Enemies would choose to fight this way, he said:

> Because they've watched CNN... They've seen the might of our technology. They're not going to fight us straight up. We're not going to see the son of Desert Storm anymore. You're going to see the stepchild of Chechnya. You're seeing it right now. It's called Kosovo. Our enemies will attack us asymmetrically. They will take us where we're weak, and they will negate our strengths, which is our technology, and so the best way to do that is to get you into close terrain—towns, cities, urban slums, forests, jungles.[16]

The 'three-block war' concept was evocative of the sort of confused tactical situations that were growing more typical: military operations against opponents who operated deliberately amongst the people in urban settings. As such, it served well also as a reminder that cities are likely to be the dominant setting of warfare for the foreseeable future.

In 1900 about a tenth of the world's population of 1.8 billion people lived in cities. Today about half of a total population of seven billion do; by 2050 it is expected that three quarters of a population estimated to be near ten billion will be city dwellers, and most of those in the new megacities of Asia, Africa and Latin America.[17] Nonetheless, three-block warfare fell short as prescriptive guidance—either tactical or strategic. Soldiers cannot be humanitarians and warfighters at the same time, and if they should try then a thinking opponent will elect simply to attack them while they are in a peaceful posture and run away from them when they are in a warlike one.[18] 'The enemy gets a vote', as is often said; and there is no reason to expect that they will elect to fight in the block chosen for them in the manner desired—quite the opposite, obviously.

In any event, this was not the direction of travel for defence policy on the whole, which was rather more impressed by the power of information networks to dramatically change the art of war to the advantage of the high-tech fighter. The basic idea at the root of such thinking is perhaps best conveyed by the aphorism variously attributed to Sir Francis Bacon and Thomas Hobbes: *scientia potentia est*—knowledge is power. In the mid-1990s the Harvard scholar Joseph Nye teamed up with Admiral Owens to write an article on 'America's Information Edge', which opened with the words 'Knowledge, more than ever before, is power.'[19] The logic in military terms has been touched upon. What Nye added to the mix was the thought that the 'information edge' was equally important as a 'force multiplier of American diplomacy, including "soft power"', by which he meant the attraction of people globally to American culture, democracy and free markets.[20]

The United States can use its information resources to engage China, Russia, and other powerful states in security dialogues to prevent them from becoming hostile. At the same time, its information edge can help prevent states like Iran and Iraq, already hostile, from becoming powerful.[21]

This addition of a 'non-kinetic' (that is, not involving physical force) psychological dimension to information age conflict was potentially useful but remained largely underdeveloped in the RMA literature.

This is not to say that 'soft power' did not also enjoy a high degree of success as a concept subsequently; it was, rather, that 'soft power' thinking and RMA thinking did not intersect again until well after the response to the 9/11 attacks put the phrase 'war of ideas' on the lips of world leaders. In the preface to his 2004 book on the subject, Nye provided a telling anecdote about Donald Rumsfeld, a champion of RMA-inspired 'transformation', which illustrates the conceptual parting of ways:

> I spoke about soft power to a conference co-sponsored by the US Army in Washington. One of the other speakers was Secretary of Defense Donald Rumsfeld. According to a press account, 'The top military brass listened sympathetically' to my views, but when someone in the audience later asked Rumsfeld for his opinion on soft power, he replied 'I don't know what it means.'[22]

For intellectual inspiration the revolutionaries were much more prone to drawing on the work of futurists and business management gurus.

Most influential were the futurists Alvin and Heidi Toffler, who very successfully popularised a variant of the knowledge-is-power theory. In their view, the way in which 'civilisations' or societal 'waves' make wealth determines the way in which they make war. Thus, 'first wave' agrarian civilisations fought agrarian wars—muscle-powered affairs fought largely by part-timers in accordance with the cycle of planting and harvesting. 'Second wave' industrial civilisations fought wars of mass—huge tests of the total mobilisation capacity of countries in terms of both men and machines. And in 'third wave' high-tech civilisations:

> a revolution is occurring that places knowledge, in various forms, at the core of military power. In both production and destruction knowledge reduces the requirement for inputs.[23]

These were not new ideas; rather they were a synthesis of a few by then reasonably well-established information age tropes such as 'de-massification', the increasing detachment of physical labour from industry, and above all the acceleration of change noted in Chapter One. This synthesis was then bolted on to a vaguely Marxist 'dominant mode of production' theory of history and applied to warfare.[24]

But the Tofflers' presentation of these ideas was engaging and easily digested, and gained much attention as a result. The RAND (Research And Development Corporation) analysts John Arquilla and David Ronfeldt came to broadly similar conclusions in the seminal article 'Cyberwar is Coming!' in which they described dramatically the advantages accruing in war to the possessor of better knowledge:

> For your [knowledge rich] forces, warfare is no longer primarily a function of who puts the most capital, labour and technology on the battlefield, but of who has the best information about the battlefield. What distinguishes the victors is their grasp of information—not only from the mundane standpoint of knowing how to find the enemy while keeping it in the dark, but also in organisational and doctrinal terms. The analogy is rather like a chess game where you see the entire board, but your opponent sees only its own pieces—you can win even if he is allowed to start with additional powerful pieces.[25]

However, being more astute observers of the development of the art of war, Arquilla and Ronfeldt dispensed with the one-dimensional concept of 'generational' developments of tactics, acknowledging that efforts to harness the power of information are found throughout military history and pointing out that amongst the best examples of their conception of 'cyberwar' was that of the twelfth- and thirteenth-century Mongols who were consummately successful conquerors.[26]

They also made, before Nye and Owens, a vital distinction between 'cyberwar', which (contrary to contemporary usage) they describe as information-enabled combined arms warfare at the 'military level'; and what they call 'netwars', which are societal-level ideational conflicts waged in part through 'internetted modes of communication'.[27] However, like Nye's soft power theory, 'netwar' proved considerably less engaging than 'cyberwar'.

Clearly, the latter presented intriguing and plausibly logically answerable questions. For instance, as one thoughtful study of information age 'principles of war' asked, 'what happens when technology allows the commanders and staff to transcend estimates and replace them with truth?'[28] Dwelling briefly on the various attempts of senior military officers, doctrine writers and defence analysts to develop these ideas into concrete policies and organisational changes serves to elucidate a few important themes.

As in business, so too in war?

Among the first of these attempts was the aforementioned 'system of systems' concept, which ultimately was articulated in American military thinking under the rubric of 'Dominant Battlespace Knowledge' (DBK). This consisted of three main elements:

I. Intelligence, surveillance and reconnaissance technologies underpinning a 'real-time' all-weather awareness in and above a wide geographical area.

II. Command, control, communications and computing technologies with which 'we translate the awareness of what is occurring ... into an *understanding* of what is taking place there, and communicate that understanding, surely, and accurately—in usable form—to combat forces'.

III. Precision force: 'the area in which the knowledge generated from the overlap of the first two areas leads to action'.[29]

DBK built upon pre-existing claims about information age warfare but it also explicitly and extensively took inspiration from voguish ideas in business and finance. For the most part, the 1990s (and much of the 2000s) was a time of great economic optimism. Gordon Brown, Britain's chancellor for much of that time (and, from 2007 to 2010, prime minister), famously declared—more than 100 times in Parliament, in fact—the 'end of the boom-and-bust business cycle'.

He was far from alone in this view that the cyclical volatility of economic life had been conquered. Around the same time, the Chairman of the US Federal Reserve Bank Ben Bernanke announced what he called the 'great moderation', a substantial decline in macroeconomic volatility that he explained was in part a result of improvements in monetary policy, which rested in turn upon a data-driven accurate real-time understanding of the structure of the economy and the impact of policy actions upon it.[30] In other words, knowledge equals power in the economic sphere; chaos can be managed. The late 1990s burst of the 'dot-com bubble', a massive overvaluation of many Internet-based companies, dented but did not demolish such thinking.

By 2005 the *New York Times* columnist Thomas Friedman declared with wonder and enthusiasm that the 'world is flat':

> We are now connecting all the knowledge centers on the planet together into a single global network, which—if politics and terrorism do not get in the way—could usher in an amazing era of prosperity and innovation.[31]

If, indeed. With that caveat stated, but not minded, it was out with the old rules of business and in with the fast and loose ones of the 'New Economy'. Key among these was the concept of the 'just-in-time' production model, which aimed to achieve efficiencies through the minimisation of inventories.

On the principle of 'as-in-business-so-too-in-war', then, 'just-in-time' war would use:

> DBK and information technology to produce real-time scheduling to cut the need for today's enormous inventories. More frequent deliveries of smaller amounts of product (i.e., destruction) allow for more flexible scheduling, quicker response, and shortened decision cycles. If the batch size of weapons and other logistics shipments into a theatre can be reduced, so will the vulnerability of logistical connections. Just-in-time suggests that forces need no longer be massed prior to attack. When mass is needed for offensive or defensive purposes, it need take place only at the point of impact.[32]

It was not that advocates of DBK were unaware of its potential shortcomings. Actually, they were acutely aware of several major ones. Thinking opponents would not remain supine, rather they would fight back creatively. High technology can also be an Achilles' heel if what it does, even in part, is introduce new information dependencies that could in turn be targeted by enemies. The theory was also especially derivative of the 1991 Gulf War and relied heavily upon that war's unique geographical and geopolitical conditions. It ignored the fog and friction of war and it defied the timeless principle that 'if it's not broken then don't fix it'.[33]

Objectively, especially with the benefit of hindsight, these all seem pertinent concerns and the literature on DBK did little to dispel them. Instead, it tended to adopt an exhortatory tone, stressing the urgency of taking action rather than firmly substantiating the premise upon which such action was predicated. Thus, concluded Owens in a rhetorical flourish at the end of his book:

> We remain 'the last, best hope' for mankind even in an era where the computer and information and communications technologies both liberate us from the past while destroying the sense of space and time that for centuries defined our context of existence. It is up to us whether we can safeguard the instruments of our protection. We must do it *now*.[34]

Notwithstanding the lacunae in its rationale, DBK achieved a high degree of currency in the American defence establishment. The concept of 'Rapid Dominance', colloquially known as 'shock and awe', nodded to the 'system of systems' and shared many of its assumptions and preoccupations.[35] Its four categories of 'core characteristics and capabilities' were cognate with those of DBK: complete knowledge of self, adversary and the environment; rapidity; brilliance of execution; and control of the environment.[36]

Its aims were also of a type with DBK, though more stridently put:

The key objective of rapid dominance is to impose this overwhelming level of shock and awe against an adversary on an immediate or sufficiently timely basis to paralyse its will to carry on. In crude terms, Rapid Dominance would seize control of the environment and paralyze or so overload an adversary's perceptions and understanding of events that the enemy would be incapable of resistance at tactical and strategic levels. An adversary would be rendered totally impotent and vulnerable to our actions.[37]

The hyperbolic quality of DBK and particularly Rapid Dominance rendered the RMA concept relatively open to refutation. Critics like Colin Gray were sharply critical of the knowledge equals (military) power theory, noting that 'information itself does not coerce or kill; it has to act on and through weapons systems of all kinds'.[38]

Others, like the Brookings Institution scholar Michael O'Hanlon, looked at the underlying technologies and pointed out that they were actually not quite as transformative as had often been made out. Most trends in defence technology, he argued, were quite slow moving—armour was becoming lighter and stronger, weapons were getting more accurate and powerful, but by increments rather than orders of magnitude. Sensors were indeed getting cheaper, smaller and more capable, but at the same time detection countermeasures, both technical and tactical, were developing at the same pace. Moreover, while communications were becoming more sophisticated they were not invulnerable, for example, to disruption with potentially catastrophic consequences by electro-magnetic pulse.[39]

'Battleshock XXI', a fictional account of a mid-twenty-first-century small, ultra high-tech American military force optimised to act as spotters for an impressive arsenal of stand-off weapons, was meant as a cautionary tale about the danger of catastrophic failure that may come with reliance on digital systems:

> Colonel Pierce's anxiety increased. Virtual was not in synch with reality. He had never been off simulation before. Simulations reduced uncertainty to insignificance. Simulations controlled the planning process. Being 'off sim' added chaos into the equation—and chaos was anathema to the twenty-first century military doctrinal tenets of precision force, target sensing, and certainty.[40]

Lawrence Freedman put forward similar points and made the larger argument that:

> If there is a revolution, it is one in strategic affairs, and is the result of significant changes in both the objectives in pursuit of which governments might want to use armed forces, and in the means that they might employ. Its most striking feature is its lack of a fixed form.[41]

None of this, however, decisively impeded the progress of the RMA—or 'Transformation' as it came to be called in the United States—towards the status of orthodoxy. In its last major iteration as 'Network-Centric Warfare' (NCW), or 'Network-Enabled Capability' in its less expansive British variant, it was more convincing. Popularised in a 1998 US Naval Institute *Proceedings* article co-written by Vice Admiral Arthur Cebrowski and John J. Garstka (a retired Air Force officer and fixture in the information age warfare literature), NCW was a sort of distillate of previous thinking with claims expressed somewhat more cautiously and systematically.[42]

Though it made no specific reference to the Tofflers, NCW repeated more or less wholly their thesis that the dynamics that were reshaping business processes would do the same thing for military operations. Thus the references of the Cebrowski and Garstka article were mostly to business literature on the 'new economy'. And the key objective was speed—specifically of closing the 'sensor-to-shooter gap' and of shortening decision cycles. In this NCW drew on a developed body of theory and practice in naval warfare, where for many years experts had already been developing such capabilities. In the United States, what was called the 'Co-operative Engagement Capability' (CEC), a system for improving the quality of a battle fleet's air defences by networking the sensors and fire control systems of all its constituent parts into a single distributed system, was already well established.

Without it, in fact, the speed and lethality of anti-ship missiles and aircraft would probably have made the operation of surface ships exceedingly dangerous, as was amply illustrated in the 1982 Falklands War. Even then unguided aerial bombs and relatively unsophisticated French-made sea-skimming *Exocet* missiles wrecked six Royal Navy ships. Many more that were damaged might have been sunk if the Argentine bombs had not failed to explode. The British could have lost the war if the losses of the amphibious landings at San Carlos (where the worst of the damage was suffered) had been much greater.[43] At its most basic, NCW was an attempt to apply to the land environment principles and systems of command and control, sensing, targeting and fire control that had been shown to be valid in naval and also in air warfare.

One of the new aspects of NCW, however, was the inspiration that it drew from the natural sciences in general and biology specifically. This is most evident in the emphasis placed in the NCW literature on the 'self-synchronisation' of forces in combat, which was regarded as something of a holy grail of information superiority:

> Self-synchronisation is perhaps the ultimate in achieving increased tempo and responsiveness. Self-synchronisation is a mode of interaction between ... two or

more robustly networked entities, shared awareness, a rule set, and a value-adding interaction. The combination of a rule set and shared awareness enables the entities to operate in the absence of traditional hierarchical mechanisms for command and control.[44]

In a quite sensible twist of the connectivity-will-lift-the-fog-of-war argument, NCW theorists observed that military synchronisation was becoming more difficult as a result of 'increasing complexity, growing heterogeneity, and a faster pace of events'—in other words, that there was more scope for friction, not less.[45] But this worry was offset by the hope that networks also permitted the development of forces that could preternaturally effectively handle the challenge of complexity—organically, without central direction:

> [T]he behaviour of an organisation can be influenced and perhaps even controlled without the issuance of detailed top-down direction. It offers the alternative of achieving the desired results in another way. That is to say that organisational behaviour could be consciously designed to be an emergent property that derives from the commander's intent, as internalised by actor entities, and the degree of battlespace knowledge available...[46]

This biological approach to the conduct of warfare was potentially very helpful. Rather than futilely working to banish complexity from situations that are inherently complex and chancy the commander and his army ought to embrace chaotic uncertainty and work with it to the extent that they are able.

By no means was this a new idea. In fact, it was essentially Clausewitz's point about chance and the art of war in the first place, nearly 200 years before; but it was among the more sensible realisations in the RMA literature, which when it stopped worrying about finding a substitute for Clausewitz had some perceptive things to say. A decade later, General David Petraeus, on taking command of NATO forces in Afghanistan, used Frederick Remington's famous painting 'The Stampede' as a visual metaphor of how he envisaged an information age force operating in a way that has a lot in common with the organic ideal of NCW:

> I use the painting to describe what we do. I use this image to tell you what I am comfortable with. The painting depicts an outrider galloping full tilt over rough terrain at the height of a violent storm while steering a wilful mount and guiding a sometimes frightened and unthinking herd to its destination. It represents getting the job done despite the challenges. Some of these cattle will get out ahead of us—that's fine, we will catch them up. Some cattle will fall back—that's fine—we will bring them on. We must be comfortable with the environment of uncertainty, challenge, risk, danger, and competing agendas. But we need to do more than simply hang onto the saddle. We must flourish in the apparent chaos and competing ends.[47]

Unfortunately, it must be said, this was a minor theme in the discourse.

Speed, always speed!

General Tommy Franks, again, is something of an exemplar of the mainstream obsession that prevailed. He records in his memoirs that twenty years before the invasion of Iraq as an artillery battalion commander, he relished experimenting with the capabilities offered by the relatively simple fire-control computers with which his unit had been issued. Stripping an old maintenance vehicle down, he built a mobile Tactical Operations Centre around a computer that allowed his unit to move and to fire much more quickly than had been possible before. 'More than ever', he wrote, 'I was fascinated by the combination of speed and firepower.'[48]

Twenty years later that fascination had been moulded into a 'basic tactical principle: speed kills... the enemy.'[49] The aphoristic fidelity here is admirable. Franks' subordinate ground forces commander in Iraq Lieutenant General David McKiernan's version was wordier, 'Fast is better than slow. Fast is more lethal than slow. Fast is more final.'[50] And way earlier Napoleon said it more elegantly than either: 'It may be that in the future I will lose a battle, but I shall never lose a minute'. The principle is sound.

Moreover, the results of its application initially seemed very positive. In the case of Afghanistan, the rapid defeat of the Taliban by a combination of Special Forces, precision weapons and indigenous allies was trumpeted as a model of future wars and a template for defence planning. In a speech in December 2001, President Bush awarded the RMA the presidential seal of approval. It is worth quoting at length as it illustrates the completeness of the concept's victory:

> The first priority is to speed the transformation of our military. When the Cold War ended, some predicted that the era of direct threats to our nation was over. Some thought our military would be used overseas—not to win wars, but mainly to police and pacify, to control crowds and to contain ethnic conflict. They were wrong. While the threats to America have changed, the need for victory has not ... Afghanistan has been a proving ground for this new approach. These past two months have shown that an innovative doctrine and high-tech weaponry can shape and then dominate an unconventional conflict. The brave men and women of our military are rewriting the rules of war with new technologies and old values like courage and honour. And they have made this nation proud. Our commanders are gaining a real-time picture of the entire battlefield, and are able to get targeting information from sensor to shooter almost instantly. Our intelligence professionals

and Special Forces have cooperated with battle-friendly Afghan forces ... And our Special Forces have the technology to call in precision airstrikes from horseback, in the first cavalry charge of the twenty-first century. This combination—real-time intelligence, Special Forces, and precision air power—has really never been used before. The conflict in Afghanistan has taught us more about the future of our military than a decade of blue ribbon panels and think-tank symposiums...[51]

But Bush's 'lessons' were nearly completely wrong. A few defence analysts were more circumspect about the lessons of Afghanistan and anxious about what further actions they would be employed to justify, arguing for the importance of context and of understanding the limits of the extent to which the 'Afghan Model' could be generalised.

Afghanistan did not represent a radical break with past experience; there was as much continuity in it as there was change, concluded Stephen Biddle in a well-regarded tactical study. It was 'neither a revolution nor a fluke' but involved a good deal of hard fighting against enemies fighting from concealed positions in complex terrain of a sort that would not have surprised the grandfathers of the Special Forces troops involved.[52] On the other hand, as was observed in Chapter Three, critics of the revolutionary new way of war said the same thing about unique conditions after the Gulf War. Perhaps these Cassandras were just wrong.

Biddle worried that the Afghan campaign would be misread as confirming the dawn of the long dreamed of way of war that could defeat enemies quickly, easily and cheaply, and would thus bolster the arguments of those in Washington eager to apply that model to Iraq.[53] He was right to worry. 'I'm not sure that much force is needed given what we've learned coming out of Afghanistan', said Rumsfeld to Franks in a December 2001 meeting to scope a new war plan for the invasion of Iraq, talking him down from a high estimate of force requirements for the operation.[54]

It is true that, when it came to it, the results of the fighting in Iraq in March–April 2003 seemed as electrifyingly asymmetrically impressive as Afghanistan had been. Senator Carl Levin, in a hearing on 'Lessons Learned from Operation Iraqi Freedom', lavished praise on Franks before he gave testimony:

> Historians will some day judge the military campaign that you led in Afghanistan and Iraq that swiftly defeated the Taliban and the forces of Saddam Hussein as brilliantly planned and executed examples of the military art and as foreshadows of future military tactics.[55]

This was only mildly over the top compared to other such encomia, which were commonplace before the course of events revealed that the tactical accomplishments of the model were less significant, easier to counter relatively cheaply by asysmmetric techniques, and, most importantly, decidedly less strategically momentous than had been made out. It is hard to imagine any of history's great commanders—Zhukov, Patton, Sharon—bothering to list the defeat of Iraq in 2003 on their resumes. The Iraqi Army was a shambolic and unmotivated wreck—a remnant of the shattered army of 1991 with twelve more years of wear and tear on its equipment and formations. Moreover, few ordinary Iraqis, brutalised by Saddam's regime, were prepared to fight in its defence as they might have done had Iraq been a normal country and the question primarily the defence of their homeland. Still, the victory seemed to offer a large measure of vindication.

The noted pundit and classicist Victor Davis Hanson, for example, said of Rumsfeld:

> Not since Secretary of War Edwin M. Stanton poked his head into every department of the Union Army and Robert McNamara tried to apply corporate business procedures to the Pentagon bureaucracy has a US official exercised such political and military influence as Donald Rumsfeld. But while Stanton was politically inept and McNamara failed at war, so far—twenty-seven months into his tenure—Rumsfeld is showing every sign of success. At home, he is steamrolling angry generals and balky diplomats; on the battlefield, he has crushed the Taliban and Saddam Hussein.[56]

Soon after, Saddam's ouster Vice President Dick Cheney concluded that Rumsfeld's success was 'proof positive of the success of our efforts to transform our military to meet the challenges of the twenty-first century'.[57] A few months later, conservative author and military analyst Max Boot concurred with that assessment in the pages of *Foreign Affairs* magazine, hailing the advent of a 'new American way of war', and listing among its characteristics more or less all of the RMA tropes.[58]

There was some justification to all this hearty backslapping. In terms of the production of raw combat power, the performance of coalition forces in Iraq in 2003 was noteworthy. The numerically superior Iraqi army was completely routed, the regime was thrown down, and most of its leaders were put to flight, captured or killed in record time at a cost of just over 100 American and British lives. But the achievement was exaggerated by the self-congratulatory rhetoric about the scale of success, which made 'fabled generals such as Erwin Rommel and Heinz Guderian seem positively incompetent by comparison.'[59]

On closer inspection, the results—particularly in the areas in which connectivity was supposed to have delivered the greatest effects—were decidedly mixed. As often as not, the fighting in March–April 2003 showed how even scarce good information could be misinterpreted, ignored or lost in the background noise while bad information in the form of a welter of gossip was able to spread through the force at the speed of light on the new information grid.

Bing West, who accompanied the First Marine Division on its march to Baghdad, described the persistence of confusion at the tactical level very forthrightly:

> Veterans and academics alike refer to the 'fog of war'—this battle [in An Nasiriyah, 22–24 March 2003] could be used as an illustration. With garbled communications and different groups of Marines fighting in different locations against different groups of enemy, information filtering up the chain of command and down to other units was fragmentary at best and misleading at worst ... The chatrooms on the secret internets at higher staff headquarters lit up with rumours. A Marine battalion had been stopped in its tracks. A Battalion! That just couldn't happen. A dozen rumours spread uncontrolled ... No one knew truth from fiction.[60]

This was by no means an isolated example. In his book *Generation Kill* Evan Wright, a *Rolling Stone* reporter embedded with a Marine reconnaissance force during the same period as West, described similar events. Though filled with cinematic passages (the book was later made into a successful television mini-series) and a somewhat bemused outsider's sense of military surreality, Wright's is one of the best first person accounts of the war.

His description of the night of 27 March 2003, when the Marines he was with reported observing somewhere between 120 and 140 lights moving about 6 kilometres away from their position, is telling. Most likely, the Marines decided, it was an Iraqi convoy that they were seeing and they called in multiple air strikes on its position over several hours. In the light of day, however, they observed bomb craters outside a nearby village but no sign of any bombed vehicles. As Wright puts it:

> What it boils down to is that under clear skies, in open terrain with almost no vegetation, the Marines don't have a clue what's out there beyond the perimeter. Even with the best optics and surveillance assets in the world, no one knows what happened to nearly ten thousand pounds of bombs and missiles dropped a few kilometres outside the encampment. They may as well have been dropping them in the Bermuda Triangle. It's not that the technology is bad or its operators incompetent, but the fog of war persists on even the clearest of nights.[61]

In other words, the soldiers' eye view of the war, against an opponent who was not working very hard to disrupt their operations and impede their progress, was a far cry from the Olympian perspective promised by DBK. Units still got lost, wires still got crossed, and equipment failed—and good soldiers got on with their missions regardless, through improvisation, good drills and gritty determination, as they always had done. West's conclusion about the sources of the Marines' success is romantic, referencing the march of Xenophon's 10,000 beleaguered Greek hoplites through Persia in 400 BC. But he is correct: 'the engine driving the campaign was not mechanical ... it was a spirit, an unspoken code, a shared recognition by all Devil Dogs that they were in this together'.[62]

Undoubtedly, the coalition forces were capable of delivering powerful blows very precisely and swiftly. In practice, however, the much-talked-about 'shock and awe' campaign produced not much of either. In part, this was because the nature of the regime rendered it immune to the paralysis followed by mute compliance imagined in Ullman and Wade's theory. For Saddam Hussein, given his nature and his crimes, surrender was really not an option— it was an all or nothing affair.[63] But it was also because it remained eminently possible to avoid detection by distant sensors with relatively simple means of camouflage and concealment. Extraordinarily, according to one account, the movement of three Republican Guard divisions around Baghdad went unnoticed by the sophisticated airborne systems designed to pick out just such operations.

One of them, the Medina Division, was thought to have been all but obliterated by air attack. The unit given the task of mopping up the survivors, however, the 2nd Brigade of the 3rd Infantry Division, found it alive and well hidden beneath the palm trees on the southern approach to Baghdad. In the words of the commander in charge, 'I fully expected I would see carnage and destroyed vehicles. But I didn't see any ... We literally came in contact with hundreds of vehicles. None of them was destroyed'.[64] Finally, if evasion was impossible then there was always the gambit of situating assets in civilian or culturally and historically sensitive areas: for a sufficiently ruthless and cold-blooded enemy, hospitals, places of worship, orphanages, museums and the like all make splendid fighting positions.[65] Sometimes, even knowing exactly where your enemy is does not ultimately solve the problem of what to do about it.

War, not a range exercise

To a large extent it was the target-centrism of NCW that proved its major undoing. The failures of this or that system in the fighting of March–April 2003 to deliver 'near perfect clarity' of situational awareness and the consequent inability to show 'brilliance in execution' is not the main issue. A fair reckoning of the performance of NCW as seen in Afghanistan and Iraq would also find startling examples of very short decision cycles indeed. The trouble is that while fast may be more lethal, it does not follow that fast is more smart. The swift sword cuts both ways.

Take, for example, an episode in the war that is frequently invoked as a showcase of the cyclical rapidity of sensing, target identification, and firing of weapons that is at the heart of NCW. On the afternoon of 7 April 2003 American intelligence believed they had firm evidence that Saddam Hussein and his sons were at a restaurant or a nearby bunker in the Al-Mansur district of Baghdad meeting with several high officials of the regime. A B1-B bomber loitering on call in Western Iraq was ordered to deliver an attack. On the fly, as it were, a strike package, composed of F-16s to provide suppression of any anti-aircraft fire and an EA-6B Prowler for electronic warfare and radar jamming, was organised around the high and fast-flying B1-B. Within just twelve minutes from the start of the operation a pair of 2000-pound GBU-31 bunker-busting bombs were falling towards the target. The bunkers were flattened; in fact, the whole city block where they had been located was obliterated. Unfortunately, Saddam was not there. But the impressively swift message of air power, as Murray and Scales put it, 'was clear enough: we can go after you anytime, day or night'.[66]

Surely, though, that was a message that Saddam already knew very well by that time. Was it not apparent in 1991? Had it not been made abundantly clear thereafter in Kosovo that when Western air forces know where to apply force they can do so with lightning alacrity and power? What is intriguing is why Saddam was not there when the bombs fell, as it raises the question of who was operating within whose decision cycle. According to fragmentary accounts, by this late stage of the war Saddam had grown suspicious that his intelligence chief Jalil al-Habbush al-Tikriti, whom he had invited to the meeting, was betraying him to the Americans. Arriving early, Saddam asked if al-Habbush was present and, hearing that he was not, immediately fled out the back of the building to a vehicle waiting there. 'Saddam had been suspicious of Tahir Habbush since the bombardments of 19 March and that is why his absence from the meeting was proof of his treachery', claimed an Iraqi official quoted later by Agence France Presse.[67]

The details are murky and highly contested. If there is nothing to the story, then it suggests that the narrowed sensor-to-shooter gap of NCW was achieved, but that owing to faulty intelligence, at least in this instance, it merely enabled a swift strike at nothing. If, however, the story is accurate then it illustrates how a clever opponent can use one's own haste to their advantage.

It comes back, really, to Baudrillard's point about the targeting mentality blinding one to the actual enemy. The striking thing about the graphic representation of the 'logical model of NCW' is that it made almost no mention of the enemy, representing it only as an 'object' which peeks out from 'behind the barricade' of electronic systems and is sensed, identified and then 'negated' by fire.[68] With this as one's conception of war the only way to arrive at victory is by accident. Ultimately, the 'need for speed' leads to a sort of *reductio ad absurdum*, illustrated marvellously by Victor Davis Hanson in his 'Postbellum Thoughts' on the Afghan and Iraq wars:

> We can take out rogue regimes within a matter of days or weeks without inflicting the level of pain, injury, and humiliation on enemy forces that traditionally rids opponents of any lingering doubts about the end of the old order and the onset of the new. In short, we win so quickly that some of the losers inevitably do not quite concede that they are defeated.[69]

But it is a truism of war that it is a test of wills and, as Clausewitz maintained, 'cannot be considered to have ended so long as the enemy's will is unbroken'.[70] An enemy who has not conceded defeat and is not disarmed is not defeated. Marine General James Mattis put it in more modern epigrammatic fashion:

> War is a human endeavour, a social problem, and we have modest expectations that technology is able to solve a problem as complex as warfare ... [N]o war is over until the enemy says it's over. We may think it's over, we may declare it over, but in fact, the enemy gets a vote.[71]

The trouble is that on the whole our expectations of technology in the contemporary Western way of war are, in practice, not modest at all—indeed, they are extraordinarily immodest.

We may see this very clearly in President Bush's speech in December 2001 in which, in so many words, he affirmed the RMA. After extolling the narrowed link from sensor to shooter he noted in passing the cooperation of Special Forces with 'battle-friendly' Afghans. An odd formulation but a telling one; effectively it says that we went into war equipped with amazing technology that blinded us not merely to the enemy as a thinking, reacting force in its own right but blithely ignorant of the goals and thinking even of our transient allies. Why? The term suggests no more than a superficial understanding of the aims, ideals, motivations and modes of operation of the people with whom one is attempting to forge common cause. It was not, after all, the first time that vastly technologically superior foreigners had attempted an economy of force operation in this region in this way, and came to grief as a result.

In his memoirs, the late-Victorian-era British Army officer Robert Warburton, who served eighteen years on the Khyber Pass as a Special Forces man (no one would have used the term then but the analogy is valid) cum diplomat, described how the entirely contingent loyalty of the local Maliks (leaders) turned on a dime, almost literally, because:

> they had no faith in the continuance of any British policy. The Caubul allowances [remittances from the Amir whom the British were supporting] were certainly small, but the tribesmen got something in the end; on the other hand, they did not know how long the war would last, and whether at its close the British Sarkar would not throw them over if it suited the Government to do so. The lessons of the first and second Afghan wars were firmly implanted in their minds and memories.[72]

If the West forgot its history when American and British troops arrived in 2001 and blew away the Taliban, the Afghans certainly had not. They were entirely switched on to the ways in which the mighty but ignorant could be harnessed to the aims of the weak but wise. The mismatch between the simplistic outsider's analysis, 'Mujahideen good' and 'Taliban bad', and the complex reality on the ground had a profound impact on the course of political and military developments.[73]

In 1999 in the foreword to a RAND study on *The Changing Role of Information in Warfare*, Andrew Marshall, the godfather of the American RMA, was already pointing to the really pertinent questions. There was already much speculation that the state would weaken in power relative to non-state groups as a result of new media and cheaper and more powerful means of communication. 'While this may be true', he noted, 'the more important question is how much and how fast?':

> Information and its associated technologies are destined to become a central focus on the battlefield. Does that mean that the offence or the defence will dominate? Will these developments favour states or terrorists? Will war become an exercise in media spin?[74]

The short answer, the answer which presented itself swiftly after the ousting of Saddam Hussein—though the Bush administration was at pains not to recognise it for months after the conclusion of 'major combat operations in Iraq'[75]—was plain: a lot and very fast.

The long answer, however, especially the degree to which war became an exercise in the media, requires another chapter.

5

WAR WITHOUT PASSION
SOMETHING OTHER THAN WAR

'I know what you're thinking about', said Tweedledum: 'but it isn't so, nohow.'

'Contrariwise', continued Tweedledee, 'if it was so, it might be; and if it were so, it would be; but as it isn't, it ain't. That's logic.'

'I was thinking', Alice said very politely, 'which is the best way out of this wood: it's getting so dark.'

A Conversation in Lewis Carroll's *Through the Looking Glass* (1871)

History does not lack for wars launched for good causes or ill ones by powers that proved badly equipped for their chosen task. Few of them, however, can match the unreadiness of the United States and its allies for the real challenges of the War on Terror. Like Alice, they had entered the wood—and they no longer knew the way back out. The problem is not material—by no conventional measure does the enemy possess but the tiniest fraction of the West's raw military power. The problem is moral—in 'war amongst the people' the West has proven profoundly anaemic and its foes comparatively strong. Partly, this is a result of the state of Western civilization, which is— independent of any external challenge—caught at a point of acute crisis in confidence, being more and more fragmented and increasingly ambivalent about its mission and purpose. Partly, it is a result of the fact that for years before 11 September 2001 it had developed a form of post-heroic warfare, precisely the opposite of and completely unsuited to 'war amongst the people', which was designed to replace the missing quality of passion in Western warfare with ersatz spectacle and long-range weapons. When it came to the test it proved highly inadequate.

In June 2009 Gordon Brown announced the launch of the Iraq Inquiry (also known as the Chilcot Inquiry after its chairman, Sir John Chilcot, a retired senior Whitehall mandarin). The war had been enormously controversial in Britain from the beginning, as indeed it had elsewhere, and was a political millstone for Brown, who had succeeded Tony Blair as prime minister by internal succession but had not yet himself been tested at a general election. Comprised of a handful of eminent academic historians and civil servants, the inquiry's purpose was, in Chilcot's words, to consider 'the UK's involvement in Iraq, including the way decisions were made and actions taken, to establish, as accurately as possible, what happened, and to identify the lessons that can be learned'.[1] In the public's mind, the task of the inquiry, which has not yet issued its judgment, is to determine whether the war, to use a phrase that has been popularised by the press, was 'sold on a false prospectus [and] delivered little but bloodshed'.[2] Did, in other words, the Bush and Blair governments cook the intelligence concerning Iraq's weapons of mass destruction programme? And why once the war had been undertaken did it all go so wrong and so badly?

No peace through superior firepower

False prospectus or not, it is clear now that the war was begun on a false premise—the premise (described in the previous chapter) that the West through superior technical means would be able to quickly and cheaply solve deep-rooted and difficult political problems with 'rogue' regimes abroad through decisive military force. A better premise, it will be argued in this chapter—the premise that ought to have formed the basis of planning and conduct of military affairs—is, broadly speaking, Rupert Smith's that the norm of warfare that now pertains is 'war amongst the people', or operations undertaken 'in order to establish a condition in which the political objective can be achieved by other means and in other ways'.[3]

To be sure, some experts have found fault with Smith's thesis. In his opening line, for instance, he declared flatly that 'war does not exist', though he almost immediately qualified that statement as referring to war as it is 'cognitively known to most non-combatants', by which he meant the sort of war that people imagine from viewing old newsreels of the world wars and watching popular films.[4]

Though eye-catching, the straw man fallacy of that initial sentence detracts from his very pertinent main argument, which is that war, as we have seen, is simply metastasising—changing its form in accordance with the ever changing conditions of its host, as it always has done. Moreover, his bold talk of a 'paradigm shift' in war also cannot fail to unsettle the large majority of scholars who have been trained not to talk that way, for the very good reason that such shifts only happen extraordinarily rarely and the fate of people who proclaim them (even when they are eventually proved correct, or at least partially correct) is generally to be ridiculed as naïve or ignorant or both.[5] The career of Norman Angell, whom we mentioned in Chapter Two, is a case in point (though on the up-side he sold many copies of *The Great Illusion*).

Moreover, to declare that old fashioned, conventional war, 'war as a battle in a field between men and machinery, war as a massive deciding event in a dispute in international affairs', is gone and not to be seen again is to leave oneself eternally hostage to the fortune of events.[6] It is not clear that even the West has seen the end of war of this kind.[7] Indeed, the eminent strategist Colin Gray concluded in his book on future war, written about the same time as Smith's *Utility of Force*, that 'irregular war may well be the dominant mode in belligerency for some years to come, but interstate war, including great power conflict, will enjoy a healthy future'.[8]

Smith's is a rather Western-centric and perhaps near-sighted vision too. A South Korean general looking north to the 10,000 artillery tubes of the antique but large and well-tended army of North Korea still pointed at him, or a Japanese admiral looking across the Yellow Sea to a still intensely nationalistic China flexing its increasingly prominent military muscles, or an Indian air vice marshal pondering Pakistan on his northwest flank and China on his northeast, would have a rather more traditional view of war's future, no doubt.[9]

Further, we might as well ask whether 'war amongst the people' represents any sort of new paradigm or is merely, as with 'fourth generation warfare', a variant of war that has existed alongside 'regular' war for as long as there has been war. If we open the floodgates of history completely why then locate the origin of 'war amongst the people' in the early nineteenth century?[10] 'War amongst the people', says Smith:

> is both a graphic description of modern war-like situations, and also a conceptual framework: it reflects the hard fact that there is no secluded battlefield upon which armies engage, nor are there necessarily armies, definitely not on all sides.[11]

However, a glance at the Israeli historian Azar Gat's survey of war in human civilisation shows us that to some degree or another this form of war has always existed; indeed, for much of the time from the 'evolutionary state of nature' (that is, pre-historic times) onwards it has been the dominant mode.[12] Smith draws a vital distinction between 'conflict', by which he means organised and purposeful violence in the form of actual battles, and 'confrontation', by which he means a state of competition and continuing hostility over a long period conducted largely by means other than war. These, he argues, are more useful concepts for understanding the world as it is today than the simpler dichotomy of war and peace.

Be that as it may, how is now different from the past? Gat's point is that the solution to the 'enigma of war', as he puts the dichotomy to which Smith refers, is that there is no enigma: violent competition is the evolutionary norm of human society; it is the belief in war as an intrinsically futile and repugnant discontinuation of the natural state of peace that is ahistoric. Nonetheless, Smith's valid preoccupation is with the current maladaptation of conventional armed forces, which are optimised for achieving objectives like 'take, hold, destroy', but tasked with the achievement of 'softer, more malleable, complex, sub-strategic objectives'.[13] That is why his book's message resonated so clearly when it was published in 2005. As Eliot Cohen, the professor of strategic studies at Johns Hopkins University's School of Advanced International Studies, wrote in a review of *Utility of Force* just before he accepted an appointment as Counsellor to the Secretary of State, 'to some extent [war amongst the people] is already the war we are experiencing in Iraq and Afghanistan.[14]

This is an old story, in other words. Is there a better example in history of a brilliant strategic raider transitioning sharply to clay-footed occupier than the great general Hannibal over 2000 years ago? The tactically brilliant but strategically indecisive Gulf War discussed in Chapter Three, or the 2003 invasion and occupation of Iraq discussed in Chapter Six, are moderate let-downs by comparison.

Hannibal famously led the Carthaginian army during the Punic Wars from Spain through Gaul and across the Alps into Italy where, in a series of battles culminating at Cannae in 216 BC, he effectively destroyed the Roman Army. The slaughter at Cannae was so great, in fact, that there are accounts in the ancient sources of Carthaginian soldiers complaining to their officers about the fatigue of mechanically chopping up so many Roman legionaries. No one really knows how many Romans were killed. Polybius says it was 70,000; Livy reckoned it was about 50,000; modern historians consider it was probably lower than that but still a large number.[15] Rome was more or less disarmed but it was not defeated. Hannibal's cavalry commander Maharbal lamented of his superior's strategic lassitude after Cannae: 'The gods have not given all their gifts to one man. You know how to win victory, Hannibal, you do not [know] how to use it.'[16]

In fact, though it took another fifteen years, Rome went on to defeat Carthage and, quite literally, to wipe it from the face of the Earth. It was the Roman general Fabius Maximus, 'Fabius Cunctator' as he was nicknamed (meaning 'Fabian the Delayer'), who saved the day for Rome. His advice after the disaster of Cannae on how to beat the apparently unstoppable Hannibal was simple: if Hannibal wants to fight, run away; if Hannibal wants to rest, then attack—then run away again. In the end, though it was his rival Scipio Africanus who led the victorious Roman counterattack on Carthage, without Fabian's insurgent tactics there would not have been a Rome to issue such a reprisal.

Indeed, it requires relatively little conceptual stretching to argue that the history of Rome from the first through to the fifth century provides an even more terrific example of 'war amongst the people'. At the start of this period Christianity was a small Jewish cult; by the end it had effectively claimed the empire, adopted many of its outward trappings and organisational structures, and preserved some of its temporal power over formerly imperial organisations. Granted, this took a long time to happen. Moreover, we are unaccustomed to thinking of the fathers of the church as insurgent commissars;[17] but the analogy is not without merit. Christianity emerged inside the Roman Empire, but also in tension with it because of the multiple contradictions between their respective worldviews, notably Rome's promiscuous polytheism as opposed to Christian monotheism, and Roman militarism as opposed to Christian pacifistic leanings.[18] By the late second century AD it had begun to offer a complete alternative to the existing Roman status quo. And the beneficiaries of that status quo were not happy about it.

For example, for Celsus, a second-century Greek philosopher and figure of the Roman establishment, Christian belief was not merely 'stupid', a cultish mishmash of other religious beliefs, it was particularly dangerous, insidious even, because of its 'worldwide coherence':

> It was a conspiracy, and one which Celsus saw as especially aimed at impressionable young people. The result of Christian propaganda would be to leave the emperor defenceless, 'while earthly things would come into the power of the most lawless and savage barbarians.'[19]

These words would have had a great significance to Romans at the time because the Empire then had reached its apogee and was beginning its slow economic, political and military contraction. Moreover, as scholars have pointed out, the mutation of Christianity over centuries of tension, confrontation and accommodation with Rome from a counter-cultural movement to a settled governing agent in its own right was in part a result of a piece of communications technology, the Bible, which helped the dispersed Christian community to maintain the worldwide coherence that unnerved Celsus.[20]

The point need not be belaboured, however. The anxiety of our own day about the ambiguity of war and peace, the fear that globally-dispersed but virtually-connected conscience communities threaten the existing and seemingly increasingly exhausted status quo, and even the apprehension about disruptive communications technologies—none of these are wholly new phenomena.

In-between war

This is not so fatal a flaw of the 'war amongst the people' thesis as might be imagined; after all, if it works as a prism for understanding war in the twenty-first century BC and the twenty-first century AD, it might just have some general merit. That war has probably always been 'amongst the people' does not mean that policymakers and strategists today need not be reminded of it, particularly since, as we have seen, many have convinced themselves that the opposite is now true. It is simply a useful reminder that in trying to navigate the turbulence of information age security we ought not to abandon history's potential contribution to understanding.

The most eyebrow-raising aspect of Smith's argument, however, is his seemingly unconscious embrace of a little postmodernism. This is a strength: he makes it, to refer back to Der Derian's 'little po-mo' from Chapter Three, go a very long way indeed. But it is unfortunate that he does not draw explicitly on a range of other ideas, including some postmodern ones, about the mediatisation of war, the confusion of actual and 'virtual' aspects of international politics, and more general societal change driven by information and communications technology. This lacuna means that he does not spell out the implications of his own argument as far as he might have. In fact, the challenge of the 'utility of force' may be substantially more fundamental than even he lets on.

Jean-François Lyotard defined postmodernism, 'simplifying to the extreme' (to the immense gratitude of some of his readers, to be sure), as 'incredulity to metanarratives'.[21] Yet the oft-cited 2002 United States *National Security Strategy*, generally reckoned to be the closest thing there is to a formal enunciation of the 'Bush doctrine', opens with a strident metanarrative in the form of a preface by President Bush:

The great struggles of the twentieth century between liberty and totalitarianism ended with a decisive victory for the forces of freedom—and a single sustainable model for national success: freedom, democracy, and free enterprise. In the twenty-first century, only nations that share a commitment to protecting basic human rights and guaranteeing political and economic freedom will be able to unleash the potential of their people and assure their future prosperity. People everywhere want to be able to speak freely; choose who will govern them; worship as they please; educate their children—male and female; own property; and enjoy the benefits of their labour. These values of freedom are right and true for every person, in every society—and the duty of protecting these values against their enemies is the common calling of freedom-loving people across the globe and across the ages.[22]

How do we attach meaning to the state's warlike endeavours when societies have grown intensely (and justifiably) sceptical of such narratives? Serious observers noted with alarm and dismay early on that the characterisation of post-9/11 security operations as a 'War on Terror' was highly problematic. How could we be at war against terror except in the rhetorical sense that we might be in a 'war on drugs' or a 'war on poverty'?[23] Who was the enemy to be defeated? Without an identified enemy how does one begin to conceive a strategy for their defeat? Others questioned the assumptions of the strategy, as well as the veracity of certain phrases employed by its proponents. 'Islamo-fascism', for instance, struck many as inapt as a description of the opponent's ideology, one that needlessly alienated a large number of Muslims whose goodwill the West desired.[24]

Few, however, were more perceptive of the long term danger than Andrew Bacevich, whose critique of the extraordinary confidence evinced in the Bush doctrine's metanarrative about America's ability to change other nations and societies in accordance with its own preferences led him to warn that:

> The ensuing collision between American requirements and a non-compliant world will provide the impetus for more crusades. Each in turn will be justified in terms of ideals rather than interests, but together they may well doom the United States to fight perpetual wars in a vain effort to satisfy our craving for freedom without limit and without end.[25]

A decade later, these fears seem justified. Despite a change in president from George W. Bush to Barack Obama, there has not been a marked shift in American policy—notwithstanding the fact that the term 'War on Terror' has been shelved. The incredible burgeoning of the security sector is being tamed not so much by strategic reassessment as by economic exigency, to the extent that it is being tamed at all.[26]

Alongside cogent criticisms of the War on Terror, however, there have also been a welter of less cogent ones, including '9/11 trutherism', which in its raw form essentially argues that the United States (or Israel, or both countries together) attacked itself on 11 September 2001, ostensibly to create a rationale for attacking Iraq and the Muslim world. More moderately dyspeptic and ignorant theories include that the United States used 9/11 as a pretext upon which to pursue a 'shock doctrine' agenda bent on realising the imposition of a 'neoliberal' economic model globally.[27] Others, such as the linguist and public intellectual Noam Chomsky, preached a rough equivalency of the belligerents. A war to (paraphrasing Bush) 'rid the world of evildoers' was all well and good, Chomsky said, so long as it was accepted that the exploits of al-Qaeda paled in scale against the West's 'state terrorism' practiced over decades in the Middle East, Central America, Southeast Asia and elsewhere.[28]

These are not really fringe ideas. Even '9/11 trutherism' theories, despite being bizarre and unfounded, are widely held and often repeated.[29] Making war on a large scale when the populations one is seeking to influence, including one's home population, reflexively generate such counter-narratives is very difficult. In late 2002 Bush reiterated the gist of his strategy at a political rally:

> You know, I laid out a doctrine—you've just got to know it still stands—it said, either you're with us, either you love freedom, and [you're] with nations which embrace freedom, or you're with the enemy. There's no in-between.[30]

The trouble is that many Americans—not to mention citizens of other countries—do feel themselves to be 'in-between'. As one critic put it, the war on terror was a case of Jihad ('disintegral tribalism and reactionary fundamentalism') vs. 'McWorld' ('integrative modernisation and aggressive economic and cultural globalisation'), with democracy the victim of both.[31]

Some of this was envisaged before 9/11 but as if through an unfocused glass that became more focused as the wars of the War on Terror developed momentum. Amongst the most perceptive of those visions was the idea of 'spectator-sport war'. With the end of the Cold War and its explicit threat to human survival, and in the absence (or at least diminishment) of passion for ruling others directly, which once animated the great powers, what was left? One thing was a public appetite for spectacle, with conflict reporting emerging as a supremely engrossing form of reality television.

Immersive media enhances already powerful stories, making the audience feel excitingly as though they are present at these important events in world affairs.[32] It does not, however, necessarily make the audience wiser or more decisive about what to do about such events—quite the opposite, for the most part. Nor does it make them committed to the long-run time-scales over which conflicts transpire. Spectacle is like a high glucose energy drink—good for a sprint but poor for endurance. Journalist Robert Kaplan described Western society at large in the 1990s as having fallen under the 'numbing and corrosive illusion of peace', in which condition peace is taken for granted and that:

> the electronic media increasingly adopt the aspirations of the mob. The mob, like the television camera, has no historical memory and is entirely reductive: it considers only what is within its field of vision, not the complicating facts beyond it.[33]

On the one hand, the mass killings in Bosnia and Somalia, and particularly the recriminations that followed the non-intervention of the international community to mitigate or forestall the Rwandan genocide in 1994, spurred demands on the part of voters to governments to 'do something' in response to eye-catchingly horrid world events.

On the other hand, the practical ability of foreign intervention to affect the trajectory of most such events was quite limited.[34] In the words of Colin McInnes, who coined the term 'spectator-sport war':

> When Western states use force, they do so from afar, involving directly only a limited number of representatives on the field of battle. Society no longer participates; it spectates from a distance. Like sports spectators, Westerners demonstrate different levels of engagement, from those who watch unmoved and soon forget to those who follow events, personalities, tactics, and strategies closely and empathise strongly with what is happening. But their experience is removed. They sympathise but do not suffer; they empathise but do not experience.[35]

The theory of 'postheroic warfare', first advanced by the strategist Edward Luttwak, pursued a similar line of reasoning, the gist of which was that the West's acute casualty-sensitivity was driving it towards this sort of low participatory warfare based on small troop numbers on the ground and heavy reliance on precision-guided munitions. The applicability of this train of thought to the 'Revolution in Military Affairs' described in Chapter Three should be obvious. While strategically suboptimal in many ways—slow, timid and able to achieve at best partial results—Luttwak argued that 'postheroic warfare' basically fit the bill in a strategic environment wherein partial results were deemed acceptable by politicians who perceived that 'doing more would be too costly in US lives and doing nothing [would be] too damaging to world order and US self-respect.'[36] Strategic and political reality, he argued, provided much justification for a form of warfare that had 'modest purposes and casualty avoidance as the controlling norm.'[37]

It could be argued that the American way of war has long (perhaps always) been exceedingly casualty averse. American political culture reveres the individual over the state and American military culture has traditionally been very keen to substitute firepower for manpower in battle.[38] Moreover, while there is considerable truth in the idea that casualty sensitivity is the Achilles' heel of Western states engaged in what their publics perceive as 'wars of choice', this has been known for a long time.[39]

Andrew Mack famously argued in the aftermath of the Vietnam War that when 'big nations lose small wars' it is because a fundamental asymmetry of will exists between the intervening foreign power and the local belligerent: for the latter, the stakes of the conflict are likely to be mortal and total; for the former they are discretional and limited.[40] As a result the level of force that the intervening power is prepared to apply as well as the pain it is prepared to endure—measured in blood, treasure and possibly infamy—is constrained. Generally, the materially weaker actor's best move is to protract the conflict in an effort to exhaust the greater power's reserves of patience to the point that the latter's own population grows convinced that even if it is possible to win the war, it is not worth it.[41]

There is a decidedly jaded and cynical aspect of both theories. Luttwak, in a later *Foreign Affairs* article entitled 'Give War a Chance', further developed his argument into the thesis that, all things considered, it would be best for all parties, especially those suffering from war, that the world allow belligerents to just get on with killing each other, the sooner therefore that small wars would burn themselves out without the need for costly and futile interventions from outside.[42]

Moreover, the casualty aversion thesis was perhaps overstated. In actuality, the tolerance for carnage and casualties in the West has proved to be flexible within a broad range—albeit highly contingent on the existence of a narrative that justifies the action and its costs. Colin Powell put it pragmatically in terms of a 'parent test' in a mid-1990s interview:

> [The American people are] prepared to take casualties. And even if they see them on live television it will make them madder. Even if they see them on live television, as long as they believe it's for a solid purpose and for a cause that's understandable and for a cause that has something to do with an interest of ours. They will not understand it if it can't be explained, which is the point I have made consistently over the years. If you can't explain it to the parents who are sending their kids, you'd better think twice about it.[43]

But none of this invalidates the essential point that 'postheroic warfare' and 'spectator-sport war' have predominated since the Cold War.

Wanting to be seen by their voters to be doing something, but unwilling to incur much cost, governments squared the circle as best they could. Arguably, this was 'low and dishonest', as the poet W.H. Auden once described the decade before the Second World War.[44] It certainly reflected a powerful (also naïve and misplaced) belief in the efficacy of technologically advanced military force. Equally, though, one might say it was a pragmatic response to the political and strategic conditions of the 1990s. The West, by and large, was content with achieving partial results because it was not directly threatened by the conflicts in which it intervened; hence determination to obtain significantly different outcomes was proportionately mushy. It could hardly have been more ill-suited, however, to the post-9/11 world—as Clausewitz might have explained.

Passion!

Undoubtedly, it is his conception of war as a political act for which he is mainly remembered; but Clausewitz was just as much concerned with what he called 'moral forces' in war. In fact, he considered them to be almost preeminently important, although whereas his views on war as a continuation of politics have an aphoristic specificity, on 'moral forces' his thoughts are generally more *passim*:

> They constitute the spirit that permeates war as a whole, and at an early stage they establish a close affinity with the will that moves and leads the whole mass of force, practically merging with it, since the will itself is a moral quantity. Unfortunately, they will not yield to academic wisdom. They cannot be classified or counted. They have to be seen or felt. The spirit and other moral qualities of an army, a general or a government, the temper of the population of the theatre of war, the moral effects of victory or defeat—all of these vary greatly. They can moreover influence our objective and situation in very different ways.[45]

Norman Gibbs, the Chichele Professor of the History of War at Oxford University (1953–77), explained Clausewitz's 'moral forces' as equivalent to ideology, defined broadly as 'something more comprehensive than simply political doctrine; something which, operating in the hearts and minds of men, moves them and inspires them to action'.[46] In modern times we would likely use the term 'psychological' to cover much of the topic. We are speaking, in other words, of that element of the trinity that Clausewitz described as 'passion'. And yet the definitive characteristics of 'postheroic warfare' and 'spectator-sport war' are dispassion and detachment respectively.

Post-mythological war

These characteristics form a profound strategic conundrum of our day, though they would be strategically burdensome characteristics of a serious way of war in any period of history. Clausewitz grasped that war requires society to cohere around the project towards which violence is aimed at advancing. That is the real and vital driving force of war. The point is sufficiently basic in principle that it was hardly a unique insight of the Prussian master. It is essentially the same truth to which Shakespeare makes Henry V give voice in his 'Cry God for Harry, England, and St George!' speech at the high point in his dramatisation of the siege of Harfleur:

> Once more unto the breach, dear friends, once more;
> Or close the wall up with our English dead.
>
> ...
>
> Now set the teeth and stretch the nostril wide,
> Hold hard the breath and bend up every spirit
> To his full height. On, on, you noblest English.
> Whose blood is fet from fathers of war-proof![47]

In soaring rhetoric here we see a straight appeal to a particular historical narrative—a grand cultural memory of 'nobility' and the consequent obligation passed on from father and mother to son and soldier—and an evocation of myth for the purposes of imbuing Henry's war with a palpable moral force. After Clausewitz, others made similar sorts of argument. The late-nineteenth- and early-twentieth-century French philosopher Georges Sorel, for example, is remembered primarily for his *Reflections on Violence*, in which he remarked:

> men who are participating in a great social movement always picture their coming action as a battle in which their cause is certain to triumph. These constructions, knowledge of which is so important for historians, I propose to call 'myths'.[48]

In a subtle variation on the 'parent test', the London School of Economics professor Christopher Coker observed in a pointed essay on 'The Unhappy Warrior' that a society which fights postheroically—without recourse to myth, one might say—will struggle to invest the deaths of its soldiers with the force of free sacrifice and will therefore deprive these deaths of nobility:

> Without an anchor to the past, to existential needs, or metaphysical hope, death really has become meaningless. Lives really are 'wasted' in both senses of the word. Death is seen not as central to war—death as sacrifice—but as a side effect of war. It has been instrumentalised as a risk to be avoided, which is profoundly at odds, of

course, with the humanist message at the heart of the warrior tradition—i.e., that the warrior takes risks to make a difference, that he hazards all, including his life, which is the supreme reason why his death is a gift to the rest of us.[49]

A soldier whose potential sacrifice cannot be reconciled by his own society, by his own parents even, says Coker, as other than a waste of life will struggle to find the risk that he is taking meaningful.[50]

And yet by the last years of the twentieth century many statesmen and soldiers in the West had come to believe that they could achieve their political aims with force alone, as though the 'moral forces' of war no longer mattered. As a result, they grossly overestimated their own strength to fight in the name of half-truths and vague hopes, while underestimating that of their opponents who in their own minds were fighting for the proverbial 'truth, the whole truth, and nothing but the truth'. This realisation is Smith's most noteworthy contribution: in his words, 'wars have become media events far away from any ongoing social reality'.[51] Into this gap—between war as media event (discussed in more detail in the next chapter) and the 'social reality' of the disparate societies differentially engaged in it—drained the utility of force.

As it happens, Smith does not explain what it is that has caused the grand shift in war that he maintains has taken place. The first two thirds of his book, beginning with Clausewitz and Napoleon, describe war's progress towards 'war amongst the people' but the reader is left to guess at what has driven the surface developments in military technique and organisation, strategic thinking and political purpose that he describes. However, as his two major preoccupations are the end of the 'industrial form' of war and the enormous impacts of ubiquitous media on contemporary warfare, it seems fair to presume that the key factors are a broader societal shift to post-industrialism and the burgeoning of connectivity.

This does not draw him away from Clausewitz, as it has done other scholars; on the contrary, it compels Smith to cling all the more tightly, and rightly, to certain of his concepts. In particular, though he actually describes the trinity of war narrowly as consisting of the people, the army and the state rather than Clausewitz's more inclusive passion, chance and political purpose, it is impossible not to observe the Clausewitzian trinity's influence on his thinking, particularly in his estimation of the vital quality of will. In support of this he quotes Clausewitz:

> If we desire to defeat the enemy we must proportion our efforts to his powers of resistance. This is expressed by the product of two factors which cannot be separated, namely the sum of available means and the strength of the will.[52]

He also invokes two Frenchmen to bolster the point. Predictably, Napoleon's well-worn aphorism that in war 'the moral is to the physical as three to one' is deployed. Less predictably, he enlists the philosopher Michel Foucault's description of power as a 'relationship, not a possession', which is odd not because it is incorrect but because Foucault is not often invoked in strategic studies and almost never in the same breath as Clausewitz.[53] This is surprising, actually, since Clausewitz had a strong influence upon Foucault and they conceived of strategy, war and the workings of power very similarly.[54] But the French philosopher whom Smith might as well have dragooned in support of his 'war amongst the people' thesis was really the aforementioned Baudrillard, for it is he who put his finger on the problem that concerns Smith through page after page: 'the lack of political will to employ force rather than [merely] deploy forces'.[55]

The ghost of UNPROFOR (the United Nations Protection Force in Yugoslavia) haunts Smith's theory. He presents Bosnia as the *locus classicus* of intervention forces being plagued by incoherent political aims and weak will.[56] Similarly, it is the unreality of the 1991 Gulf War which animates Baudrillard's fury: the West, Baudrillard argued, combined mastery of war as a physical struggle with near total ignorance of war's function as a means of 'symbolic exchange' or 'commerce' in which, as Clausewitz put it, battle is the equivalent of 'cash payment'.[57]

In Baudrillard's words, the Gulf War was all *trompe l'oeil* (an art technique meaning to 'deceive the eye'):

> It is as though there was a virus infecting this war, which emptied it of all credibility. It is perhaps because the two adversaries did not even confront each other face to face, the one lost in its virtual war won in advance, the other buried in its traditional war lost in advance. They never saw each other: when the Americans finally appeared from behind their curtain of bombs the Iraqis had already disappeared behind their curtain of smoke ... The conquered have not been convinced and have withdrawn, leaving the victors only the bitter taste of an unreal made-to-order victory.[58]

Smith and Baudrillard both recognised that wars were increasingly of a sort that could not be decided by military force, that an element of the trinity, 'moral forces', understood as an amalgam of will and identity expressed as myth, was increasingly absent from the equation. A materially weak actor who nonetheless does not believe in his powerlessness possesses a paradoxical strength which can out measure that of a materially greater opponent who does not believe in his power.

The profound problems that this presents for the contemporary conduct of war exist in two dimensions, the pragmatic and the virtual. In the pragmatic (the actual field of battle where bullets fly, bombs explode and blood is shed), if you see military action from the lowest tactical level to the upper echelons of policy as necessarily constituting an integrated (and ideally coherent) whole, then the prevailing state of affairs is intensely problematic. The more that force is used for 'sub-strategic' goals the more important it is that commanders:

> have their actions firmly nested in a context that includes the political, economic, and social factors local to the achievement and exploitation of their objective. Without this wide context commanders at all levels will not be able to achieve their objectives, nor therefore enable the final attainment of the desired political outcome—the overarching purpose of all activity.[59]

In the absence of a coherent Clausewitzian 'moral force' in which to embed their military actions, every theatre commander, and especially every non-American national contingent commander, in Iraq and Afghanistan has wrestled—largely unsuccessfully—with this problem.

In the virtual dimension, the informational realm in which belligerents contend with words and images to manufacture narratives that are more resonant and better at structuring the responses of others to the development of events, the situation is much worse. In Chapter One we saw that Rumsfeld, Gates and others have been perplexed that the West should be losing a 'War of Ideas' with al-Qaeda, or more specifically with the 'moral force' that drives it and its adherents. But the essential reason is uncomplicated: one side is better at convincing itself that the work in which it is engaged is serious, formidable and sublime than the other; and so the Islamists have been better able, to paraphrase George Sorel's comments on the revolutionary socialists of the early twentieth century, 'to raise themselves above our frivolous society and make themselves worthy of pointing out new roads to the world'.[60]

The above is not a value judgment; it is simply the case that connectivity makes establishing narrative coherence very difficult, and the problem is worse the greater the degree of incredulity to metanarratives in a society. Material considerations notwithstanding, a civilisation that does not much believe in war anymore will, naturally, struggle to prevail against a civilisation that does. As the marketing and propaganda expert Nicholas O'Shaughnessy has warned:

> Any society needs its myths, and if we aggressively and systematically demolish them we may be doing real damage, for myths are intimately bound up with a society's identity, its ability to transmit a coherent culture and moral code to cadet

generations and to inspire pride and a sense of community ... It is necessary for a regime to keep myths in being to guarantee its survival.[61]

As surprising as it may seem, this chariness about myth, indeed the destructive urge that Western society exhibits towards myth, is integral to its serial martial failures in the last half-century and especially since 11 September 2001.[62]

Let us now look at the way that these forces played out in the Iraq and Afghan campaigns, which illustrate well the new realities of both the pragmatic and virtual dimensions of conflict.

6

THEATRE OF WAR

A sahib has got to act like a sahib; he has got to appear resolute, to know his own mind and do definite things. To come all that way, rifle in hand, with two thousand people marching at my heels, and then to trail feebly away, having done nothing— no, that was impossible. The crowd would laugh at me. And my whole life, every white man's life in the East, was one long struggle not to be laughed at.

George Orwell, former Imperial Policeman, 'Shooting an Elephant' (1936)[1]

Very few people can look upon the Iraq and Afghanistan wars and see success. Iraq has effectively ceased to exist as a unitary state within its titular borders. In the south of the country a Shiite regime openly backed by Iranian force rules. In the Sunni regions to the north of Baghdad Islamic State has wrested control; while further to the north the Kurdish territories battle to maintain their *de facto* independence. We have yet to see the denouement of the withdrawal of Western forces from Afghanistan, though there is precious little evidence that the stability and friendliness of the new regime will be long lasting. For the United States, the wars have cost around 7500 dead soldiers (with many more having suffered life-changing injuries) and between $4 and $6 trillion.[2] The British death toll sits around 650 (again, with many more badly wounded and requiring long-term care), while monetary costs are proportionately vast.[3] For the British Army, Iraq in particular was an embarrassing failure, injuring both its reputation and to some extent its self-belief. At the outset of the war it reckoned itself (and was reckoned by others) to be a master of the arts of counterinsurgency and to be up to the job in southern Iraq. It proved not to be. The United States Army, by contrast, was quite unprepared for counterinsurgency at the outset and messed things up extremely badly before adapting to it spectacularly on the fly. That is the story, at any rate, and there is some truth to it. The war may have been a debacle but the battle to adapt the US Army for counterinsurgency operations was a triumph. In fact, neither the British nor the American army's highly publicised efforts to 'win the population' made as much difference to the outcome as did the methodical wrecking of insurgent networks by equally networked high-value target teams on the ground. They made excellent theatre, however, and this was not unimportant.

The assumptions guiding the 2003 invasion of Iraq were predicated on the idea that this was a 'regular' war. The conflict was between states and was justified, however inadequately and unconvincingly, in terms of necessary measures taken in support of the rules of the international system, specifically Iraq's obligations under UN resolutions concerning its weapons of mass destruction programme.[4] As Tommy Franks put it in a 'Freedom Message to the Iraqi People' distributed on 16 April 2003:

> Coalition forces in Iraq have come as liberators, not as conquerors. We have come to eliminate an oppressive and aggressive regime that refused to comply with UN Security Council resolutions requiring the destruction of weapons of mass destruction.[5]

The assumed means of achieving this political objective was a lean military force designed to effect a decisive physical defeat of Iraq's army as quickly as possible—and then to depart as quickly as possible having created the conditions for democracy to take root and to flourish. This and similar assumptions did not long survive actual contact with the enemy. In October 2006 the then Chief of Staff of the British Army, General Sir Richard Dannatt, explained his disillusionment plainly in a wide-ranging interview with the *Daily Mail*:

> The original intention was that we put in place a liberal democracy that was an exemplar for the region, was pro-West, and might have a beneficial effect on the balance within the Middle East. That was the hope. Whether that was a sensible or a naïve hope, history will judge. I don't think we are going to do that. I think we should aim for a lower ambition. ... [O]ur presence exacerbates the security problems. We are in a Muslim country and Muslims' views of foreigners in their country are quite clear. As a foreigner, you can be welcomed by being invited into a country, but we weren't invited, certainly by those in Iraq at the time. Let's face it; the military campaign we fought in 2003 effectively kicked the door in.[6]

The failings of the post-2003 occupation have been extensively covered in the press and in academic and popular literature. The root problem was that, as Dannatt observed, the professed initial political objective was beyond practical reach. The failure to quickly achieve it turned what was assumed to be a 'regular' war with a definable physical end state into an 'irregular' one with what proved to be a rather fluidly defined and unrealistic political goal.

The high price of ownership

Constructing a liberal, West-leaning democracy out of the wreck of Saddam Hussein's Iraq was clearly the work of a generation or two, not a year or two. In the lead-up to the war CIA analysts, a large project on the 'Future of Iraq' organised by the State Department, and experts at the Army War College's Strategic Studies Institute all warned against the irrational exuberance of those contemplating regime change.[7]

Arguably, it was historically illiterate to expect that the invasion would be long popular with Iraqis, however much they wished to be rid of Saddam Hussein (and dreaded being ruled by his sons in future). The West's hopes for catalysing peace were based on their mistaken belief that Arabs' ill-feeling towards the West was rooted solely in their dislike of their own miserably inadequate leaders: regime change, it was hoped, would neutralize anti-Western sentiment.[8]

The US Administration, however, was not without significant scholarly backers of its chosen course of intervention. In August 2002 Vice President Cheney, in an address to the Veterans of Foreign Wars, acknowledged the critics in one breath and dismissed them in the next:

[An] argument holds that opposing Saddam Hussein would cause even greater troubles in that part of the world, and interfere with the larger war against terror. I believe the opposite is true. Regime change in Iraq would bring about a number of benefits in the region. When the gravest of threats are eliminated, the freedom-loving peoples of the region will have a chance to promote the values that can bring lasting peace. As for the reaction of the Arab 'street', the Middle East expert Professor Fouad Ajami predicts that after liberation the streets in Basra and Baghdad are 'sure to erupt in joy in the same way the throngs in Kabul greeted the Americans.' Extremists in the region would have to rethink their strategy of Jihad. Moderates throughout the region would take heart. And our ability to advance the Israeli-Palestinian peace process would be enhanced, just as it was following the liberation of Kuwait in 1991. The reality is that these times bring not only dangers but also opportunities. In the Middle East, where so many have known only poverty and oppression, terror and tyranny, we look to the day when people can live in freedom and dignity and the young can grow up free of the conditions that breed despair, hatred, and violence.[9]

In 2006, probably the low point of the war, Fouad Ajami re-entered the debate, this time directly, describing the war as morally right, albeit politically costly. 'The Saddam regime would have lasted a thousand years had the Americans not come in and decapitated it', he said.[10]

But if one millennium is the benchmark judgment period then it will be a long time before history can judge the veracity of Cheney's theory. In the meantime, however, the signs have not been good. In the prologue to his colourful account of the effort to install democracy in Iraq, Rajiv Chandrasekaran describes the scales falling from the eyes of an American official involved in the reconstruction, interviewed somewhere in Baghdad's walled Green Zone. Having arrived filled with optimism for what might be achieved in the country, after a few months he was describing himself as 'a neoconservative mugged by reality'.[11]

Plainly, the war failed the 'parent test' of whether it could be explained to the parents of soldiers in terms of a cause that was understandable and deemed acceptable. Kanan Makiya, also a noteworthy academic supporter of the war, reflecting upon its connection with the 'Arab Spring' revolutions in the Middle East, admitted:

> I could not in good conscience tell an American family grieving for a son killed in Iraq that the war was 'worth it'. We didn't know then what we know today. Some, including many of my friends, warned of the dangers of American hubris. I did not heed them in 2003.[12]

Perhaps the most poignant appraisal, though, was that of Kadhom al-Jabouri. Imprisoned by Saddam for eleven years, al-Jabouri was the instigator of the toppling of the statue of Saddam Hussein in Baghdad's Firdos Square hours after the regime had fled. The iconic images of the closing of the invasion feature al-Jabouri, built like a circus strongman, pounding the statue's pedestal with a sledgehammer. Speaking a decade after he lamented the country's fate:

> I was extremely optimistic. The Americans would do something for us. They would push our country forward ... [But now] this government is a curse. Saddam's regime was much better—a dictator left but one hundred dictators came. A looter left but one hundred looters came instead. So, honestly, I regret it.[13]

Whether it is for the invasion in the first place, or the bungling of the post-war stabilisation effort, regret is a most common feeling about Iraq typified by a sort of buyer's remorse, the unshakeable sense that one has purchased not very much at a very substantial cost. Consider the implications of Colin Powell's 'Pottery Barn Rule' warning to President Bush before the invasion of Iraq:

You are going to be the owner of twenty-five million people. You will own all their hopes, aspirations, and problems. You'll own it all.[14]

The cost of ownership, however, as the economist Dan Ariely has explained, can be very high indeed—and this applies not just to material things but also to ideas. Once we take ownership of a thing or idea we tend to prize it beyond its objective worth. As a result, we experience difficulty letting go of it and cannot stand the idea of its loss. 'What are we left with then?' asks Ariely. 'An ideology—rigid and unyielding.'[15] The differential in the perceived burden of ownership of the war would prove to have big effects on strategic behaviour within the coalition. America, having led the march to war in the first place, evinced a greater need to actually win it—or perhaps more precisely a greater difficulty backing out of it even after the point of seriously diminishing returns had obviously been passed. Its allies, by contrast, willingly adopted a subaltern role, to a greater or lesser degree, happy to be along for the ride provided that costs could be maintained below a threshold, which was only defined from country to country as the conflict progressed.

As Greece to America's Rome[16]

Readers of Clausewitz often conflate what might be called the primary trinity (of passion, chance and reason) and the secondary trinity (of people, army and government) because he himself drew a connection between these 'predominant tendencies' in war and these particular actors. As ever, though, Clausewitz hedged an ideal in principle with a *caveat* in practice. In this case, he explained that each member of the primary trinity is normally manifested in a specific member of the secondary trinity, but that occasionally the member it is manifested in can vary.[17] The Iraq War provides an excellent example of this occasional oddity, as does Afghanistan to an extent. Passion for the Iraq War, mixed from the beginning (though less so in the United States than its allies), was more manifest in the White House—the government—than the people.

The 2006 *Iraq Study Group Report*, compiled by a group of former American defence and foreign policy luminaries under the auspices of the United States Institute for Peace, described how international support for the war was tepid, while attitudes in the Middle East varied from actively and officially hostile to merely quietly and unofficially so:

Despite a massive effort, stability in Iraq remains elusive and the situation is deteriorating. The Iraqi government cannot now govern, sustain, and defend itself without the support of the United States. Iraqis have not been convinced that they must take responsibility for their own future. Iraq's neighbours and much of the international community have not been persuaded to play an active and constructive role in supporting Iraq. The ability of the United States to shape outcomes is diminishing. Time is running out.[18]

Moreover, the report pointed out, at that time 66 per cent of Americans reported disapproving of the war's conduct and more than 60 per cent felt that there was no clear plan for moving forward: 'US foreign policy cannot be successfully sustained without the broad support of the American people', it remarked.[19] Their conclusion was that all things considered it was best to beat the retreat—not a hasty retreat, necessarily, but a retreat nonetheless and a more precipitate one than any contemplated by the president. It was a well-reasoned and dispassionate assessment.

In January 2007, therefore, when Bush laid out a contrary new strategy that increased the size of the American contingent in Iraq by 20,000 troops, he was gambling against the house, as it were, that his own personal passion for the war would suffice to sustain it until more agreeable conditions for withdrawal could be achieved. His closing remarks in a televised speech on the subject were not quite Shakespearean but shades of Henry V beneath the breach in the English wall at Harfleur were apparent:

Fellow citizens: The year ahead will demand more patience, sacrifice, and resolve. It can be tempting to think that America can put aside the burdens of freedom. Yet times of testing reveal the character of a nation. And throughout our history Americans have always defied the pessimists and seen our faith in freedom redeemed. Now America is engaged in a new struggle that will set the course for a new century. We can and we will prevail. We go forward with trust that the Author of Liberty will guide us throughout these trying hours.[20]

In rhetorical form, it contained all the same elements of mythic narrative, an appeal pitched to resonate emotionally first and foremost and to engage reason only secondarily. Bush's 'gamble', as the journalist Thomas Ricks put it, effectively turned the fate of his presidency over to his military commanders, leaving it to them, more or less, to pull his feet from the fire.[21]

Leaving aside whether the project was doomed before it even began, there were other failings of execution that made it even more difficult. The divisive diplomacy that preceded the war alienated many allies and lost their support for the ensuing occupation: Rumsfeld's derisive description of France and Germany as 'old Europe' effectively sealed off the possibility of support from that quarter.[22] Even Britain's contribution was reckoned superfluous in the beginning, as the Americans, frustrated with the Blair government's desire to obtain a 'second resolution' from the United Nations Security Council backing the invasion, let it be known that the United States could get on without them if necessary.[23] While certainly true in the military sense, the remark bruised the Blair government and exacerbated British public's anti-war feeling, adding weight to the millstone that the occupation became for British governments faced with explaining the war to a sceptical population.

The disbanding of the Iraqi army and the de-Baathification of the whole civil service right down to low levels were perhaps the most consequential acts of all. When Paul Bremer, the head of the incoming Coalition Provisional Authority, announced these policies as practically his inaugural initiatives General Jay Garner, who at that point was heading the Office of Reconstruction and Humanitarian Assistance, thought 'Holy Christ. We can't do this'.[24] Taken together, these acts had the effect of throwing out of work about half a million people, many of whom were either blameless or crucial to the running of the state bureaucracy and social services, or both. Also, many were trained soldiers and police with extensive knowledge of weapons and tactics. That was the day, one army planner recalled, 'that we snatched defeat from the jaws of victory and created an insurgency'. Or in the words of another, 'we expected to be able to recall the Iraqi Army. Once CPA [Coalition Provisional Authority] took the decision to disband the Iraqi Army and start again, our assumptions for the plan became invalid'.[25]

Ironically, as it turned out it was a British officer, Brigadier Nigel Aylwin-Foster, who in a sharply critical essay (republished in the *Military Review*, the American Army's major professional journal) pointed out how ill-prepared in regard to both training and temperament the American military was for the sort of war in which it had become embroiled. The thrust of his argument was that the root of the problem was 'moral and conceptual' in nature rather than material and physical—it was only this that could explain the 'apparently paradoxical currents of strength and weakness' that he observed while serving with American forces in Iraq in 2004.[26]

'Wars amongst the people' such as that in Iraq were more dislocating for the American military than others, he argued, because no other military was focused with such relentless intensity on regular, large-scale, firepower-orientated modes of warfare. As such, it lacked, in Aylwin-Foster's words, two skills that were suddenly crucial to successful operations: first, the ability to 'see issues and actions from the perspective of the domestic population'; and second, an understanding of the 'relative value of force and how easily excessive force, even when apparently justified, can undermine popular support'.[27]

These criticisms were not beyond challenge. The argument that the American military was poorly prepared for 'Phase IV' (that is, post-major operations, or 'stabilisation' operations) was not incorrect but contained telling inaccuracies. As one thoughtful respondent—actually the same planner quoted above about invalidated planning assumptions—put it in the *Military Review*:

> Aylwin-Foster is wrong in claiming that we did not plan for Phase IV. The challenge was translating the plans into action while dealing with guidance and assumptions from higher echelons of command, the deployment process, and evolving policy. As a result, our plans never quite evolved to link ground operations to logical lines of operation that would lead to setting solid military conditions for policy objectives.[28]

This is, of course, more or less exactly the problem that Rupert Smith pointed out as the predominant one at the pragmatic level of contemporary warfare when he spoke of the need for actions to be nested in a coherent strategic context (as discussed in Chapter Five).

Drawing on John Nagl's comparative research on the American and British armies in counterinsurgency, in which he juxtaposed the latter's putative capacity for organisational cultural learning against the former's allegedly more hidebound adherence to the precepts of large-scale conventional warfare, Aylwin-Foster criticised the American army's ability to adapt to the situation. There is something to be said for this line of argument, which he advanced cautiously and with due regard for American 'can-do ethos, self-belief and resilient optimism'.[29]

It is also true that America's firepower orientation, which ill-suited it to the challenge at hand, has long been deeply entrenched. Indeed, after the Vietnam War the American military effectively defined counterinsurgency as outside the army's *métier*. The 1976 edition of Field Manual *100–5 Operations*, written at a time when South Vietnam's resistance to the armies of North Vietnam was crumbling, did not even mention counterinsurgency, as sure an indicator of the concept's Siberian exile from the American military mind as it is possible to imagine.[30]

Moreover, it is true that the British Army's history includes a strikingly large number of small wars, first in its hyperactive phase of imperial expansion, followed by myriad wars of imperial maintenance, and finally those of its post-Second World War withdrawal from empire in the face of various wars of national liberation. In staff colleges worldwide, when the syllabus turns to counterinsurgency it is C.E. Callwell's work on small wars, as well as post-war quasi-doctrinal British books by the likes of Robert Thompson and Frank Kitson, which form the heart of the canon.[31]

In short, Britain was widely considered to have an army shaped by history to be relatively small and decentralized and, therefore, ideally suited by temperament and training to such warfare.[32] In testimony to Congress in July 2004 the thoughtful and well-written American Major General Robert Scales claimed:

> Even today the British Army has an advantage over the United States in that they possess officers with the ability to move comfortably between and within the inner circles of foreign militaries. Great Britain's relative success in Basra is due in no small measure to the self-assurance and comfort with foreign culture derived from centuries of practicing the art of soldier diplomacy and liaison.[33]

British attitudes did sometimes display an unattractive tendency toward smugness and arch superiority, which was bound to, and did, rankle the Americans.[34] But this was not the case with Aylwin-Foster's essay, which, though pointedly critical, was a fair assessment of the state of affairs as he saw them from 2003–5. Nonetheless, the considerable irony of his piece was that in Britain's patch of Iraq, in the southern predominantly Shiite city of Basra where the situation in 2003 and 2004 was moderately good (particularly compared to the increasingly chaotic violence in the north), the situation was rapidly deteriorating. Criminal gangs and Shiite militias effectively took over the city from the British.

By the autumn of 2005 the situation was so bad that an armoured attack had to be made on a police station in Basra to release two Special Forces men who had been arrested while conducting undercover surveillance in the city. A crowd gathered throwing rocks and petrol bombs at the British Warrior armoured vehicles surrounding the building, from one of which a British soldier with his uniform on fire was pictured exiting in what became an iconic image.[35] In December that year, British forces returned to the police station, which by then had been taken over by militias, and blew it up. Over the next year they withdrew further and further into just two bases, a small one at Basra Palace in the city, and a larger one at Basra airport where effectively they were besieged. Then on 3 September 2007 they pulled out of the city entirely, leaving just the airport outpost occupied.

It was not a glorious finish, although the British spokesman did his best to put a positive spin on it:

> [T]his is the point, really, where we ask the Iraqis, the Iraqi security forces, to start to take the responsibility for the security of Basra themselves. I think that's the right thing to do, because the longer that we're here, the more they are—well, the less inclined that they are to run things for themselves.[36]

The Basra police chief's description of his inheritance was a stinging indictment of British operations there: 'They left me militia, they left me gangsters, and they left me all the troubles in the world'.[37]

Counterinsurgency: The Movie!

By contrast, the American army was about to complete one of the most striking reversals of mindset in the history of large organisations. Arguably, by the time Aylwin-Foster's essay was published the insurgency in Iraq had already passed its 'tipping point', the point beyond which in theory no amount of effort could win the population back to the side of the government. The authors of the Iraq Study Group report were quite realistically pessimistic in their assessment of the situation and the wisest course of action. Yet the Americans did 'learn counterinsurgency', and they did so on the fly, as though changing the tires on a moving car.[38] In light of its previous marginalisation in American military thinking, the reorientation of the military around counter-insurgency was a remarkable story.

In fact, the story of this transformation became the story full stop and the subject of extensive, and often worshipful, recounting. Generally, these accounts feature three key themes. The first is that the first two years of the occupation were essentially lost to incompetence: progress on the political front was slow to non-existent, while the returning of Iraq to some semblance of normal civil life and economic vitality was impossible given the dire security situation of the country.[39]

The repeated and intrusive sweeps of towns and villages by soldiers resulted in the killing, wounding and capturing of few insurgents but many civilians who, naturally enough, grew more alienated and angry as time went on. The cruel and humiliating abuse of Iraqi prisoners in Abu Ghraib prison, much of it captured in snapshots taken by the soldiers involved, was perhaps the nadir. The first battle of Fallujah in early April 2004, launched hastily at the urging of a very angry President Bush in response to a classic insurgent provocation (the murder of four civilian contractors whose burnt and mutilated bodies were then hung from a bridge over the Euphrates River), was also a deep low-point. The result was a display of futile strength that did more harm than good. The city was badly damaged but also ultimately left under the control of the insurgency. 'By attacking frontally', said the Marine commander General James Conway who led the assault, 'we unified the city against us'.[40]

Images of the depraved abuse of prisoners by their American military gaolers, the ghoulish dangling display of mutilated bodies by insurgents, and then ultimately the pounding of Fallujah, which was portrayed in the Arab world as though it were the second coming of the rapacious Mongols, flashed around the world. In the case of Fallujah, concluded the Arab media analyst Marc Lynch, 'Al Jazeera's reporting ... contradicted the coalition's narrative so graphically and dramatically that it determined the outcome of that battle'.[41] Though poorly recognised at the time, Lynch's observation underlined the way that the virtual dimension of the conflict, into which the insurgents were pouring their main effort with resolute intensity, was superseding the pragmatic dimension where the counterinsurgents were investing theirs.[42]

The second theme is the importance placed on the new *Counterinsurgency Field Manual* (FM3–24) published on 15 December 2006.[43] Never has a piece of military doctrine received such lavish and sustained attention outside of military circles. One and a half million people downloaded the online edition, and a civilian version with a foreword by John Nagl, one of the authoring team, made it to the *New York Times* bestseller list. It is not just the content of the doctrine that attracted attention and debate. The doctrine itself acquired a sort of iconic status in the story of America's adaptation to the new counter-insurgency era.[44]

It was as though, as the author and journalist Fred Kaplan described it, there were two sorts of insurgencies going on—the bitterly fought ones in Iraq and Afghanistan that dominated the global mediascape, but also another within the military itself, bitterly fought in the pages of professional journals, in the outpourings of doctrine writers, and behind closed doors in promotion boards and budget committees. The key figure in both was the charismatic general David Petraeus whose idea it was to rewrite the existing, widely regarded as inadequate, doctrine for two reasons:

> First, he wanted to have an Army doctrine on counterinsurgency in place by the time he went back to Iraq, so that he would have official cover for the new strategy he was intent on imposing ... Second, over the long haul, he wanted to force a change in mind-set, to drive a wedge into mainstream Army thinking, to broaden and overhaul the official definition of war in a way that he had been thinking about and advocating for over twenty years.[45]

Out went the old strategy developed by General George Casey to hand over responsibility to Iraqis and get American troops out as soon as possible. In came the new strategy developed by Petraeus and his 'brain-trust', an idiosyncratic group comprising his military protégés, like-minded long-time colleagues, and a number of outsiders mostly from academia and the NGO community, many of whom were involved in the writing of FM3–24.[46] 'The surge', as it came to be known, involved more troops on the ground, but more importantly it involved troops actually operating in accordance with a different mind-set encapsulated by what are referred to in the Field Manual as the 'paradoxes of counterinsurgency'. There were nine of these, generally variations on the ideal that violence should be used discriminately because the protection of the population was paramount and that the counterinsurgent force had to be as adaptive and nimble as their insurgent quarry.[47]

The third theme, following from the second, is the ostensibly electrifying effect that Petraeus had on the campaign. As Thomas Ricks put it: 'The answer for what to do in Iraq would come largely through one person, General David Petraeus, who ... would lead the way in determining how to revamp the US approach to the war'.[48]

False memory syndrome

Each of these themes, however, is to a greater or lesser degree inaccurate or misleading. They are also to a large degree based upon a false historical narrative of counterinsurgency and a belief in the applicability of British military competence in its myriad wars of imperial withdrawal, as well as domestically in Northern Ireland, to the expeditionary campaigns of the War on Terror.[49] It is indisputable that from a relative high in 2004 the trajectory of British operations in Iraq was downward, with retreat from contesting control of the streets and markets with the insurgents followed by isolation and effective besiegement on its fortified base on the outskirts of Basra city, and ultimately ignominious withdrawal. By March 2008, when the Iraqi Army launched Operation Charge of the Knights to retake the city, the British had effectively sidelined themselves.[50] By contrast, from the low of 2004–5 the trajectory of American operations was generally upward from isolation on its bases to greater and greater engagement with 'war amongst the people' and if not to victory in Iraq then at least to a reasonably dignified withdrawal. Why the difference?

It beggars belief to suggest that it was the arrival of a new doctrine. After all, it is not a slur on the authors of FM3–24 to say that it is largely a codification of counterinsurgency 'best practice' derived in large part from British sources with a few adjustments for contemporary context and American military institutional sensitivities and internal turf wars.[51] The importance of coordinated government machinery, the need to focus on the population and not the insurgents *per se*, the use of minimum force, adherence to the law, operations designed to 'clear and hold' rather than 'search and destroy', the vital importance of intelligence, and the pursuit of political settlement of the conflict—all these were established elements of British counterinsurgency doctrine and practice. Even if the links to the classic 'British way' in counterinsurgency had eroded in the British Army (a possibility for which there is a good deal of evidence), why did they not relearn them as speedily and put them back into practice as adroitly as did the Americans?[52]

Moreover, accounts of the Iraq War turnaround that emphasise 'population-centric' security often tend, consciously or unconsciously, to diminish the signal contribution of enemy-centric action to success. For instance, David Kilcullen, an Australian army officer and academic anthropologist who went on to be General Petraeus's senior counterinsurgency advisor, wrote:

> In 2007, we successfully turned Iraq back from the brink of total disaster by applying a strategy of protecting the population, co-opting and winning over the reconcilables, expanding the 'centre' of Iraqi politics, marginalising the extremes, and eliminating the irreconcilables.[53]

This would seem, though, to reflect the orthodoxy of post-war counterinsurgency theory more than it does the actual practices that were evident on the ground. This is not to say that population-centric techniques (not a 'strategy') were unimportant but rather that they put the cart before the horse; the fact is that the coalition forces, in particular 'interagency' teams of Special Forces plus other intelligence, police and foreign service officers, became extremely good at finding and capturing or killing insurgents, which opened up space for other measures to advance the pacification of the country. In part this depended on connectivity.

Soldiers learned that to be successful they had to be able to hit targets identified within forty-five minutes of receiving a tip. Advanced communications and decentralised leadership made this possible—and not simply with relatively easy to task fast-moving bomb-delivering aircraft but with teams of soldiers actually on the ground 'swarming' the insurgents.[54] This in turn meant that force could be applied quite discriminately—if not, as the famous Vietnam era counterinsurgent John Paul Vann urged, literally 'with a knife' then at least more or less face-to-face and not from the security and anonymity of a pilot's seat.[55] Other developments in technical and signals intelligence, long-endurance unmanned systems for surveillance and attack, biometric census, and computer-aided data analysis also provided potentially significant tools.[56]

Interestingly, given the failings described in the previous chapter, this was a sort of continuation of the ideals behind Network-Centric Warfare in the form of 'network targeting', which proved vital. In the words of one critical assessment of 'high-value target teams':

> Christened collaborative warfare by one proponent, the new capability reportedly captured or killed enemies so fast that it put their clandestine organisations on the defensive and gave population security measures a chance to shift public support to government forces. Unlike the unmanned drones that kill terrorist suspects from afar, the new capability was not a high-profile breakthrough, but rather an underappreciated organisational innovation.[57]

Basically, the insurgents initially confounded the coalition by dropping their profile below the engagement threshold of the major sensors and weapons systems arrayed against them; in return, the coalition went down the rabbit hole after them and learned to fight there, more or less effectively. The key innovation, then, was not technological, but rather an organisational adaptation that took account of technological possibilities. Most of military history looks this way in one form or another: whether a small war or a great war, action is followed by reaction, innovation by adaptation and re-innovation in a continuous cycle where no particular weapon or technique remains permanently irresistible or immutable.

This may be seen, however, to challenge the narrative given voice by General Petraeus, amongst others, that 'you don't kill or capture your way out of an industrial-strength insurgency. Rather, it takes a mix of every aspect. It takes a comprehensive approach, and not just military but civil–military'.[58] The problem is that this is more truism than truth. In counterinsurgency as in war generally, much depends on context and in particular the idea that one is trying to defeat; hence Clausewitz's point about war being an extension of politics enacted violently. Contemporary strategic thinking in many ways has regressed in respect to this point.

For example, in a 2008 speech to the Royal United Services Institute, General Dannatt pinned the problem in an interesting way. Putting the blame for Britain's poor performance in Iraq partially upon a politically correct historical sensitivity, he noted that, 'In a desire not to be considered still colonial, I sense that we lost the mindset and skills across government that our fathers and grandfathers instinctively understood'.[59] He then name-checked the aforementioned Victorian-era guru of small wars, C.E. Callwell, as an example of this wisdom of the ages. But Callwell did not say you cannot kill your way to victory in small wars. In fact, he said completely the opposite thing, clearly and categorically. He insisted that the insurgent must be shown at 'every turn that he has lost [the initiative]' and that 'the forces of civilisation are dominant and not to be denied'.[60] To the reader of contemporary doctrine the stridency of such pronouncements is striking, for this is no longer the current teaching.[61]

Ironically, though, while Callwell and his fellow Victorians made less reference to a 'civil–military' approach than we do today, they actually practised it much more than do their descendants (who make constant reference to it). The casualty lists from the British retreat from Kabul in 1842 are evidence of this, revealing the vast number of civilian 'Britishers' then involved in Afghanistan: 4500 soldiers died compared to 12,000 civilian administrators and engineers, family members and assorted hangers-on in that debacle.[62]

It comes back to 'moral forces', which Callwell, like Clausewitz, elevated to a position of primary importance in war. Moreover, he conceived of this moral force as an approximation of what we might describe as 'civilisational confidence'—a confidence he simply assumed, *a priori*, that the intervening power possessed and was in no danger of losing.[63] Compare this to the attitude betrayed by Mark Urban's observation, in his detailed account of British involvement in the 'secret war' fought by SAS units and American Special Forces to take down insurgent networks, that the 'truly disturbing (to those of a liberal mind, in any case) things about the special operations campaign in Iraq is that it suggests a large terrorist organisation can be overwhelmed under certain circumstances by military force'.[64]

Why would this be disturbing, except that it conflicts with the narrative that counterinsurgencies are not won with force? Post-Second World War wisdom on counterinsurgency, especially that of the French practitioner-cum-theorist David Galula, holds that the counterinsurgent force's strengths are 'congenital' and in large part unusable. As he put it, for a regular force 'to adopt the insurgent's warfare would be the same as for a giant to try to fit into a dwarf's clothing'.[65] In Iraq at least, this was flatly wrong—the giant's donning of the dwarf's clothing was the key to success. In a way, though, Aylwin-Foster put his finger on perhaps a more salient issue:

> US Army personnel, like their colleagues in the other US services, had a strong sense of moral authority. They fervently believed in the invasion's underlying purpose, the delivery of democracy to Iraq, whereas other nations' forces tended to be more ambivalent about why they were there. This was at once a strength and hindrance to progress.[66]

Aylwin-Foster focused on the palpable negatives of American 'moral righteousness combined with emotivity', which undoubtedly contributed to some of the major missteps of the war, from the wilful refusal at the top to even say the word 'insurgency' let alone to contemplate how to counter one for over a year after the initial invasion, to the counterproductive tactics of corporals and privates in their daily operations.[67] Yet Callwell never talked of 'winning the population'. The 'object to be sought for', he argued, 'clearly is to fight, not to manoeuvre', or in other words, to bring the insurgent to battle and defeat him there in battle.[68] He did enjoin his readers, however, to use force purposefully and, in a sense, discriminately, so as not to 'exasperate' the population.[69]

Compare this with journalist William Langewiesche's searing 2005 'letter from Baghdad', which painted a picture of life in the city that epitomised the exasperation of the population:

> The Iraqi people are far from stupid or unaware. But in the isolation and arrogance that have characterized the American occupation, never have we addressed them directly, explained ourselves honestly, humbly sought their support, respected their views of solutions, of political power, of American motivations, or of the history and future of Iraq. Even short of the killing we have done, we have broken down their doors, run them off the roads, swiveled our guns at them, shouted profanities at them, and disrespected their women—all this hundreds or thousands of times every day.[70]

It was, of course, quite necessary that the American military learn to operate in this environment in a less abrasive manner; to do otherwise would be to simply invite backlash after backlash in a downward spiral of pointless violence. Considering the case of the British, however, serves to illustrate the power of the Americans' sense of moral authority—not their sense of righteousness *per se*, but the relative lack of ambivalence in their belief in the cause of the war, and their straightforward abhorrence of the looming spectre of defeat.

It was not simply, as Andrew Garfield observed in 2006, that 'the British generally have lower ambitions abroad than Americans and would normally avoid seeking more lofty and problematic societal change'.[71] The differences went deeper. Basically, Britain's aims had little or nothing to do with Iraq or Afghanistan. It simply sought in both campaigns to fulfil its traditional role as the transatlantic link between the United States and Europe, as well as to demonstrate to its long-term ally that it was fully committed to the 'special relationship' at a crucial time. This suited the United States because Britain's presence helped to keep other coalition members, most of whose populations were even more sceptical, involved in the campaign.[72] Ultimately, the British government lacked President Bush's willingness to escalate the situation in the hopes of achieving 'victory' (however defined), but was also unwilling to bear the diplomatic costs of cutting and running. In effect, they were committed enough to lose but not to win because they did not feel nearly so much burden of ownership of the problem.

The British Army is much more phlegmatic about this pattern of strategic thinking than one might expect. That is because Britain is conditioned by history to subscribe to the belief (outdated, as we shall see in the next chapter) that tactical defeats in small wars abroad do not represent strategic crises at home.[73] The British Army has consequently developed a habit of mind and practice typically described as 'cracking on'. This is a major strength, in many respects—particularly in terms of tactical fortitude, small unit cohesion, durability of morale, and the quality of 'extreme self-control'. Martin Van Creveld has argued that it was this that underpinned British success in Northern Ireland where, unlike practically every other army under similar conditions, the British Army:

> did not become demoralised. They did not take drugs, did not go AWOL or desert, did not refuse to fight, and did not turn into a danger to themselves and their officers as had happened in Vietnam, where any number of the latter were 'fragged'—blown to pieces—by their own subordinates. Instead, they were as ready to give battle on the last day of the hostilities as they had been on the first—a fact that the terrorists learned to their cost.[74]

It can, however, be something of a weakness, as seen in senior officers' willingness in Iraq and, arguably, Afghanistan to commit to operations while knowing they lacked the necessary resources and had no realistic chance of success.[75]

In a nutshell, while Bush was gambling his government's credibility on his army the British government was gambling with its army too. What both campaigns threw into stark relief was that British governments behaved strategically rather in the manner of an inveterate gambler with a small pile of chips. They wish to stay in the top game of global players and they perceive that in order to do so they need to place a stake on the table. That stake was the army. And its job was to do 'just enough to satisfy the Americans while limiting where possible both financial cost and exposure to casualties'.[76]

Moreover, it was not just the British government that calculated the strategic cost/benefit of expeditionary campaigning in the war on terror in this way.

7

STRATEGIC NARRATIVE
AND STRATEGIC INCOHERENCE

'Still no word from the garbage men?'

'No. They're no shows. Three months of preps down the tube, and I dragged you out of retirement for nothing.'

'This is fun. I like this. You've taken over the reins, all the worries. You're loosey goosey. I'm just along for the ride.'

A conversation in the film *The Italian Job* (2003)

Britain's strategic behaviour vis-à-vis the United States in both Iraq and Afghanistan was atypical of other coalition members only in that it was actually more than averagely willing to take on major responsibilities (albeit as a junior partner under American leadership with access to American resources where necessary) and to pay the price. Most coalition members were less willing and many were considerably less willing. Restrictions on what the military contingents of some states would and would not do proved to be a considerable operational headache. The most vexatious problem, however, was the inability of the coalition to articulate a compelling strategic narrative that could retain its coherence amongst all the disparate audiences who, while physically separated, share the same global mediaspace. In many ways, the experience of the Canadian forces in Afghanistan, like Britain a serious contributor to the fighting, illustrates the new salience of strategic narrative coherence and the perils of its absence. Too much responsibility is invested in the local theatre commander for managing the perception of conflict and maintaining the narrative. Politicians are largely to blame for avoiding the issue. Publics readily pick up on the disconnect of rhetoric and reality and consequently lose any passion they might have for the war, even though they may be proud of their armed forces.

If one looks at this situation through the prism of Clausewitzian passion, the structural incongruities within NATO's International Security Assistance Force in Afghanistan become readily apparent. Arguably, the British government is quite right to go to war for the purposes of showing solidarity with its major ally and of bolstering the 'special relationship', such as it is. Patrick Porter has argued that this is a sort of false consciousness, that Britain cannot secure a 'uniquely privileged relationship with the United States in this way.'[1] On the other hand, if only for the lack of credible alternatives, no British government has shown any inclination to change this plank of its defence and foreign policy.[2] The trouble is the 'parent test'. No British defence minister or prime minister has been willing to go before the grieving mother of a soldier slain in Iraq or Afghanistan and say that he or she died for the purpose of preserving American-British intelligence sharing, military interoperability, access to defence technology, diplomatic collaboration, and a commitment to a more or less common vision of global order.

Though true, this is a politically unpalatable message that ministers have shied away from voicing. They have preferred to be rhetorically vigorous, framing the conflict either as an existential, values-driven fight that it is vital to win, or as an essential step in preventing terrorism at home. Unfortunately, both messages failed to resonate because the rhetoric of the government and its actual behaviour rarely dovetailed.

Whose hearts and minds?

Overall, sweeping objectives were paired with plainly inadequate resources and strategic drift that imparted to the whole effort a painfully unsettling ambiguity felt not only by civilians but in the military too. As an illustration, Major General John Cantwell, an Australian officer with thirty-eight years of service encompassing three wars from Operation Desert Storm in 1991, through Iraq in 2006, and Afghanistan in 2010 where he headed the Australian contingent, recorded in his memoirs his struggle with post-traumatic stress disorder. He was troubled by a gnawing doubt:

> As I paid a final salute at the foot of yet another flag-draped coffin loaded into the belly of an aircraft bound for Australia, I found myself questioning if the pain and

suffering of our soldiers and their families were worth it. I wondered if the deaths of any of those fallen soldiers made any difference. I recoiled from such thoughts, which seemed disrespectful, almost treasonous. I had to answer in the affirmative, or risk exposing all my endeavours as fraudulent. I had to believe it was worth it. But the question continues to prick at my mind. I don't have an answer.[3]

Moreover, in Europe especially, but also increasingly in the United States, it grew ever clearer that expeditionary campaigns abroad exacerbate the radicalisation of poorly integrated Muslim minorities at home, some of whom feel so strongly about supposed offences against their co-religionists that they are moved to murder their compatriots in large numbers. The 'martyrdom speech' of the 7 July 2005 (or '7/7') London bomber Mohammed Siddique Khan exemplified this phenomenon. In a broad Yorkshire accent he declared in a posthumously released video:

> Your democratically elected governments continuously perpetuate atrocities against my people all over the world. And your support of them makes you directly responsible, just as I am responsible for protecting and avenging my Muslim brothers and sisters. Until we feel security, you will be our targets. And until you stop the bombing, gassing, imprisonment and torture of my people we will not stop the fight.[4]

In war, it is perfectly acceptable—indeed, it is actively desirable—to mislead and confound one's enemy. It is also sometimes necessary to dissemble amongst one's allies, or at least to paper over contradictions in respective aims and objectives with artful rhetoric, provided the overall goal is sufficiently mutually vital. The Second World War alliance of Britain, the United States and the Soviet Union provides a case in point, with each pursuing a different and contradictory vision of the post-war peace. It is wholly undesirable, however, to deceive oneself. This is the essential gist of the oft-quoted remark by Clausewitz that the supreme and most far-reaching act of the statesman and commander is to establish 'the kind of war on which they are embarking; neither mistaking it for, nor trying to turn it into, something that is alien to its nature'.[5]

The trouble is that the post-9/11 expeditionary campaigns have rested on faulty premises, half-truths and strategic self-deceptions. In the first place, it was misconstrued as a war that could be decided by the kinetic blows of a military campaign, rather than as a confrontation with something more formless, insidious and implacable than a regular army. Michael Howard described what the war was about as a mood of 'sullen resentment' in the Muslim world: 'a state of mind that has to be transformed; a task demanding skill, sagacity, determination, empathy, and above all patience'.[6] Unfortunately, even while armed forces were relearning old skills of 'winning hearts and minds' as they operated amongst local Iraqis and Afghans, they were simultaneously exasperating segments of their home populations and those of onlooking nations.

Then there was the basing of the campaigns upon *ad hoc* 'coalitions of the willing' in which nations committed their armed forces without first establishing clearly understood and agreed foundational principles. This deprived the campaigns on the ground of coherence, particularly in Afghanistan. This was first and foremost an artifact of impatience, that sense of urgency that has had an enormously compromising effect on the quality of strategic thinking. But there was also a large degree of politicking behind the coalition's formation that was never dealt with openly. History, unfortunately, does not record any successful counterinsurgencies by a coalition. The ideal of unity of effort is very difficult to achieve even within the military, intelligence, police, and diplomatic and other agencies of a single country.

The International Security Assistance Force (ISAF) in Afghanistan has involved contributions of one sort or another from thirty-nine countries, including all of the major democracies—not all of which were perfectly honest with themselves, let alone others, about their intentions and aims. As a result, there were massive differences in levels of commitment to operations, often expressed in the form of 'national caveats' restricting how troops could be employed, which caused a major headache for the overall theatre commanders.[7]

In fact, in Afghanistan operations were pervaded by a lethal cocktail of blind optimism and neglect from 2002 through 2005, while the United States turned its attention to Iraq, taking ownership there, as described in the last chapter. In the meantime, nobody took similar ownership in Afghanistan—as a result of which the once-defeated Taliban got the breathing space it needed to reconstitute itself as a military and political force and charge back into action in 2006. Since then strategic clarity and narrative coherence have not been much in evidence, despite some effort on the part of the Obama administration after the 2008 American presidential elections. As one hard-hitting analysis concluded, there have been just two consistent themes in the Afghan campaign: first, the 'mismatch between the dominant policy fashions pursued at particular points in time and the cycle of events in Afghanistan itself' and, second, the flawed execution of those policies 'suggesting that even if there had been a closer alignment of approach with conditions on the ground, "success" would have been elusive'.[8]

The most strategically debilitating thing, however, was always the incoherence of the overall strategic narrative, not so much in the eyes of the local population, the populations of neighbouring countries and Muslims worldwide (though all these were important) as in the eyes of the populations of the coalition members. There is nothing unusual about mutable war aims, but consistent answers to the questions 'why are we in Afghanistan?' (let alone Iraq) and 'what is this war about?' never really established themselves in the public consciousness after the intervention. And few people were more acutely aware of the squishiness of support and the confusion of the public than those officers in theatre struggling with the practically impossible task of translating faulty policy and incoherent strategy into something meaningful on the ground.

All for one and none for all

As one senior American officer involved in ISAF's information operations put it when interviewed in Kabul, 'We entered Afghanistan after September 11 for one limited reason—to get Bin Laden and punish those who attacked us and those who sheltered them. And then we just… stayed'. War needs a firmer plot than this; otherwise everything—policy, strategy, action—lacks foundation. In the words of another ISAF official, 'we've lost [the narrative] and the international audience has grown lost and uncommitted'.[9]

The problem is not lack of strategic narrative *per se*; it is rather the lack of any overarching narrative that unifies the diverse and often contradictory communications and audiences involved. For the United States, the problem of narrative coherence is arguably less acute: the war is about 9/11, punishing the perpetrators and preventing the cancer of al-Qaeda which once metastasized in Afghanistan from rooting there again. Also, for better or worse, if the United States did not shoulder the task then no one else would. For most of the coalition, however, the war was about various subsidiary objectives, primarily their relationship with the United States and more generally the coherence of NATO, and the obligations entailed were often eminently shirkable. No coalition members truly bought the Bush administration's 'War on Terror' metanarrative.

General Rick Hillier, Canada's Chief of the Defense Staff through much of this period, described in his memoirs the dire effect that these problems have had on NATO, which he described as having:

> reached the stage where it is a corpse, decomposing, and somebody's going to have to perform a Frankenstein-like life giving act by breathing some life saving air through those rotten lips into those putrescent lungs, or the Alliance will be done.[10]

This, it must be recalled, is from the pen of the most senior military officer in one of the most stalwart and committed NATO member states. For a war embarked upon by most of the coalition in the spirit of Article Five of the NATO Charter, which holds that an attack on one member state is as an attack on all of them, and after claims from two NATO Secretary Generals that nothing less than the credibility of the military alliance was on the line, this is a startling admission of failure.[11]

Although much of the 'blowback' of expeditionary campaigning in Iraq and Afghanistan has, in the form of domestic Muslim radicalisation and terrorism, been focused on Britain, this country is perhaps not the most representative of the dynamics in the coalition more generally. Arguably Britain is an outlier because of its longstanding commitment to Atlanticism and its ideal of 'punching above its weight' internationally, closely tied as those things are to its national self-image. The presumption of policy in Britain has for many decades been that the United States should always be supported when it is acting on behalf of the 'free world'. Britain alone, for example, joined the United States in the four-day December 1998 'Desert Fox' bombing campaign launched by President Bill Clinton. For Britain, the general lesson of its post-Second World War military campaigns has been that the degree of American support is almost always crucial to the outcome, and successive prime ministers, not least Tony Blair, have been wary of letting a gap over policy develop between London and Washington.[12]

Canada's role in the coalition serves better to highlight a number of significant points. Also a tight ally of the United States, Canada's own 'special relationship' with Washington is rooted more in trade, culture and the defence of North American airspace. There is little to none of the 'where you go we go' automaticity in their military relationship that is present in the British-American relationship. In fact, the deployment in 2003 of Canadian troops to Afghanistan in an explicitly peacekeeping role was more or less openly conceived as an inspired diplomatic and strategic ploy by then Prime Minister Jean Chretien. Exceedingly loath to be a part of the invasion of Iraq, the deployment to Afghanistan was reckoned to be an ideal way to 'placate its American neighbour, while appeasing the "peaceable kingdom" at the same time'.[13] It was the best of both worlds, allowing Canada to contribute to the war effort in a way that did not offend the perceived sensitivities of the generally pacific but also exceedingly penny-wise Canadian public, which had been not keen on foreign military adventures for many decades.

Things changed drastically in 2005 when about 2500 Canadian troops deployed to Kandahar where Canada took control of the local Provincial Reconstruction Team. The mission did not stay in the peacekeeping mould for long as the Taliban for the first time since 2002 were about to attempt to challenge ISAF forces in the south of the country in open battle. In one forty-eight hour battle with the Taliban in early September 2006, Charles Company of the 1st Battalion Royal Canadian Regiment lost its company commander, company sergeant major, one of three platoon commanders, all three platoon warrant officers, five out of nine section commanders, and all their section seconds in command. In total, five were killed and forty wounded. The Canadian Forces had not seen fighting like this since the Korean War and although they acquitted themselves extremely well throughout that fall's Operation Medusa, a major offensive to clear the Taliban from the area, which they headed, the transition to war was unexpected and jarring.[14] 'Canada slipped into war in Afghanistan, step by step, incrementally, without fully understanding that it was going to war', concluded the Canadian political scientist Janice Gross Stein.[15]

Great pride, little passion

While the Canadian public evinced a great degree of pride and interest in their long-neglected armed forces, as seen for example in the large and apparently spontaneous public demonstrations that occurred during the repatriation of the bodies of dead soldiers, the government perceived (in a study of 'Public Perceptions of Canada's Role in Afghanistan' conducted by the Department of Foreign Affairs in 2006) a downward trend in support for the mission overall. The study advised an aggressive information campaign aimed at the winning over of Canadian hearts and minds, in particular what it termed 'soft supporters' of the mission, using 'concrete examples of progress (focusing on women and children), UN and NATO involvement, and clarity around the need for security and stability in order to provide aid and undertake diplomacy'.[16]

The results were not good and opinion continued on a downward trend. Interestingly, where they had success was in reinforcing the feelings of pride in those parts that were predisposed to pride in the mission in the first place, whether as a continuation of Canada's peacekeeping tradition or as a sort of rebirth of its martial tradition. By and large, the public was engaged in the debate and receptive of their government's narrative. It was, however, not persuaded. The reason, according to one study of the campaign, was that the 'government failed to connect on an emotional level. As a consequence they won some minds but too few hearts'.[17]

In 2007 the government commissioned an independent panel on Canada's role in Afghanistan, a sort of Canadian Iraq Study Group report. The chair's foreword to the report published in 2008 laid out the basic problem: what is the war about and is it worth it? With surprising honesty about the ambiguity of the objective of what by then was already a six-year-old deployment in which over 100 soldiers had been killed, the report declared:

> We find ourselves, with our allies in a situation of conflict in a land that is far from us, little known by us, and where our interests do not seem self-evident. We are trying to help a country whose recent history has been one long, unending tragedy, and whose prospects still appear bleak. The question of Canada's future role defies a simple answer. It is complicated by the challenging nature of the mission and by the difficult neighbourhood in which Afghanistan is situated ... It is made more complex because we assumed responsibility for fighting an insurgency in a danger-ous province of the country and we did so with little political debate and not much public engagement. And that insurgency is far from defeated.[18]

As it happened, Canada did not withdraw precipitately—as no few voices argued that it should. The panel concluded it would do more harm than good, risking 'undercutting international confidence in Canadian commitments and impos[ing] new burdens on others obliged to take our place in Kandahar'.[19] The flag came down on Canada's deployment in a main combat role in Afghanistan in December 2011, by which point the surge of 30,000 American troops into the area ordered by President Obama shortly after his first election was in full swing.

One could argue that the case of Canada exhibits a degree of strategic per-spicacity. Given the choice between Iraq and Afghanistan, it chose the right war, the war that President Obama declared, in open contrast to Iraq, to be 'not a war of choice [but] a war of necessity ... a war worth fighting [and] fundamental to the defence of our people'.[20] Moreover, when it was seemly to depart that doomed exercise in nation-building it did so in good order. Over 150 Canadian soldiers had been killed and four times that number wounded. Yet while each of these was a tragedy for the families involved, as a country and even as a very small professional army, that rate of loss was in no physical sense unsustainable. In fact, the morale of the Canadian Forces and its esteem in society was higher at the end of the deployment than it had been at the beginning.[21] It had been a good war. Why not carry on?

Ultimately, it was the tenuousness and tepidity of the war's narrative com-bined with the raw immediacy and emotional resonance of the war's televisual costs that dented enthusiasm. The steady flow of flag-draped coffins along the highway between the air base at Trenton (to where the bodies of dead soldiers were flown home) and the mortuary facilities in Toronto, renamed the 'Highway of Heroes', became the story of the war. Hillier noted that early in the campaign he discontinued his initial practice of personally telephoning the grieving families of servicemen, which had to be synchronised with others making their condolences 'from the Governor General and the Prime Minister right down to their local member of parliament or mayor', because he recognised in his own conscience that his phone calls did not always help.

If Hillier had a point to prove it was not that the small community of Canadian Forces honoured its dead. For the military, the logic of the situation was relatively simple:

> If we were going to take casualties and we were going to grieve, our nation was going to grieve with us. If Canada as a nation was to continue to ask young men and women to go out and put their lives in jeopardy on its behalf, then it owed us that recognition.[22]

Politically, however, this was untenable as Hillier described vividly with an anecdote about the May 2006 death of Captain Nichola Goddard, Canada's first female combat arms casualty. An artillery forward observation officer, she was mortally wounded in a ferocious engagement with the Taliban while directing fire from the turret of her light armoured vehicle. Officials in the prime minister's office clearly sensed the electrical importance of the event. 'Look, don't bring the Airbus [repatriating her body] in, or if you bring the plane in, turn it away from the cameras so that people can't see the bodies coming off or do it after dark or do it behind the hangars or just bar everybody from it', they implored.[23]

The government's instinct in this example was not unusual, nor, indeed, in a less densely mediatised strategic context, would it have been an unwise one. Historically, small wars have gone more smoothly the less interested the media has been in dramatising them. Keeping them simmering along just below the threshold of public attention is a time honoured technique.

Ramparts of willed incomprehension

Unfortunately for governments it is precisely this distance between the war abroad and the views on it at home that of late has become impossible to maintain. Disconnection is not an option. Smith captured the situation well with an arresting simile:

Whoever coined the phrase 'the theatre of operations' was very prescient. We are conducting operations now as though we are on stage, in an amphitheatre or Roman arena. There are two or more sets of players—both with a producer, the commander, each of whom has his own idea of the script. On the ground, in the actual theatre, they are all on the stage and mixed up with people trying to get to their seats, the stagehands, the ticket collectors, and the ice cream vendors. At the same time, they are being viewed by a partial and factional audience, comfortably seated, its attention focused on that part of the auditorium where it is noisiest, watching the events by peering down the drinking straws of their soft drink packs—for that is the extent of the vision of a camera.[24]

To understand why this is so important to the conduct of today's wars it is useful to take a step back to view the problem in perspective. C.E. Callwell, upon whose major work, *Small Wars: Their Principles and Practice*, we have already remarked, and the naval strategist Julian Corbett are perhaps Britain's greatest strategic thinkers. Rarely, however, are they mentioned in the same breath. The concern of the former was with the myriad brushfire wars of imperial enterprise, whereas the latter concentrated on the principles of maritime strategy. Both, however, realised that command of the sea is merely a means to the 'furtherance or hindrance of military operations ashore' and that this is because wars are won in the minds of humans and humans live on land.[25]

But one of Corbett's keenest observations was that Britain's former naval supremacy gave it the wonderful advantage of being able to engage in as much or as little small war as it wished. In his words:

> limited war is only permanently possible to island Powers or between Powers which are separated by sea, and then only when the Power desiring limited war is able to command the sea to such a degree as to be able not only to isolate the distant object, but also render impossible the invasion of his home territory.[26]

Essentially, at the height of Britain's Empire, when both Callwell and Corbett were writing, it was still possible for small wars abroad to be kept small and contained more or less at the leisure of the intervening power for the simple reason that the sea's vastness provided a potent barrier to the internationalisation of the conflict. Connectivity, however, it is said, causes the 'death of distance'.[27] It is important not to overstate the case here. The legendary war reporter William Howard Russell's dispatches on the Crimean War of 1854–56 was a major headache for the British government and military because it publicised their bungling of operations, major command inadequacies, and the appallingly poor provision for the welfare of their own troops.[28]

The Second Anglo-Boer War of 1899–1902 provided another sharp test for the containability of small wars. Boer political leaders worked with a good deal of success in foreign capitals from where they hoped to draw support to bring attention to harsh British measures against Boer non-combatants. In the French press, for instance, Field Marshal Horatio Kitchener was pictured as a monster feasting on Boer corpses, Britain was accused of genocide, and the Empire as a whole was characterised as a dim and overweight bully.[29] The British government was very concerned about the fragility of domestic opinion about the war. The 'hysterical, euphoric relief' that followed the breaking of the siege of the British garrison at Mafeking and the subsequent lionisation of the commander Colonel Robert Baden-Powell were testament to the public's fear of national humiliation and sense of ownership of the war and was similar to more recent hagiographic treatments of celebrity generals.[30]

There was also a good deal of domestic upset over the harsh tactics against Boer civilians employed by the British, which offended Victorian sensibilities. The Fawcett Commission, for instance, which looked into the conditions in the British concentration camps where Boer civilians died of disease by the thousands, was a result of public outcry over such measures.[31]

Moreover, it is not simply that the traditional media is now more present on the battlefield to report bad news. In fact, since Vietnam the military has become increasingly confident in its management of the media's coverage of operations. Before the 2003 invasion of Iraq the American military had stopped seeing journalists as a source of vulnerability and learned to think of the media as a force multiplier.[32] As it turned out, that confidence was not misplaced. The media, for instance, eagerly portrayed the toppling of Saddam's statue in Firdos Square as a dramatic and spontaneous event dominated by Iraqis 'jubilantly roaring their approval' when in fact between a quarter and a half of the crowd was composed of journalists and Marines.

Many editors happily dialled up the triumphalism and downplayed the ambiguity of the scene because it made good television.[33] A 2005 study by American University's School of Communications based on a survey of 210 journalists involved in the coverage of Iraq summarised its findings as follows: 'Many media outlets have self-censored their reporting of the conflict in Iraq because of concern about public reaction to graphic images and details about the war'.[34] In other words, the traditional media—for so long the *bête noire* of uniformed military men, an object of cultural 'loathing', as one observer put it—cannot be blamed for the failings of the 'war on terror'.[35] In actuality, they proved quite happy to go along with a good story.

There is a more fundamental problem here that resides in the explosion of connectivity which the popular author James Gleick has compared to a 'rising, churning flood ... [calling] to mind bombardment, data impinging in a series of blows, from all sides, too fast ... [making] the truth seem harder to find amid the multitude of plausible fictions.'[36] The traditional media is as caught up in this maelstrom as are states and their armed forces. Indeed, they may be more imperilled by the emerging global mediascape, which is dynamic and cheap to access at any time of the day and from any place in the world. Ideas can take on a self-generating life of their own in this new arena, without help or hindrance from the editorial preferences of media corporations and political elites.[37]

By and large, it was possible while the density of connectivity was lower, the movement of information from one place to another was slower, and populations were more homogeneous and unified to keep such pressures under control. Nowadays, small wars are more likely to 'spill their banks' and spread out along the network flows of globalisation as a multitude of spatially distant actors are added into the strategic mix. This is not simply academic theorising. The same argument has been made by senior figures in Britain's military establishment such as General David Richards, who was commander of ISAF in Afghanistan at the point that historians are quite likely to determine the war's outcome became apparent. As he put it:

> Conflict today, especially because so much of it is effectively fought through the medium of the Communications Revolution, is principally about and for the people—hearts and minds on a mass scale.[38]

The trouble is that in Iraq and especially in Afghanistan it fell upon the local theatre commander to adopt the role of 'producer' or 'commanding spokesman' of the conflict, charged with in some sense embodying its direction and purpose in the minds of observers, and contextualising the events, good or bad, which occurred in its conduct. Few, however, are suited by training or temperament for this role. By all accounts, David Petraeus was a preternaturally media savvy commander and showed great political acuity. Accounts of the Surge in Iraq usually credit his performance in two days of congressional hearings on the war in September 2007 as having altered the course of the war, adding much needed 'time on the clock'. Perhaps the most aggressive questioning came from then Senator Hillary Clinton who remarked, accurately, 'You have become the de facto spokesman for what many of us believe to be a failed policy.'[39]

This was not as it should have been. Generals are not meant to articulate policy—that is the job of government. It is a dreadful failure of political leadership and an inversion of strategic logic when the onus to answer the question 'why are we there?' rests most heavily on the theatre commander. The question is perfectly legitimate but, as Canadian General Andrew Leslie lamented, it is not really within the power of the soldier to answer:

> I often get asked ... why are you there? We're there because you sent us. As a soldier, it's not my job to explain why you sent us. Soldiers don't do that. We tell you what we're doing, we tell you how we're doing it, but we should not be in the position of explaining to the people of Canada why we're there. The responsibility for that lies with the political leadership and those who sent us.[40]

The communications expert Philip Taylor wrote in the epilogue to his classic history of propaganda through the ages that 'In the war against terrorism there is a need for western liberal democracies to package their very value systems'.[41] This would be a challenge for a large society in any time. Walter Lippmann, a noteworthy journalist and intellectual as well as a wartime propagandist, described as the 'democratic El Dorado' the eternal search for the 'perfect environment ... where the innate good will and instinctive statesmanship of every man could be translated into action'.[42] Connectivity today makes that El Dorado all the more distant and unobtainable, while the politics of coalition operations puts the wrong people at the head of the search.

Traditionally, strategic narrative or propaganda rests on a combination of myth, as already noted, rhetoric and symbolism.[43] Together, these are employed to achieve a 'common will', as Lippmann called it: an 'oversoul ... a national mind, a spirit of the age which imposes order upon random opinion'.[44] The perfect environment of strategic narrative, as one can imagine it, is homogenous, total and continuous. As Jacques Ellul put it in his seminal work on propaganda, a strategic narrative:

> tries to surround man by all possible routes, in the realm of feelings as well as ideas, by playing on his will or on his needs, through his conscious and his unconscious, assailing him in both his private and his public life. It furnishes him with a complete system for explaining the world, and provides immediate incentives to action. We are here in the presence of an organised myth that tries to take hold of the entire person. Through the myth it creates, propaganda imposes a complete range of intuitive knowledge susceptible of only one interpretation, unique and one-sided, and precluding any divergence.[45]

In this conception, simple overarching messages are meant to 'ring true' or 'resonate' because they harmonise with policies that in turn are attachable to beliefs that already exist in the individual and which express the 'fundamental currents of the society [the propagandist] seeks to influence'.[46] Everything is orchestrated and coherent, from the eschatological/cultural narrative at the very top all the way down to the local and individual narratives at the bottom.[47]

Paradoxically, though it clearly satisfies the criterion of ubiquitous presence, connectivity overall has the effect of subverting and undermining every aspect of the perfect environment. Instead of homogeneity, the reality of the network society is extreme heterogeneity of community, identity and viewpoint. Instead of totality—a message that is unified and sustained across media—the environment is characterised by multiplicity, fragmentation and boisterous cacophony. Information is cheap and bountiful; therefore attention is expensive and limited. And the only constancy is the flux of one story after another in a kaleidoscope of words and images blurring constantly across the public consciousness, robbing it of sustained belief.

Obviously, under such conditions there can be no 'oversoul' for the War on Terror. What prevails instead is a multitude of narratives, variously contradictory, incomplete or unconvincingly rendered. In the case of Afghanistan, which serves as a microcosm of the larger project, one finds a basic failure to communicate an answer to the oft-asked 'why are we here?' question amongst the populations of the contributing member states of the coalition. We lack a message of resolute determination to prevail until the Taliban is beaten or forced to reasonable compromise upon which Afghans might bet their lives; and we lack a picture of 'victory' that is accompanied by a compelling rationalisation of the costs.

Without these, the war lacks 'productive' force in the sense of purposeful shaping of the beliefs and ideas of populations.[48] 'Warfare', argued the British journalist Andrew Marr writing after the breaking of stories in 2004 (false, as it turned out, but all too plausible at the time) about the mistreatment of Iraqi prisoners by British troops, 'has depended on a rampart of silence, a wall of willed incomprehension, between civilians at home and those killing'.[49] That wall has come down and there is no Henry V beneath the gap filling it with convincing strategic communications.

Deploying rhetoric in place of actual passion proved to be no better at lifting war out of the miasma of indecision than did fighting as though technology had lifted the fog of war. There was, however, one more way to try.

8

WAR WITHOUT REASON

SOMETHING JUST SHORT OF WAR

Zeppelin, flieg,
Hilf uns im Krieg,
Fliege nach England,
England wird abgebrannt,
Zeppelin, flieg.

[Fly Zeppelin! Help us in the war. Fly to England! England shall be destroyed with fire!]
'Fly Zeppelin', a German children's song by Anonymous (1914)[1]

In recent years the strategic assessments of the major powers have considered increasing global connectedness to be a major new source of threat to security. The imaginations of policy-makers and strategists have been exercised in particular by cyber security—both the new terror that it represents and the opportunity it provides for them to exercise coercive power in seemingly new and effective ways. The extant debate on the subject is voluminous but also highly superficial. It resembles nothing so much as the interwar air power debate and the related search for an 'indirect approach', a period that was filled with overblown claims and distracting alarmism. The debate over cyberpower is prone to the same mistakes. The issue is not the potential significance of cyberpower as a multiplier of combat force but its all too frequent characterisation as a strategically decisive new weapon on its own. There is no reason to doubt that cyberpower is an important addition to the combined arms arsenal. But there is also no reason to believe that it heralds a decisive new form of war.

In October 2010 the United Kingdom published a new National Security Strategy. It was long past due. The previous Strategic Defence Review had been conducted twelve years before. In the years since then most of the assumptions underlying British strategic thinking had been undermined by events. It was not simply that the 9/11 al-Qaeda attack signalled the arrival of a virulent new form of non-state threat to the moral power of great nations on their home territory. Nor even was it the embarrassing failings of the Iraq and Afghan campaigns, or the financial crisis of 2008, although that was an especially heavy blow to British economic confidence, especially given the important place of financial services in the British economy. Together these things portended distinctly uncongenial realisations: that conventional military strength presented little obstacle to the metastasising threat of domestic radicalism and terror; of the salience of the old and unsubtle rule of thumb that great powers ought not to rush into small wars, for they are invariably strategically unfavourable to the intervening power; and that the existing defence procurement programme was unaffordable, possibly by an order of magnitude.[2] But underlying these serious concerns was a new, more fundamental, and paradoxical one, which was precisely expressed at the beginning of the prime minister's foreword:

> Britain today is both more secure and more vulnerable than in most of her long history. More secure in the sense that we do not currently face, as we have so often in our past, a conventional threat of attack on our territory by a hostile power. But more vulnerable, because we are one of the most open societies, in a world that is more networked than ever before.[3]

Britain was not peculiar in this apprehension that networked societies faced threats that previous societal forms did not. In its 2010 National Security Strategy the United States employed similar language, warning that 'the very technologies that empower us to lead and create also empower those who would disrupt and destroy'.[4] Indeed, practically all developed states are grappling with the same question of how they might adapt to an apparently new and unsettling reality of connectivity coupled with economic uncertainty.

A new terror, another silver bullet

It is recognised in both Washington and London that the security concerns that issue from the new connectedness, the 'dark side of this globalized world', as the American strategy puts it, encompass a broad range of ills from terrorism, through nuclear proliferation, to the knock-on effects of climate change.[5] At present, foremost among them is 'Cyberwar! The threat from the Internet', to quote from the cover of the July 2010 *Economist* magazine where these words were emblazoned across an illustration of a mushroom cloud looming over a burning city below, lest any reader underestimate the gravity of their digital peril.[6] 'Be afraid, be very afraid,'[7] is the not too subtle message spread by the burgeoning cyber security industry and echoed in policy circles. Critical national infrastructures are said to be vulnerable to cyberattack; the vitality of the economy is said to be threatened with enervation through cyber espionage and cyber crime, which plunder intellectual property and pose a risk to electronic commerce; and the property and wellbeing of citizens are claimed to be endangered by cyberwar. In June 2010, the then incoming Secretary of Defence Leon Panetta advised the Senate Armed Services Committee that 'the next Pearl Harbour that we confront could very well be a cyber attack'.[8]

It bears mentioning that these are not peculiarly Western preoccupations. The Chinese strategists Qiao Liang and Wang Xiangsui, authors of the much cited late 1990s future war text *Unrestricted Warfare*, were equally impressed by the potential power of new non-kinetic forms of attack to achieve powerful strategic effects and the need for conventional defence establishments to adjust to deal with a new 'severe reality' of war:

> The battlefield is next to you and the enemy is on the network. Only there is no smell of gunpowder or the odour of blood. However, it is war as before, because it accords with the definition of modern warfare: forcing the enemy to satisfy one's own interests. It is very obvious that none of the soldiers in any one nation possesses sufficient mental preparation against this type of new war, which completely goes beyond military space. However, this is actually a severe reality that all soldiers must face. The new threats require new national security views, and new security views then necessitate soldiers who first expand their fields of vision prior to expanding their victories. This is a matter of wiping away the long narrow cloud covering of war cast over one's eyes.[9]

Even then, before 11 September 2001 the attention of the Chinese strategists was drawn very clearly towards non-state actors as a key source of threat. Their list of the most dangerous global 'lunatics' included the international financier and currency speculator George Soros, the Islamist terrorist Osama Bin Laden, Chizuo Matsumoto who founded the Japanese cult *Aum Shinrikyo* that in 1995 attacked the Tokyo subway with nerve gas, the Colombian drug dealer Pablo Escobar, and the 1990s-era hacker Kevin Mitnick. In their words:

all of the new warfare methods and strategic measures which can be provided by all of the new technology may be utilized by these fanatics to carry out all forms of financial attacks, network attacks, media attacks, or terrorist attacks. Most of these attacks are not military actions, and yet they can be completely viewed as or equal to warfare actions, which force other nations to satisfy their own interests and demands. These have the same and even greater destructive force than military warfare, and they have already produced serious threats different from the past...[10]

However, the most interest in recent years has been focused upon 'pure play' digital attacks.[11] Like the shock paddles of a defibrillator on the chest of a heart attack victim, the prefix 'cyber' has had an electrifying effect on policymakers and strategists wrestling with the complexities of information age security—or more commonly today, 'cybersecurity'. Thus, while in practically every other aspect of public expenditure the talk is all of austerity and budget cuts, there has been a bonanza of resources dedicated to countering or mitigating cyber threats.

The UK's National Security Strategy reckoned the possibility of cyberattack to be a 'tier one' threat of the highest priority. In fact, in 2013, in the context of swingeing cuts to the defence budget that had already seen the ranks of the army cut from 102,000 to just over 80,000, the Chancellor of the Exchequer announced, 'We're not going to reduce the number of soldiers, sailors, airmen [any more]. In fact we're actually going to be able to spend some money on things like cyber, which is the new frontier in defence'.[12] Similarly candidly, the United States Deputy Secretary of Defence Ashton B. Carter declared in a speech on defence priorities in an era of constrained spending that 'I dare say we'd spend a lot more [on cyber] if we could figure out where to spend it'.[13] In the information age, it seemed, God no longer favours the side with the bigger battalions, as Napoleon once quipped; it was the side with the bigger databases that would prevail.

We are, in other words, in the midst of a cyberscare in which politicians, the media, and the mushrooming cyber security industry feed off each other in a self-reinforcing engine of anxiety and alarm. Philosophically, this 'shock of the new' is perhaps no surprise.[14] In general consternation about cyberspace is perhaps best explained by Marshall McLuhan who as long ago as 1967, drawing on Søren Kierkegaard's mid-nineteenth century monograph *The Concept of Dread*, observed that 'wherever a new environment goes around an old one there is always new terror'.[15]

But there is also something of a cybermania at work here too—a craze not unlike the seventeenth century's 'tulipmania' in Europe during which the cost of the humble tulip bulb (then a recent arrival from Turkey) exploded beyond all measure of utility and common sense. In Charles Mackay's classic mid-nineteenth century treatment of the general phenomenon of 'extraordinary popular delusions' he observed that:

> In reading the history of nations we find that, like individuals, they have their whims and their peculiarities; their reasons of excitement and recklessness, when they care not what they do. We find that whole communities suddenly fix their minds upon one object, and go mad in its pursuit; that millions of people become simultaneously impressed with one delusion, and run after it, till their attention is caught by some new folly more captivating than the first. We see one nation suddenly seized, from its highest to its lowest members, with a fierce desire of military glory; another as suddenly becoming crazed on a religious scruple; and neither of them recovering its senses until it has shed rivers of blood and sowed a harvest of groans and tears, to be reaped by its posterity... Men, it has been well said, think in herds; it will be seen that that they go mad in herds, while they only recover their senses slowly, and one by one.[16]

The analogy ought to be taken loosely. Still, it serves to remind us of two things that are useful for placing the importance of cyberpower in strategic affairs accurately.

First, popular discourse on cyberspace tends to exhibit to a large degree the one-dimensional superficiality of history's great crazes. For instance, as with war itself, which we noted in Chapter One is now an essentially contested concept, there is no generally accepted definition of what cyberspace is and is not.[17] In common with land, sea, air and space, cyberspace is reckoned to be a domain of conflict, as will be discussed further below. Yet there is little consistency between definitions of it, either in the academy or, in particular, in doctrine and policy. The 2009 United States Cyberspace Policy Review, for instance, called it the 'globally-interconnected digital information and communications infrastructure [that] underpins almost every facet of modern society'.[18] In comparison, the contemporaneous British Cyber Security Strategy defined it more broadly as including 'all forms of networked digital activities; this includes the content of and actions conducted through digital networks'.[19]

Amongst an increasingly large group of scholars the term is thought to be anachronistic, redundant, or even an active impediment to thinking clearly about the broader challenges of information age security.[20] Indeed, the dominant metaphors of cyber security discourse have the potential to channel our thinking into a 'walled garden' modality in which perfect internal security is achieved by perfect external separation that is neither desirable nor necessary.[21]

Science fiction writer William Gibson, who coined the term cyberspace in a 1982 short story 'Burning Chrome', later said of his creation that 'it seemed like an effective buzzword... evocative and essentially meaningless'.[22] To a large extent so it remains. It has been described rather poetically as the 'place between the phones. The indefinite place out there, where the two of you, two human beings, actually meet and communicate'.[23] It is also often described prosaically in terms of its physical infrastructure, as in the American Cyberspace Policy Review. Howsoever we define it we are confronted with its multidimensionality and artificiality. Perhaps the best available model is long-time American analyst of information technology and security Martin Libicki's three-layered one which interposes a 'syntactic layer' (the software and protocols that govern how information flows in the network) between cyberspace's 'physical layer' (that is, routers, wires, and computers) and its 'semantic layer', which is where humans extract meaning from data on the web in the form of natural language.[24]

The issue of defining cyberspace is far from a quotidian detail from the point of view of strategy because whether one takes an exclusive view of it as encompassing just the physical and syntactic layers or an inclusive view which includes in its conception the semantic layer of ideas has a large effect on decisions concerning resources and the planning of operations. It is this ambiguity that underpins the recurring question of whether operations in cyberspace are best understood as a variant of electronic warfare or psychological warfare, or an amalgam of both, as we shall see in the next chapter.

Also, when air forces describe cyberspace as an environment in which one may 'fly, fight, and win' or pursue 'cyber superiority' and 'cyber dominance' in ways analogous to actions in conventional domains such as air and space there is an implicit claim being made on responsibilities and resources for these tasks.[25] Sometimes this is made explicitly, as in the argument for the putatively unique salience of 'air mindedness' to the unravelling of contemporary warfare's complexities:

As warfare has evolved, so has the definition of air mindedness. First and foremost, it implies an offensive mindset. During the interwar years, air-mindedness described a strategic vision of air power that produced the concept of daylight precision bombing in World War II. During the Cold War, it provided the rationale for nuclear deterrence, deep strike bombers, and ballistic missiles. Air mindedness has never been platform-centric, so it enables today's Airmen to think first about desired effects and then about the means of attaining them. Consequently, it enables Airmen to express the concepts of space and cyberspace as easily as they expressed air power concepts only a few years earlier. Thus Airmen are better equipped to exploit the other global commons of space and cyberspace since they view them as domains rather than as tools.[26]

More often, though, the hotchpotch of agendas, biases and assumptions that underlie the debate are unstated or, worse, unrecognised even by those involved in it. Thus the current fascination of policy-makers and soldiers with cyberpower is best seen not simply as a reflection of the threat that they apprehend it represents. Equally powerful is the potential they see in it for the same will o' the wisp discussed in the last chapter: victory without battles or bloodshed—a new 'silver bullet', in other words, only shinier and even cheaper and maybe more decisive.

The 'indirect approach', version 2.0

What is important here is not so much the definition of cyberspace *per se*; it is rather, at least for the moment, that judging whether this or that claim about the 'threat from the Internet' is over-inflated scaremongering or under-inflated complacency depends in part on understanding what conception of cyberspace the analyst is working with in the first place. Generally speaking, this is not made clear in the academic literature or, especially, in the doctrinal and strategic outpourings of the world's major governments and ministries of defence. Equally, threats cannot be evaluated merely technically. They need to be understood in the round, with greater attention to the social processes that are affected by technology and with an eye to historical context—not merely the period since the invention of the microchip or the World Wide Web but the more than a century-long period in which the decisiveness of major war for a mixture of political, economic and technological reasons is thought to have been gradually diminishing.

Connectivity has not had any single, overarching effect on all fields of human activity—cultural, economic or military. Nor are its effects the same at all of its levels. The best advice is not to generalise and to seek a degree of objectivity because processes that appear existentially threatening and profoundly disruptive at close hand take on different hues with a degree of historical distance and the objectivity provided by a sound theory of war. Thus equipped, for instance, when we hear it said portentously, as in a recent BBC documentary on *The Virtual Revolution*, that 'The Web is shifting power in ways that we could never have imagined [and is] reinventing warfare' we are able to recognise that such things have been said before, perhaps even with more reason, and found to be exaggerated.[27]

In fact, similar claims typified the interwar period when in the shadow of the muddy and bloody slaughterhouse of the First World War there was a great ferment in military circles about how to restore the decisiveness to wars amongst militarily competent powers that seemed to many to have been lost. The Polish banker-cum-strategist Ivan Bloch grasped the basic problem even before the war, when he argued that war between the great powers was no longer viable because of the power of modern weapons, which made the strength of defences too great to be overcome by Napoleonic methods. As he predicted of future war, between 'the two armies there will be a belt a thousand paces wide, separating them as by neutral territory, swept by the fire of both sides, a belt which no living being can stand for a moment'.[28]

As so often is the case with prediction in military affairs, Bloch was acutely perceptive of some things and profoundly wrong about many others. In answer to his own question 'is war impossible?' he ventured to say that it was indeed possible (inevitable, even, given the configuration of European politics and the state of military preparedness at the time) but that the 'quick and final decision of future battles was improbable'.[29] Ultimately, this proved to be untrue. Over time, and at a vast cost of deadly and destructive experimentation, military ingenuity prevailed over the interacting effects of accurate, rapid-firing direct and indirect fire weapons combined with cheap surface fortifications that Bloch had seen as unalterable impediments to battlefield decision.

The way out of this dilemma was the aforementioned mixture of tactical adaptation and developments in weapons technology, notably the airplane and the tank (and the radio), sometimes called the 'modern system' or more commonly combined arms.[30] In fact, as with Bloch perceiving the basic problem even before the war, there were a few before who also grasped the solution. In 1907, Gerald Gilbert, a British Army Major, admonished his fellow officers:

> We have gotten into the fashion of talking of cavalry tactics, artillery tactics, and infantry tactics. This distinction is nothing but a mere abstraction. There is but one art, and that is the tactics of combined arms.[31]

Before the war many paid lip service to this idea, but few understood the extraordinary importance of the combined arms principle impacting everything from the top generals all the way down to the lowliest infantry section commander. Even after the harsh task mastering of the war, what in the main captivated the military minds of the English-speaking world at this time was the technology. The British Army officer and theorist of armoured warfare J.F.C. Fuller provides an unimpeachably clear example of this technophilia in one of the most strikingly exaggerated passages of one of his most influential books:

Tools, or weapons, if only the right ones can be discovered, form ninety-nine per cent of victory ... Strategy, command, leadership, courage, discipline, supply, organisation, and all the moral and physical paraphernalia of war are nothing to a high superiority of weapons—at most they go to form the one per cent, which makes the whole possible ... [W]ar is primarily a matter of weapons.[32]

Overall, Fuller's contribution to military thought was large and impressive.[33] His thoughts on the mechanisation of land warfare and more generally on what he termed the 'law of military development' in particular are justifiably lauded. According to the latter, all military adaptation is akin to Darwinian evolution—armies adapt competitively to changes in their environment in order to remain fit for war. The 'constant tactical factor' at work in this ever-changing conduct of warfare is the equally ever-swinging balance between offence and defence, driven largely in accordance with broader developments in civilisation.[34] In other words, logically, there could be no technological 'silver bullets' or at any rate no permanently operative ones because war is too dynamic and innovative by nature to allow them to exist.

Fuller, however, was not always consistent in his thoughts and for a time during the interwar period he attached a special significance to one technology in particular, air power, which he invested with enormous strategic consequence:

Armies and navies are lethal instruments of security, but the true object, as I have frequently stated, is not to kill soldiers or sink ships, but to change a policy, which these soldiers and ships are protecting. If, in the event of war, an air force can change this policy with less physical destruction than in the past it has been possible to attain by means of armies and navies, and this may be the case, then the air force will not absorb the military purpose of navies and armies, which in nature is tactical, but will instead establish a new conception of war, a conception in which naval and military forces will have either no place at all or one which is subordinate to their present purpose, and by subordinate I mean the occupation of land and sea after a moral victory has been won on land by aircraft.[35]

Even more impressed by the apparent puissance of air power was Fuller's contemporary and compatriot Basil Liddell-Hart, originator of the concept of the 'indirect approach' in warfare. The gist of the indirect approach was that the aim in war is to subdue the enemy's will to resist with the least loss of life and wealth as possible. In essence, he argued, the function of strategy is to identify an enemy nation's most vulnerable point and strike there. This amazingly obvious point, which in no way contradicts the dictums of Clausewitz, Liddell-Hart's chosen *bête noire*, was twinned with an acute sense of the new fragility of modern industrial society.

The modern state, he reckoned, was so complex and interdependent that it was hugely vulnerable to enemy disruption because of its connectedness. The economic achievements in which they gloried, their industrial power, and their vast material and cultural wealth also made modern states hopelessly weak in the face of some sorts of attack. As he described it in his 1925 book, *Paris, Or the Future of War*, the title an allusion to the slayer of the near-invincible Greek champion Achilles in Homer's Trojan war epic *The Iliad*, brought down by a poisoned dart to the heel, his only point of weakness:

> A nation's nerve system, no longer covered by the flesh of its troops is now laid bare to attack [from the air], and, like the human nerves, the progress of civilization has rendered it far more sensitive than in earlier and more primitive times.[36]

And the key instrument of power, the poison dart, to continue the analogy, was aerial bombardment, an attack vector that would allow an aggressor to leap over a country's surface fortifications and attack its vulnerable innards (their industrial, cultural and population centres as well as their transport and communications links), directly causing a disarming and irresistible bedlam:

> Imagine for a moment that, of two centralised industrial nations at war, one possesses a superior air force, the other a superior army. Provided that the blow be sufficiently swift and powerful, there is no reason why within a few hours, or at most days from commencement of hostilities, the nerve system of the country inferior in air power should not be paralysed ...

> Imagine for a moment London, Manchester, Birmingham, and half a dozen other great centres simultaneously attacked, the business localities and Fleet Street wrecked, Whitehall a heap of ruins, the slum districts maddened into the impulse to break loose and maraud, the railways cut, factories destroyed. Would not the general will to resist vanish, and what use would be the still determined fractions of the nation, without organisation and central direction?[37]

Liddell-Hart's firmest friends were candidly critical of his theory and urged him to tone it down. T.E. Lawrence observed that it was something of a truism: 'you establish your thesis; but I fear that you could equally have established the contrary thesis'. Others noted that it was a perilously circular argument: the indirect approach is what leads to decisive victory and decisive victory is what is secured by the indirect approach; also that it was historically weakly grounded and, moreover, exceedingly unfair to Clausewitz.[38]

In his later work, the uniquely decisive importance of aerial bombardment was a less prevalent theme. For a time, however, it was an influential and widely held view. Nowhere was this more evident than in a famous House of Commons speech by three times Prime Minister Stanley Baldwin in

November 1932 entitled 'A Fear for the Future'. The speech is generally remembered for the flat warning he gave to 'the man in the street' about the irresistible quality of the preeminent anxiety of the day, 'that there is no power on earth that can protect him from being bombed, whatever people may tell him. The bomber will always get through'.[39]

As it turned out, though, this was far from true. When Baldwin said these words, as Liddell-Hart's critical friends pointed out to him when he had made the same pronouncement, defences against air attack were still in their infancy and would inevitably improve. Indeed, during the Second World War the most attritional battles the United States and Britain faced were in the skies over Germany as their huge bomber fleets learned painfully the lesson that air forces could not 'always get through' to wipe out enemy 'nerve centres' without incurring savage losses to defending fighters and anti-aircraft artillery along the way. In one illustrative example, in the United States Army Air Force's raids on the German ball-bearing industry in and around Schweinfurt in October 1943 they lost sixty out of 291 attacking bombers with 138 badly damaged.[40]

Moreover, even when they did get through the expected paralysing effect of their bomb loads on the population on whom they were dropped did not materialize. In January 1919, Major General Sir Hugh Trenchard, father of the Royal Air Force, in a hyperbolic reference to Napoleon's more famous injunction on the point, asserted that, 'At present, the moral effect of bombing stands undoubtedly to the material effect in a proportion of twenty to one'.[41] This was artful marketing. It was known at the time through post-war British surveys that the material results of bombing had been meagre across the board.[42]

Furthermore, it flew in the face of hundreds of years of military history that suggested attempts to terrorise civilian populations actually bolster popular resistance if their armed forces in the field are undefeated. There is probably no surer way to convince people that a war is necessary, even sublime, and to get them to willingly shoulder the costs of it than to blow away the homes and lives of a visible fraction of them indiscriminately. Consider the power of Churchillian rhetoric, such as this speech made in the dark days of May 1940 with the Battle of France raging and going badly for the Allies:

> I have nothing to offer but blood, toil, tears, and sweat. We have before us an ordeal of the most grievous kind. We have before us many, many long months of struggle and suffering ... You ask, what is our aim? I can answer in one word: Victory. Victory at all costs—Victory in spite of all terror—Victory however long and hard the road may be, for without victory there is no survival.[43]

The exhortatory call to collective self-sacrifice that we see here is a perennially popular one with politicians in all countries to this day. The problem is that it does not work very well without the actual *Wehrmacht* or its equivalent serving as an object reminder of the scale and immediacy of peril nearby. Baldwin's 1932 speech was no less suffused with straight talk of the public's endangerment than Churchill's; but shorn of a visible threat its tone was more of formless and tentative anxiety, 'fear held instinctively and without knowledge', as he put it. In that respect it is more exemplary of a number of preoccupations highly germane to current debates about security and connectivity. Foremost among these is the aforementioned immanent threat of speed:

> I doubt if many of those who have that fear [of bombing] realise one or two things with reference to its cause. One is the appalling speed which the air has brought into modern warfare. The speed of air attack, compared with the attack of an army, is as the speed of a motor car to that of a four-in-hand and in the next war you will find that any town which is within reach of an aerodrome can be bombed within the first five minutes of war from the air, to an extent which was inconceivable in the last war...[44]

No issue is more consistently mooted as the cyber security dilemma above all others than this: 'Events in cyberspace can happen at immense speed, outstripping traditional responses', says the UK's 2011 Cyber Security Strategy.[45] In Baldwin's day destruction came winging towards hearth and home at 300 or so miles per hour. In our day, it is said that it comes at the velocity of electron vibrations in copper. In October 2009, American Deputy Defence Secretary William J. Lynn explicitly drew a parallel between the century-long history of military aviation, noting its beginning in the United States with the flying of a biplane around Fort Myer, Virginia in 1908, and the initial stirrings of military cyberpower: 'By that measure, it's only 1928', he noted:

> This year marks the twentieth year of the World Wide Web. In other words, in terms of cyber security, we're still in the era of biplanes and dirigibles. We're still in the dawn of the Information Age. We still have decades of change and challenge ahead of us: Decades of innovations and technologies we can't even imagine.[46]

There is a slightly upbeat quality to the above—an awareness of the opportunity as well as the threat of cyberpower. Baldwin's speech on air power was darker but he too apprehended its Janusian quality—on one face was civil aviation, a powerful symbol of national technological sophistication and economic achievement, and on the other face was military aviation, portending remorseless and irresistible death from above:

As long as the air exists, you cannot get rid of the fear of which I spoke, and which I believe to be the parent of many troubles. One cannot help reflecting that, after the hundreds of millions of years during which the human race have been on this earth, it is only within our generation that we have secured the mastery of the air. I certainly do not know how the youth of the world may feel, but it is not a cheerful thought to the older men that, having got that mastery of the air, we are going to defile the earth from the air as we have defiled the soil during all the years that mankind has been on it.[47]

The interwar period air power debate was characterised by this tension. As Michael Sherry observed in his masterful account of the rise of American air power, 'aviation enthusiasts tended to view flight as a "holy cause", and with religious fervour they outlined its potential to democratise, uplift, and pacify the nations that touched it'.[48]

Exactly the same mix of apprehension and enthusiasm pervades the debate over cyberpower today. The constituent technologies are essentially civilian. Nations consider the sophistication of their information and communications technology to be integral to the advancement of their prosperity. Countries pump resources into increasing the speed and bandwidth of their digital networks, attentive to the social and economic benefits that may accrue as a result. They also invest great efforts into observing what their people do with all this connectivity, attentive to the harm that can be done by enemies hiding in plain sight and using those self-same digital tools for nefariousness. And there is that same urge to pacify.

The closing remarks of British foreign secretary William Hague at the inaugural 2011 London Conference on Cyberspace generally placed a positive spin on the state of affairs:

> Many speakers in particular welcomed [cyberspace's] contribution (especially through social media) to freedom of expression and association and its ability to expose human rights abuses as they happen and give the unheard a voice. In bringing citizens and government closer together, the Internet is a powerful engine for empowering citizens and driving government accountability.[49]

The revealing in June 2013 of a massive American National Security Agency data collection and electronic surveillance programme known as PRISM was not an unexpected development to technology watchers. Notwithstanding the public's disquiet over the apparent intrusion by the state into their private lives and the scale and granularity of data collected on them, people's expectations of anonymity and privacy are at least a decade out of alignment with technological possibilities.[50] Nonetheless, Hague's remarks about bringing government and people 'closer together' are tinged in the light of PRISM with an Orwellian overtone that was not so apparent (and almost certainly not intended) at the time the words were spoken.

In short, there is a striking similarity between the rhetoric that surrounded the emergence of military air power and that which now pervades in the discussion of cyberpower. This is not to say that what was or was not true of air power seventy years ago is necessarily true of cyberpower now; it is simply to inject some notes of caution into discussions about a technology-driven reinvention of warfare.

Most important is to be sceptical of claims made for the independent war-winning effects of any one weapon or arm of service—claims that all the early prophets of air power were wont to make to one degree or another. Indeed, General William 'Billy' Mitchell, the key figure in the early days of the United States Air Force, was so impressed by the relative superiority of air power over other arms as to describe it in almost utopian terms: '[air power represents] a distinct move for the betterment of civilisation because wars will be decided quickly and not drag on for years'.[51] It is not surprising that they were so impressed when, compared with war on the ground, war in the air is so much clearer and less cluttered. The early air power theorists possessed a faith in its unique decisiveness that has proved remarkably durable in their descendants. Actually, it has been so durable that in the early 1990s the historian Eliot Cohen considered it necessary to caution policy-makers against the 'mystique' of air power—'an unusually seductive form of military strength, in part because', he said, 'like modern courtship, it appears to offer gratification without commitment'.[52]

In other words, he might have said, war does not work that way. It requires commitment precisely in accordance and proportion with the aims to which it is applied. For at least two thousand years, since Sun Tzu described all war as a 'beginningless circle' of the direct and indirect or orthodox and unorthodox, strategists have understood the art of war to be one of combining the effects of different means.[53] As one piqued modern strategist put it:

> Super Weapons plague warfare. They are the enemy of clear thinking and good tactics. What is a Super Weapon? It has two components: a technologically advanced weapon system, and an overly zealous proponent. They are found in every age and, although endlessly discredited in practice, they reemerge from year to year, turning out doctrines and budget wars.[54]

Cyberpower is today's Super Weapon. In a recent profile of General Keith Alexander, head of both the American National Security Agency and the military's Cyber Command (and thus the most powerful figure in this domain of conflict and a worthy successor to 'Billy' Mitchell), he was described as being 'jokingly referred to' by his colleagues 'as Emperor Alexander—with good cause, because whatever Keith wants, Keith gets. We would sit back literally in awe of what he was able to get from Congress, from the White House, and at the expense of everybody else'.[55]

The trouble is that, as, ironically, Liddell-Hart knew perfectly well, war is not won in the air, or in cyberspace, or on the ground for that matter. Wars are won by imposing on one's opponent the belief of an insuperable dilemma in which all the other possible courses of action he might take are worse than rendering to you whatever political object it is that you are demanding of him:

> Man in war is not beaten, and cannot be beaten, until he owns himself beaten. Experience of all war proves this truth. So long as war persists as an instrument of policy, the objects of that policy can never be attained until the opponent admits his defeat ... [T]he survivors, who alone retain the power to admit defeat, must themselves feel the superiority of the opponent.[56]

If this acceptance of defeat can be forced on an opponent indirectly or, perhaps more pertinently, at very small cost to oneself, then that is all for the better. But there have always been distinct limitations to the extent that this can be achieved, and air power is an example of this, having never quite lived up to the dreams of its most enthusiastic advocates. Cyberpower, though, possesses a quality that has led some strategists to imagine that this time things are different—a newer, better, even more indirect approach is possible.

Reason!

That quality is anonymity, or perhaps more accurately ambiguity of identity, in cyberspace. This is a fundamental aspect of the basic architecture of the Internet, amusingly captured in a 1993 cartoon in *The New Yorker* by Peter Steiner that featured two dogs sitting in front of a desktop computer with one saying to the other 'On the Internet, nobody knows you're a dog'.[57] The 'attribution problem', as it is commonly called, boils down to it being difficult for various reasons to identify the origin of many forms of cyberattack in the manner, say, that one would very easily determine the perpetrator of an aerial bombardment by the make or markings on the attacking aircraft or the route of their coming and going.[58]

The effect of this on the strategic affairs of states has been much ballyhooed both as a threat to one's own security, as well as a seductive means of delivering discreet blows against others. Cyberpower, as its proponents frequently emphasise, appears to promise the ability to deliver almighty strikes without the possibility of return in kind or, to paraphrase Cohen's remark on air power, it offers gratification without the commitment even of a one-night stand. But this contradicts Clausewitz's very simple definition of war:

> War is ... an act of force to compel our enemy to do our will. Force, to counter opposing force, equips itself with the inventions of art and science ... Force, that is physical force, for moral force has no existence save as expressed in the state and the law—is thus the *means* of war; to impose our will on its enemy is its *object*.[59]

The issue here is not the potential or actual puissance of the means. It is entirely likely that the security of 'knowledge economies' whose intellectual property, creative industries, high-tech sector, financial services, and increasingly electronic commerce, thrive on connectivity is imperilled by threats to and from cyberspace that could be considered acts of war.[60] It is, rather, that war is still an act of force the object of which is to compel our enemy to do our will. Connectivity may alter the way that pain and the destruction of value is applied (bear in mind that Clausewitz wrote at a time before even the abacus had been reintroduced to Western Europe via Russia) and perhaps (though it remains to be seen in practice) it enables an attacker to compel another bloodlessly. But it does not obviate the necessity to declare, or quietly insinuate, one's will, even if after the event.

War, as a purposeful political act, and anonymity simply do not get along. Clausewitz's foundational definition of war is that it is a purposeful act; an act of force intended to compel an enemy to do one's will. There must be a reason—a purpose or objective—for the use of force and the subject of it must know what it is, assuming it is not simply annihilation. Ultimately, the subject of an attack needs to know whose thumb they are under; otherwise to whom do they surrender? Equally, the aggressor needs to communicate the object to which the submission of the enemy's will is aimed; otherwise the act of force (however applied) is rendered meaningless.

The sound of two hands clapping[61]

History provides us no grand disarming digital attacks to analyse and from which to draw firm conclusions about cyber warfare. The literature is rich, however, in imagined scenarios of cyberwar in varying degrees of apocalyptic magnitude. There have also been a handful of relatively small and well-reported attacks. There are things to be learned from both.

One of the most persistent concerns among those who study cyberwar is that it flattens the existing asymmetry of conventional power among nations. For example, American military spending and commensurate power currently outstrips not just its most likely military competitors but the combined total of nearly all other states combined, many of whom are allies of the United States. It is a gargantuan military power on an unprecedented scale. And yet, as it was put in *Joint Force Quarterly*, the American military's premier national security and strategy journal, as opposed to the 'vastly more complex and expensive appurtenances of air and space warfare' the instruments of cyberwar are cheap, allowing 'Lilliputian adversaries' to generate 'catastrophic cascading effects through asymmetric operations against the American Gulliver':

> America's vulnerabilities in cyberspace are open to the entire world and are accessible to anyone with the wherewithal and determination to exploit them ... [A]ny loss of cyberspace dominance on our part can negate our most cherished gains in air and space in virtually an instant.[62]

Such warnings cannot be gainsaid too lightly. True, there are echoes here of the Sputnik-era fears of a 'missile gap' when it was said that the United States was in danger of being leapfrogged in weapons technology, concentrating resources on an older generation of weapons, in that case heavy bombers, while the Soviet Union skipped a generation, jumping straight to missiles and satellites. As it happened, the gap was a myth, but the concern at the time of being outflanked by an enemy more nimble and better adapted to the new environment created by a disruptive technology was real and plausibly valid.

In 1958, General James Gavin, a highly decorated commander of the 82nd Airborne Division during the Second World War and subsequently a prominent figure in the post-war redesign of the army for operations in a nuclear-armed world as Chief of Research and Development, retired early in order to write *War and Peace in the Space Age*, a book explicitly aimed at frightening and awakening his countrymen to the peril that they faced. The West, he argued, had lost the 'technological initiative' and needed an 'all out effort' and a 'strategy of technology' in order to regain it. 'Of one thing we may be sure', he said: 'the nation that first achieves the control of outer space will control the destiny of the human race.'[63]

But hyperbole about the destiny of mankind aside, it would be foolish to deny the enormous enabling effect of air and space power on warfare over the last century and half century respectively. Indeed, virtually untrammelled air supremacy has become more or less the *sine qua non* of the Western way of war since 1945. Rommel, for example, only credited Allied victories over his

German forces in the Middle East in 1941 and later in Normandy in 1944 to air power—of German military superiority on the ground his confidence was essentially boundless. Of the Middle East campaign he wrote evocatively:

> Anyone who has to fight, even with the most modern weapons against an enemy in complete command of the air fights like a savage against modern European troops, under the same handicaps and with the same chance of success.[64]

Of the Normandy battle he declared flatly that ubiquitous Allied air patrols caused 'the movement of our troops on the battlefield [to be] almost completely paralysed, while the enemy can manoeuvre freely'.[65] Space power has also proved massively advantageous as a multiplier of power in other domains of conflict.

The history of war testifies to its invasiveness and tenacious ingenuity: when a new environment, or 'niche' in the evolutionary biological sense, opens up then war soon enters into it; when new tools and processes are developed by science and engineering then generally some way is rapidly found of weaponising them or of using them to enhance the power potential of existing weapons. It is entirely likely, then, indeed probably inevitable, that in the twenty-first century an army that attempts to fight without an 'umbrella' of military cyberpower against an enemy equipped with this capability will suffer as did Rommel's panzers. Notwithstanding their tactical acumen, *esprit de corps*, and the sophistication of their other weapons it will be as though they were the proverbial knife fighter in a gun battle, hopelessly outclassed and doomed to defeat by an opponent whom they will struggle to touch.

As yet, however, actual examples of the use of 'weaponised software', as Thomas Rid and Peter McBurney describe cyber weapons, as part of a combined arms package are few.[66] Israel's 6 September 2007 attack on a Syrian nuclear reactor site suspected of being part of a nuclear weapons programme is the best example that is currently known of. Details of the attack are classified but the general picture has been widely reported. An attack force composed of non-stealthy Israeli F15 and F16 aircraft penetrated deeply into Syria's airspace, blew the reactor site to smithereens, and slipped back out again wholly unmolested. What made the attack remarkable was that Syria's Russian-made air defence radar and missile systems, reckoned to be well maintained and capably operated, never lit up with any sign of detection of the Israeli aircraft.[67] They had been blinded by cyberattack so thoroughly that they did not even know they had been blinded. The operators of Syria's air defences assumed that no one was there because that is what their otherwise perfectly serviceable digital systems had been directed to tell them.

The attack is highly suggestive of cyberpower's contribution to warfare. It is significant that the attack was a combined one: actual high-explosive bombs delivered by physical aircraft destroyed the facility; brute force electronic jamming of a key radar site was employed alongside the more subtle cyberattacks to infiltrate communications; and, it is suspected, Special Forces were on the ground near the site to conduct an intelligence assessment after the strike. We should consider this, then, not as an example of a new form of warfare separate from the strictly kinetic warfare of the past but rather as the latest chapter in a sort of warfare that is in fact quite old and filled with such notorious exploits from which can be drawn some useful thoughts on where things might be headed.

In the American Civil War, for example, Confederate cavalrymen not only regularly conducted raids to destroy Union telegraph communications (a technology that was then barely twenty years old) where they could, they also intentionally switched enemy communications to the wrong destinations, transmitted false orders to Union forces, and generally acted in order to 'shape the information environment' of the war, as contemporary jargon would put it.[68] Similarly, during the 1870–71 siege of Paris in the Franco-Prussian War Prussian military intelligence tapped and, when that was discovered, severed the secret French telegraph cable hidden in the waterways from Paris to Tours. They also conducted observation of all possible sites of signal exchange between the outskirts of the city and semaphore stations on the Arc de Triomphe, the Pantheon and the roof of the Paris Opera, and used specially trained falcon squadrons to intercept carrier pigeons exchanged between Paris and the provinces before the outbreak of hostilities.[69]

Yes, more than thirty years before Orville and Wilbur Wright's first powered flight at Kittyhawk, North Carolina, before even Hugh Trenchard and 'Billy' Mitchell, let alone the Royal Air Force and the United States Army Air Force had been conceived, the Prussian Army had already weaponised predacious birds.

It is Britain, however, most especially the Royal Navy, that has traditionally excelled at this form of warfare. Indeed, it hardly goes too far to say that without a preternatural talent for it the country would not have prevailed in either of the World Wars against larger, and largely more strictly militarily capable, continental foes. As Nicholas Rankin observed in the opening lines of his study of the British 'genius for deception':

> When the Prussian strategist Carl Von Clausewitz defined war in 1833 as 'those acts of force to compel our enemy to do our will', he missed out the dimension that

the British political philosopher Thomas Hobbes had spotted nearly two centuries earlier: 'force and fraud are in war the cardinal virtues.'[70]

Rankin's book is popular history meant to amuse and enlighten but there is a deadly earnest point to the above, which is exceedingly relevant to contemporary strategic debates about cyberpower.

Consider Britain's coordinated use of radio interception and direction finding, code breaking, and radar, in conjunction with a superb system of intelligence analysis and dissemination during the Battle of the Atlantic against Germany's submarine fleet. If that battle had been lost Britain would simply have been starved into submission and the world quite likely would have witnessed Hitler triumphant. The Allies did not win by blanketing the Atlantic Ocean with ships and aircraft that could intercept German U-boats wherever they might appear. Rather they used their superior information systems to send their limited assets of radar-equipped aircraft and ships to the right places at the right times to catch individual U-boats on the surface and to methodically and relentlessly sink them.[71]

In other words, pasting the word 'cyber' onto descriptions of activities undertaken to confuse and misdirect one's enemy and direct one's own forces efficaciously merely because they are conducted by people sitting in front of computer screens and not, for instance, training falcons to kill carrier pigeons does not necessarily add much to understanding. In fact, by severing such operations from their historical antecedents it obscures more than it illuminates. It is worth noting, too, that the seminal 1993 article by Arquila and Ronfeldt 'Cyberwar is Coming!' in which the term was coined described it as essentially tactical in orientation:

> Small numbers of your light, highly mobile forces defeat and compel the surrender of large masses of heavily armed, dug-in enemy forces, with little loss of life on either side. Your forces can do this because they are well-prepared, make room for manoeuvre, and have superior command, control, and information systems that are decentralised to allow tactical initiatives, yet provide the central commander with unparalleled intelligence and 'top sight' for strategic purposes.[72]

As they pointed out, the above has little in principle to do with technology, surprisingly enough. Their preferred example of cyberwar in practice was the world-conquering Mongols, but one could as well populate a history of it with any number of incidences of noteworthy military organisational competence. Alternately, one might flip the lens around to study military disasters to find that since the middle of the nineteenth century, if not earlier, the scale of war in all dimensions—physical, temporal and moral—has expanded to such an extent that failings in the 'organisational dimension' of war may be blamed for the worst defeats.[73]

This limited conception of cyberwar, however, it must be said, is not the one that has really fascinated policy-makers and some strategists. Much more alluring has been the possibilities of nobody-knows-you're-a-dog warfare. In his 1998 book, *The Next World War*, one of the earliest treatments of the subject, James Adams proclaimed the arrival of a digital 'War by Other Means'.[74] In this imagining cyberwar was almost wholly electronic, virtually bloodless, and decisive—almost the epitome of Liddell-Hart's indirect approach.[75] Adams illustrated this ideal with a hypothetical conflict between the United States and China.

The scenario he described rested on the now familiar premise that the computer networks controlling China's industrial control systems, communications and public utilities had been infected with Trojans (malicious hidden software) during their installation by Western manufacturers, allowing the United States to control them at a distance in wartime. In the story a Chinese fleet was steaming towards the Straits of Malacca to assert a territorial claim there that Washington wanted to prevent by some other means than physically sinking it, or threatening to sink it. At its climax, after American cyber warriors had hijacked Chinese power generation facilities, seized control of its communications networks, and threatened it with 'catastrophic cascading effects' in agriculture and industry, the reality of their situation was brought home to the Chinese leadership:

> The phone in front of the General Secretary rang. The President offered his condolences on the unfolding agricultural crisis in the Yangtze valley, and said if China needed help, the people of the United States stood ready to do what they could. Mystified, the General Secretary thanked the President, and then hung up. With internal communications dead, he had no idea what the President had been talking about. Miraculously, phone service between the Yangtze region and Beijing was restored, and the grim news of the breakdown at the dam was relayed to the Politburo. The General Secretary quickly understood that he was not in as much control of his nation as he had thought. He ordered the Malacca-bound battle group home.[76]

Fifteen years later, cyber security experts are more likely to imagine the shoe on the other foot, given Chinese dominance of the manufacture of electronic components and computers. Indeed, one Chinese company connected to the People's Liberation Army, the telecommunications manufacturer Huawei, has alarmed many with the prospect that its products might be used (or already are being used) to allow Chinese spies to eavesdrop on communications and that they may have been equipped with hidden 'kill switches' rendering them vulnerable to remote destruction or control in time of conflict.[77]

Strict followers of Clausewitz might also be unsettled by (or at any rate highly sceptical of) the lack of a lethal dimension of 'War by Other Means'. After all, Clausewitz was clear that 'the destruction of the enemy's force underlies all military actions; all plans are ultimately based on it, resting on it like an arch on its abutment'.[78]

Thomas Rid, for instance, avers that 'All war, pretty simply, is violent. If an act is not potentially violent, it is not an act of war'.[79] This seems, however, rather too proscriptive a reading of the words 'act of force', which is a more flexible concept in On War than a rigid definition requiring the shedding of blood allows.[80] Thomas Schelling, the American Nobel Prize-winning economist who did much to expand our understanding of the strategy of conflict through game theory, described the 'bargaining power' of strategy more generally as the ability to cause pain and destroy value.[81] Undoubtedly, breaking things and killing people is the most efficacious way of creating these effects but given the ever increasing value that modern societies place on intangible digital assets it is not unreasonable to suggest that attacks on them could be significantly painful and wealth-destroying and therefore strategically compelling.

In abstract strategic terms, leaving aside the technological capability, Adams' scenario has to it the ring of plausibility—more so, in fact, than more recent ones. Richard Clarke, for instance, former US National Coordinator for Security, Infrastructure Protection, and Counterterrorism, now a popular and widely quoted expert on cyber security, rather like James Gavin a half century before, warned of a growing 'cyber war gap ... [America's enemies] can use cyber war against us and do great damage, while at the same time they may be able to withstand a US cyber war response'.[82] Most alarming to Clarke was that:

> unlike with nuclear weapons, where an attacker may be deterred by the promise of retaliation or by the radioactive blowback on his own country, launching a cyber attack may run fewer risks. In cyber war we may never know what hit us.[83]

This is implausible, not so much as a matter of technical possibility but in the sense of a deliberate instrumental act of policy. In Adams' scenario, by contrast, there was a clear policy in evidence, in that case the preservation of the status quo with respect to sovereign borders in the Malacca Straits. There was also a recognisable strategy in the form of a credible threat of pain and the destruction of wealth through the seemingly viable means of electronically disrupting vital hydro and irrigation systems. Moreover, the Chinese General

Secretary was under no misapprehension about whose thumb he was under and what course of action he was being compelled to undertake as a result.

In effect, there was no real ambiguity about it. The only curiosity was that the conflict was *sub rosa*, that is invisible to third parties—probably most importantly the populations of the belligerent parties themselves. There are several reasons why states should wish to conduct *sub rosa* warfare, as was discussed in the last chapter, but one of the most fundamental is their well-founded fear of the escalation of the scale of and means employed in war beyond a rational cost-benefit summation, which in turn is an ineluctable product of the interaction of the war's political object with the violent passion that sustains it. Clausewitz called the latter a 'blind natural force': it is a sort of 'wild card', unpredictable and potentially uncontrollable.[84] In order to control the development of conflict, policy-makers may intentionally work to keep the people out of it, so far as possible. Libicki's explanation of the strategic logic of *sub rosa* warfare is to the point:

> The attacker believes that while the state's elites may be able to handle things rationally—for instance, understand when they have been backfooted and thus retreat from some position—the same cannot be said for the target's publics. Thus, informing such publics will put pressure on the state to retaliate publicly when state elites may think other courses are less costly to the state.[85]

This only works, however, if the political object of the attack is very carefully calibrated not to exceed the 'red lines' of the target state's decision-makers. After all, in the scenario noted above, the Chinese leader might not have withdrawn his fleet thus forcing escalation of the conflict from the virtual to the physical plane; alternatively, he might have applied counter pressure in some other way such as, for example, escalating tensions with Taiwan. The point is that states have large and diverse capabilities and the wounded party of a 'pure play' cyberattack would likely retain, or have the ability to reconstitute, other means of reprisal.

Moreover *sub rosa* wars are undoubtedly injurious to democratic civil-military relations and probably also inherently unstable given the amount of guesswork that surrounds unstated national 'red lines' as well as the increasing difficulty of governments keeping secrets. How much greater might be the public's ardour if they have been subject not only to a downright digital attack in the first place but their own government has surrendered on their behalf without clueing them in to the game?

Nonetheless, arguably, this might already be the norm of warfare in the world today, although it bears noting that the tactics of *sub rosa* warfare encompass a range of non-obvious instruments, including cyberattacks but not exclusive to them. In many ways, the aforementioned Chinese future war text *Unrestricted Warfare* is a meditation on this theme, particularly in its discussion of the precise tailoring of limited objectives to a diversity of standard and non-standard means, or what it describes as 'Beyond-Limits Combined War'.[86]

In short, we might already be in the midst of all manner of such wars but, as citizens, be unaware of them. And that, as one close observer of the security policies of the Obama Administration has explained, is exactly the point:

> the expansion of drone and cyber technology has dramatically transformed Obama's strategy in ways that few—perhaps including Obama himself—expected when he was elected president. Without the use of drones, Obama and his aides are convinced al Qaeda would not be near strategic defeat in Pakistan. Without the development of cyberweapons, they believe, Iran would be years closer to the capability to build an atomic bomb. Taken together with the greater reliance on Special Forces—not just for the Bin Laden operation but for the ten to fifteen raids they now run every night—these new weapons dramatically expanded the president's ability to wage nonstop, low-level conflict, something just short of war, every day of the year.[87]

It is at this point that the example of Stuxnet, the 'weaponised code' that was used to disrupt Iran's suspected nuclear programme by targeting the industrial control systems that managed the centrifuges being used to enrich uranium to weapons-grade, becomes very important. Again, although the details are classified, the broad parameters of the story are relatively well reported. Stuxnet, or 'Olympic Games' as the project was codenamed, had two main objectives. The first, obviously, was to forestall for as long as possible Iran's progress towards a nuclear weapons capability. The second, almost as obvious, was to convince Israel, the nation most worried about a nuclear-armed Iran, that there was a better way to deal with the situation than by a conventional airstrike.[88]

Washington's concerns about the second and third order effects of a conventional attack were both manifold and well founded. A wounded Iran might strike back by, *inter alia*, attacking oil shipping in the Persian Gulf with missiles, mines and small boat attacks, by stepping up its support to groups fighting the United States and its allies in Afghanistan (perhaps supplying them with advanced shoulder-fired anti-aircraft weapons, which would seriously hamper coalition air movements—just as American-supplied Stinger missiles had done to the Soviets three decades before), by encouraging Hezbollah in Lebanon to attack Israel with rockets precipitating another war in that area, or by stoking revolution in the predominantly Shiite regions of Sunni-led Gulf monarchies. At the very least, these efforts would have caused a spike in oil prices; more than likely, however, they might touch off a much larger Middle East war.

Also of concern was the disposition of Iran's population towards the West and its own leaders, which is best described as paradoxical. On the one hand, there are points of friction and resentment between Iranians and the West that are historically rooted and go beyond mere occidentalist posturing.[89] On the other hand, as Michael Axworthy, former head of the Iran section in the British Foreign Office, explained:

> there is also a liking and a respect for Europeans and Americans among many ordinary people, that goes well beyond what one finds elsewhere in the Middle East (and to some extent is again a function of the Iranians' sense of their special status among other Middle Eastern nations). Plainly, different Iranians combine these attitudes in different ways, but the best way to explain this paradox is perhaps to say that many Iranians (irrespective of their attitude to their own government, which they may blame for the situation to a greater or lesser extent) feel snubbed, abused, misunderstood and let down by the Westerners they think should have been their friends.[90]

Nothing would have served more swiftly to galvanise the faltering support of Iranians for the existing regime in their country—to allow the Mullahs to make a Persian 'blood, sweat and tears' appeal to collective self-sacrifice, and make it count—than for Western bombers to kill and potentially irradiate large numbers of them. Policy has often in history been made in the 'land of lousy options', as one presidential adviser put it.[91] But the range of options with Iran was, and still is, especially lousy. Hence the attractiveness of the non-obvious cyberattack option.

Initially, on discovery of the attack the Stuxnet virus was heralded as a significant and powerful cyberweapon. It was reckoned to have achieved relatively cleanly what a large air force might have struggled to accomplish very messily. Ralph Langner, a German industrial control systems expert who was catapulted to celebrity status for being the first to recognise Stuxnet as a covert cyberattack, judged that it 'was nearly as effective as a military strike, but even better since there are no fatalities and no full-blown war. From a military perspective this was a huge success'.[92] In hindsight, though, this appears to have been an exaggeration. In actuality, Iran's enrichment capability was not substantially or enduringly impaired by the attack. Indeed, according to a more recent technical analysis, during the period of the attack 'Stuxnet or no

Stuxnet, *ceteris paribus*, Iran's uranium enrichment capacity increased and, consequently, so did its nuclear weapons potential'.[93]

Rather than a 'success' it is more correct to say that from a military perspective the Stuxnet attack was interesting as a harbinger. Its closest historical equivalent might be the nighttime German *Zeppelin* and *Gotha* bomber raids on Britain throughout the First World War, evidence of which is still to be seen in bomb fragment damage to Cleopatra's needle on London's Victoria Embankment, collateral damage of attacks aimed at nearby Charing Cross Station. These contributed very little materially to the war effort through 1914 to 1918, though undoubtedly they provoked psychological distress in Britain's cities at the time.[94] Probably more relevant, however, is that the German public held a very high opinion of what the *Zeppelin* raiders could accomplish on their behalf, which was completely out of step with reality—a view in which they were encouraged by German propaganda. A German cartoon of the time showed John Bull cowering beneath an umbrella trying to tow Great Britain out of the range of a German airship flying above.[95]

There is every reason to believe that cyberpower is likely to be an efficacious means of war, capable of causing much pain and destruction. There is no reason to believe that it will do so on its own. Claims, such as that of the 1994 American commission on protecting national infrastructure, that 'this technology is capable of deciding the outcome of geopolitical crises without the firing of a single weapon' have not come true after nearly twenty years of further development.[96] For conflict among nation states, cyberpower, on its own, is the sound of one hand clapping—silent and somewhat pointless. Moreover, it is not even the case that it undermines asymmetries of power, as has been suggested. Actually, if anything, cyberpower makes strong states stronger and weak states weaker.

9

THE NEW AGE OF ANXIETY

'Then there is electricity—the demon, the angel, the mighty physical power, the all-pervading intelligence!' exclaimed Clifford. 'Is that a humbug too? Is it a fact— or have I dreamt it—that by means of electricity, the world of matter has become a great nerve, vibrating thousands of miles in a breathless point of time? Rather the round globe is a vast head, a brain, instinct with intelligence! Or, shall we say, it is itself a thought, nothing but thought, and no longer the substance which we deemed it!'

'If you mean the telegraph', said the old gentleman, glancing his eye toward its wire, alongside the rail track, 'it is an excellent thing—that is, of course, if the speculators in cotton and politics don't get possession of it.'

Two gentlemen debate connectivity and the pace of change in Nathaniel Hawthorne's *The House of the Seven Gables* (1851)

The burgeoning of connectivity has brought with it a great deal of anxiety amongst states, particularly those in the West, which fear that it is bringing with it a number of profound challenges to the status quo that defy easy resolution. It seems to be changing the configuration of the global commons by overlaying on it an informational 'domain' that is as empowering of non-state actors as it is confounding of state ones. Revolutionary social movements have proliferated using the new means provided by connectivity, and some are experimenting with new forms of digital coercion that could prove potent. For the time being, the situation is best described as pregnant with latent strife. But if economic and social conditions amongst youth in society, the demographic most embedded in and familiar with the new elements of power in the putative new international order, continue to worsen then this could change rapidly. Some think that it already is changing, profoundly and inevitably. It is not so clear that this is true, or that the change would be for the better if it were true. The opportunities to disrupt the functioning of society, however, are clearly increasing. Not so apparent are convincing ideas of how to construct a better one. This has the effect of buoying the status quo, lending it a quality of solidity that is somewhat artificial.

The arrival of the information age has not been much like the advent of the nuclear age ushered in at Alamogordo, New Mexico on 16 July 1945. On the occasion of the latter, J. Robert Oppenheimer, the scientific director of the Manhattan Project to build an atomic bomb, was moved by the awesome power of the weapon he had created to think:

> the world would not be the same. A few people laughed, a few people cried. Most people were silent. I remembered the line from the Hindu scripture, the *Bhagavad-Gita*; Vishnu is trying to persuade the Prince that he should do his duty, and to impress him, takes on his multi-armed form and says, 'Now I am become Death, the destroyer of worlds.' I suppose we all thought that, one way or another.[1]

Some of the rhetoric surrounding the handful of recent cyberattacks, such as that on Estonia in late April 2007 following the decision to relocate a Soviet war memorial in Tallinn from the town centre to a less prominent suburban spot a few weeks before the annual celebration of the victory of the Soviet Union over Nazi Germany, employed similar imagery—although less poetically. In the words of Ene Ergama, speaker of the Estonian parliament:

> When I look at a nuclear explosion and the explosion that happened in our country in May, I see the same thing ... Like nuclear radiation, cyberwar doesn't make you bleed, but it can destroy everything.[2]

But the parallel between the two is overdrawn, to say the least. Would history have bothered to record it if in August 1945 the United States had contrived to interrupt postal deliveries and close the banks of Hiroshima and Nagasaki for a couple of days? The question answers itself. In fact, it is not all that easy to say when the information age even began—it has rather crept up incrementally instead of revealing itself in a blinding fission blast. As we have seen, many of its structural elements have been firmly in place for half a century, if not a century or more.[3] For purposes of convenience, however, let us concentrate on the period since the arrival of the Internet.

Utopia to dystopia

The pioneers of today's Internet were also moved to awe by the power of their creation, adopting a self-consciously positive and socially constructive tone.

A perfect illustration of this is to be found in the 'Declaration of Cyberspace Independence' written by the Internet activist John Perry Barlow, a founder of the Electronic Frontier Foundation. Addressed to the world's governments on behalf of the denizens of cyberspace, the declaration intoned:

> Governments of the Industrial World, you weary giants of flesh and steel, I come from Cyberspace, the new home of Mind. On behalf of the future, I ask you of the past to leave us alone. You are not welcome among us. You have no sovereignty where we gather.[4]

That Perry Barlow later retreated from this view to an extent, admitting with some embarrassment that it was written in the Web's relative early days in haste and in a consciously Jeffersonian manner, is not surprising.[5] Reality is actually quite complicated and the state's adaptability and significance in the information age have often been underestimated.[6] Nonetheless, it is useful to point out that the initial appraisal of connectivity was largely that it was decidedly a good thing. Subsequently, as we have observed, people grew more and more impressed with its potential for war; but by and large, as we shall see below, they have been worried about the wrong sort of war.

Part of the problem is that the emergence of cyberspace coincided with a period in which the West went from a rather rosy post-Cold War high to a considerably more uncertain present. It is no coincidence that the high times of connectivity paralleled periods of exuberant growth in the economy. From its earliest days, cyberspace was infused with an ideology born of a mix of technical pragmatism and a desire to improve the world. It is sometimes missed that the roots of cyberculture are to be found in the 1960s era counterculture:

> Fully in keeping with the scientific ethos of the era, young members ... of the counterculture ... imagined themselves as part of a massive, geographically distributed, generational *experiment*. The world was their laboratory; in it they could play both scientist and subject, exploring their minds and bodies, their relationships to one another, and the nature of politics, commerce, community, and the state.[7]

If Shakespeare were alive today and writing television miniseries about hubris and tragedy it seems certain that the line 'don't be evil', the unofficial motto of the Internet giant Google, would feature somewhere. For, unfortunately, it seems that connectivity makes it relatively easy to be evil. Jaron Lanier, one of the most well-known Web theorists, put it this way:

> I worry about the next generation of young people around the world growing up with Internet-based technology that emphasises crowd aggregation, as is the current fad. Will they be more likely to succumb to pack dynamics when they come of age? The recipe that led to social catastrophe in the past was economic humiliation

combined with collectivist ideology. We have the ideology in its digital packaging, and it is entirely possible we could face dangerously traumatic economic shocks in the coming decades.[8]

These are good things to be worried about. They make John Perry Barlow's barb about 'weary giants' stick all the deeper—for this is how many states feel nowadays as their debts mount seemingly irresistibly, austerity budgets fail to deliver growth, and unemployment, especially youth unemployment, explodes.[9]

To be sure this is a fairly long running theme in Western political thought. One detects it very obviously in the aforementioned foreword to Britain's National Security Strategy, where the prime minister writes that 'we are entering into an era of uncertainty', ironically, for a Conservative, without mentioning John Kenneth Galbraith's 1970s television programme and book of that name which called for a new socialism.[10] Similarly, a popular recent book declares that a 'new world disorder' heralds the 'Age of the Unthinkable' in which '[the old] logic can't even begin to contain dangers' from such things as millenarian terrorism, financial panics, and changes in the global economy:

> In some respects, these sorts of undeterrable wildfire scenarios are not new ... But what is new is that such threats spread more quickly and wildly than ever, mashing up into new dangers when we try to regulate or control them.[11]

It would be mad to discount these dangers. In his landmark work on international order and strategy, *The Shield of Achilles*, Philip Bobbitt argued that within the lifetime of most readers of this book it is entirely likely that a non-state group will produce a cataclysm—obliterate the heart of a major city with a nuclear device, or simply irradiate it with a 'dirty bomb', perhaps release some natural or engineered lethal pathogen killing God knows how many, there are multiple options—and that others will follow. In view of this threat, he says, our views on international security today are both too narrow and too ambitious:

> They are narrow because they have up to now excluded the non-territorial threats to the state that are becoming increasingly dangerous; they are too ambitious because they do not recognise that the power of states to ensure their own security by conventional strategies is rapidly waning.[12]

Paradoxically, an effect of connectivity is to have created a global society that is increasingly homogeneous and interdependent, but which also empowers heterogeneous fractions against whom no state, however large and powerful, is immune to attack.

It is impossible to see beyond the occurrence of a megadeath event such as those noted above with assurance, though a few such as Bobbitt have tried.

We see here, again, in the expectation of relentless cataclysm the overweening fear of speed and wild connectedness combined with the belief that this is all extraordinarily unprecedented, which it is not. Consider that within the living memory of many Europeans today several countries suffered wartime deaths totalling 10 per cent or more of their total populations. Whole cities full of women, children and the elderly were deliberately blasted to kingdom come. These were state on state attacks, though. It is not a happy thought but are we truly less resilient now? Probably not: modern societies are capable of absorbing a great deal of misery and carnage—but not without change.

Bobbitt's worry is that after a massive attack by a non-state actor society itself may call for measures that are highly intrusive and potentially extremely repressive.[13] This seems a very real possibility—not that we face external societal destruction but that as a result of an attack we shock ourselves into a new, considerably less free political order very different from the one imagined by the cyber-utopians just a few years ago. On the other hand, it is all too easy to make too much of the scale of the current societal shock. The long-time technology and society watcher Bruce Sterling attempted to put the scaremongering over the information age in its place with a reminder that:

> For the average citizen in the 1870s, the telephone was weirder, more shocking, more 'high-tech' and harder to comprehend than the most outrageous stunts of advanced computing ... In trying to understand what is happening to us today, with our bulletin-board systems, direct overseas dialling, fibre-optic transmissions, computer viruses, hacking stunts, and a vivid tangle of new laws and new crimes, it is important to realise that our society has been through a similar challenge before— and that, all in all, we did rather well by it.[14]

In short, the topic is ridiculously easy to over-dramatise and hideously difficult to keep in perspective.

Take, for example, the extract above with its talk of 'bulletin-board systems'. Very few people born in the year those words were written, not two decades ago, would have had the faintest idea of the nature of a 'bulletin-board system'. Was it made of cork? Did it come with chalk or push pins? And yet social media, the successor to electronic bulletin boards, is not new, and nor is hacking, or even the popular inclination to consider the evolution of computing and political revolution (that is, the need to 'improve the world') as being intertwined. As early as 1984 Steven Levy's history of hacking took pains to redress what he saw as the unfair characterisation of his subjects as misfits and antisocial oddballs: 'they were adventurers, visionaries, risk-takers, artists ... and the ones who most clearly saw why the computer was a truly revolutionary tool.'[15]

Discussions of the informationalisation of society often reference George Orwell's dystopian novel *Nineteen Eighty-Four* in which he imagined a highly repressive society so thoroughly and ubiquitously monitored that maintaining even one's own private thoughts, let alone voicing them or acting on them contrary to the wishes of 'Big Brother', was a vast challenge. Another of his essays, however, written in October 1945 and entitled 'You and the Atom Bomb', took a slightly different approach, raising a very timely question:

> I think the following rule would be found generally true: that ages in which the dominant weapon is expensive or difficult to make will tend to be ages of despotism, whereas when the dominant weapon is cheap and simple, the common people have a chance. Thus, for example, tanks, battleships, and bombing planes are inherently tyrannical weapons, while rifles, muskets, longbows and hand grenades are inherently democratic weapons. A complex weapon makes the strong stronger, while a simple weapon—so long as there is no answer to it—gives claws to the weak.[16]

Is connectivity a weapon of the weak or of the strong? Is it complex or simple? The answer is, of course, somewhat complicated. It is complex and simple, as well as useful to both the strong and the weak in different ways. The main effect of it on the present international order is subversive: it changes the relative relationship of power among states not very much; but it is reshaping relations between state and non-state actors quite a lot in ways that empower revolutionaries to mobilise while at the same time, thus far, impairing their ability to focus on a specific political agenda.

Cyber and the sea

As we saw in the last chapter, actually producing effective weaponised code is quite difficult and expensive. Moreover, integrating cyberpower into an over-arching combined arms capability is likely to be beyond the capabilities of those states that have found it difficult to integrate even just the conventional arms of the domains of land, sea and air. Armies that are able to defend their networks will accrue distinct advantages from network-enabling them, while armies that do not possess such ability will enjoy no such advantage—indeed they will be punished harshly for trying to network-enable anything.

It would be misleading and incomplete, however, to look at the impact of cyberpower on strategic affairs through the prism of airpower and combined arms alone. True, if we conceive of cyberspace narrowly in terms of electronic devices then cyberwar is just the latest phase in electronic warfare; but if we take a wider view of cyberspace as a realm of ideas then there is more to it than that.

A good way to start to get to grips with this wider conception is to consider connectivity in the context of the 'global commons' as a whole. An amalgam of the maritime, air, space, and now cyberspace domains, the global commons is well described as the 'connective tissue of the international system'.[17]

Particularly useful is to consider the contribution of sea power to international order over the long term. This is because, as the beginning of the 2008 United States National Security Strategy notes, 'For more than sixty years, the United States has secured the global commons for the benefit of all. Global prosperity is contingent on the free flow of ideas, goods, and services.'[18] This is surely true. However, as the historian Walter Russell Mead has argued, world politics has been shaped by a 'maritime system' for the last 400 years, not just the last sixty. This system was dominated by Britain's Royal Navy until the world wars effectively bankrupted Britain in the twentieth century, at which point the United States Navy took over.[19] There is some evidence that connectivity does change the configuration of the global commons, creating a dense and immersive 'information environment', which parallels and to some degree subverts the workings of power in other domains, as was touched upon in Chapter Seven. Control in the sense normally understood in conventional domains—having unfettered usage of a domain while being able to deny one's enemies the same usage—is practically unachievable in this new environment, and certain forms of resistance are empowered by this fact.

There are good reasons why policy-makers and strategists describe cyberspace as a domain of conflict alongside the physical domains of the global commons. In the minds of its leading developers the Internet was explicitly conceived as a sort of commons in which, as Tim Berners-Lee (perhaps the person most deserving of the title: inventor of the Internet) put it, 'anything [could be] potentially connected with anything' with a sort of immediacy and verisimilitude that conventional communications could not match.[20]

Moreover, from the perspective of politicians concerned with how their countries will succeed in the twenty-first century world of 'knowledge economies', dependent on such things as intellectual property rights, creative industries, well-functioning financial services and safe electronic commerce, it makes a certain amount of sense to view cyberspace as the sea and the nation's wealth as traversing it like the treasure ships of the Spanish Main of olden times.

This is plainly the case with Britain's National Security Strategy with its talk of the country being at the 'heart of many global networks' with an 'outward looking disposition ... both a geographical and virtual centre of global activity'.[21] Britain has long been an entrepôt nation with a maritime orientation and it is well placed to profit from the accelerated transactional flows of digital goods, finance and services particularly—if it can secure them. After all, these things are vulnerable to electronic plunder at potentially great cost, and protecting them is therefore important to national prosperity. The analogy, however, fails on other grounds.

For one thing, cyberspace is not really akin to a domain of the global commons insofar as geographers use the term to refer to tangible 'resource domains outside the jurisdiction of any one state', such as the high seas and deep sea mineral beds, the atmosphere, space and Antarctica.[22] Nor does it meet the legal requirements of a global commons.[23] Also it is not free as are the oceans and the atmosphere, because the private citizens, companies and governments that have built and paid for its material components own it.

For another thing, there is its inherent weirdness, which cannot be dealt with in a straightforward way and is sometimes therefore merely omitted in official documents. It is not just that cyberspace lacks conventional three-dimensionality; it is also infinitely more mutable than other domains. Its 'geography' is not static; rather it can be altered by destruction or compromise of its physical layer, or by programming new instructions at the syntactic layer. It is a construct, says Martin Libicki, and as such:

> there is little hard-and-fast physics of the sort that dictates what can and cannot be done in, say, outer space. What can and cannot be done in cyberspace need not follow the laws of physics or the laws of man—although violating the latter may have real world repercussions. There is no inherent 'there' there except as mutually agreed.[24]

This lack of 'there-ness' is both a philosophical problem and a bureaucratic one when considering it alongside other domains, all of which possess at least some sort of integument that can be used to demarcate service responsibilities. The sea has the shore; the air has the land; land has the sky; space has the upper edge of the atmosphere. Cyberspace, however, overlaps everything. It does not possess an edge, if one allows that it is composed of more than electronic systems but also the ideas in them. Cyberspace resides in, or more precisely its edge penetrates into, the minds of the humans who use it. Basically, there is really no clean distinction between cyberspace and real space, and pretending that there is clouds understanding of its full effect on strategic affairs. The technology and social theorist Clay Shirky put it this way:

> The old view of online as a separate space, cyberspace apart from the real world, was an accident of history. Back when the online population was tiny, most of the people you knew in your daily life were not part of that population. Now that

computers and increasingly computerlike phones have been broadly adopted the whole notion of cyberspace is fading.[25]

This fact is not of secondary importance: it is the primordially salient reason why cyberspace is different from other domains in a way which simultaneously sets it apart and makes it inseparable from them. In the same text in which they introduced the term cyberwar, Arquilla and Ronfeldt also drew a vital distinction:

> In our view, the information-age conflict spectrum looks like this: What we term 'cyberwar' will be an ever-more-important entry at the military end, where the language is normally about high-intensity conflict ... 'Netwar' will figure increasingly at the societal end, where the language is normally about low-intensity conflict ... Whereas cyberwar will usually see formal military forces pitted against each other, netwar is more likely to involve non-state, paramilitary, and other irregular forces.[26]

The key point is the aforementioned 'information environment', which we might consider the primary setting of today's wars whether we call them 'netwars', 'information wars', 'wars of ideas', 'discursive wars', 'cyberwars' or any one of a dozen new portmanteau war types invented to describe war in our densely mediated times. What does it mean?

The 2010 Quadrennial Defence Review defines it as 'the interdependent networks of information technology infrastructures, including the Internet and telecommunication networks', which is typical of the tendency to focus on devices rather than ideas.[27] The definition is not so much incorrect as incomplete to judge from the way that doctrine writers actually use the term elsewhere. The new American *Counterinsurgency* field manual, for instance, says:

> The information environment is a critical dimension [of insurgency] and insurgents attempt to shape it to their advantage ... by carrying out activities, such as suicide attacks, that have little military value but ... are executed to attract high-profile media coverage ... and inflate perceptions of insurgent capabilities.[28]

In this view, the 'information environment' is something that is 'manipulated' or 'shaped' by both sides in a conflict not so much in terms of the physical structures of the network (though that may be a part of it) but of the ideas in the minds of the people whom the network touches. Clearly, then, in actual usage 'information environment' carries a strong connotation of simply 'what people think' and it is shaped by non-kinetic propaganda as well as kinetic propaganda by deed.[29] It bears a strong resemblance to media scholars Andrew Hoskins and Ben O'Loughlin's concept of a 'media ecology', which they describe as an 'interaction order composed of both what appears in news media and what happens beyond the media text—"out there" in the world'.[30]

Global commons to global village

As was noted in Chapter One, and further developed in Chapter Seven, perception has never been incidental to the outcome of wars. The argument now is simply that informationalisation, the increased density of connectivity, has elevated the importance of perception beyond that of previous eras. Of course, this has been a popular argument amongst postmodernists for quite a long time. Paul Virilio, for example, building on Foucault's work on power, declared: 'the history of battle is primarily the history of radically changing fields of perception. In other words, war consists not so much in scoring territorial, economic or other material victories as in appropriating the "immateriality" of perceptual fields.'[31]

Apart perhaps from the obscurity of the language, a sin for which he also sometimes is blamed, none of this would have offended Clausewitz who was quite aware of the importance of war's symbolic dimension, as 'commerce' he described it, meaning thereby to embed it in broader social reality.[32] It is only recently, however, that senior leaders in Western defence establishments have begun to argue the same thing in similar terms. When Britain's Chief of Defence Staff lectured on 'People and the Information Age' in 2010 he threw down the gauntlet to the army, challenging it to replace the old 'paradigm' of war and grapple with a new one:

> Future wars of mass manoeuvre are more likely to be fought though the minds of millions looking at computer and television screens than on some modern equivalent of the Cold War's North German Plain. Indeed some might argue the screen is our generation's North German Plain, the place where future war will be won or lost.[33]

To put into perspective why this change of thinking has come about it is helpful briefly to take a step back to observe in perspective a few basic things about the evolution of the information environment. Before literacy, the information environment was necessarily highly circumscribed because knowledge could only be transmitted orally, by demonstration or to a small extent by drawing. Thus communication was 'one-to-one', or at best one-to-a-few. Moreover, the possible range of transmission of complex ideas was no further than the thinker could speak them to another person who would in turn have to hold them in memory.[34]

Logographic writing, initially on tablets of mud inscribed with a pointy reed, appeared about 7000 years ago.[35] The information environment in this era would have been of very local significance and very prosaic in content—generally being confined to the keeping of inventories of foodstuffs, bills of sale, tax receipts and the like. There would have been little point in communicating such information elsewhere even if that were possible, and just a tiny fraction of the population was literate. Over the next 6500 years, however, the importance of writing to governance and the law, science and philosophy, commercial enterprise, and war grew enormously with recognisably modern political order flowering in various places including Rome (where after a few centuries it declined for a few centuries more) and particularly China.[36]

The most important effect of the invention of the mechanical printing press in the mid-fifteenth century was not, at first, so much that books could be produced cheaply in mass (as there were at that time still so few readers) but was rather the machine-made books' relative orderliness and uniformity. Hand-written texts were by definition one-offs and never identical; they also frequently comprised fragments of older works. A printed book, on the other hand, was always the same and, once disseminated, could become an authoritative text (that is, the same whether you read it in Rome or Riga).

What is important here is that an information environment was emerging where information was formed in consistent politically resonant narratives that could be widely distributed to publics that were increasingly capable of receiving them—albeit no more quickly than before. This had a bridging and unifying effect in science, which recovered and systematised the ancient Greek and Roman texts and then rapidly began to build upon them. Its impact in politics and religion, by contrast, was divisive and fragmenting, 'making possible pamphlet wars and doctrinal polarisation'.[37] The early modern period was shot through with religious wars fired up and sustained by pamphleting and propaganda. The French Wars of Religion in the 1500s, for instance:

> were media wars as well as conflicts with swords and guns, conflicts in which pamphleteering, image-making, image breaking and oral communication were all important ... The [Catholic] League conducted what we would call a media campaign in which verses posted on walls, satirical images, fiery sermons and incendiary pamphlets all played a part.[38]

Over the ensuing centuries the information environment expanded as literacy grew and the volume and diversity of publications increased to feed the new appetite for information in a self-reinforcing cycle. The German sociologist Jurgen Habermas described what emerged from this process as the 'public sphere' meaning essentially the arena in which public debate takes place in society.[39]

Mass communication is often associated with the invention of radio and television in the early twentieth century but its actual advent was at least

100 years before then with newsprint, which was at the forefront of the new one-to-many paradigm of communications. Moreover, the giant leap in the velocity of communications was a nineteenth century phenomenon—a direct consequence of the telegraph, as may be seen in the opening quote to this chapter. The major importance of electronic media was not really its speed or mass but the injection of verisimilitude and consequently enhanced emotional impact. In 1889–90 the American inventor Thomas Edison toured European capitals demonstrating to the great and good his recording phonograph. One of those whom he recorded was German Field Marshal and strategist Helmuth Von Moltke, then almost in his nineties, who remarked with probably unintended but nonetheless eerie prognostic accuracy:

> This newest invention of Mister Edison is indeed astonishing. [It] makes it possible for a man who has already lain long in the grave once again to raise his voice and greet the present.[40]

Sound and image-based communications are qualitatively very different from text because they convey a functional facsimile of reality as opposed to a mere description of it. It is one thing to read the words of Von Moltke, a man born when Napoleon was still running roughshod over Europe; it is another thing to hear his voice. Perhaps a better illustration of the effect for those less impressed by old soldiers is to consider the difference between a piece of information such as Beethoven's 'Ode to Joy' conveyed as a written score as opposed to a digital recording of it played on a device. The same basic information produces a completely different subjective experience.[41]

Enter cyberspace, causing another step change in the information environment. Now anyone with a laptop and a network connection can transmit information, whether 'one-to-one' or 'one-to-many', effectively globally and instantaneously in a variety of forms; process information (that is, copy, cross-reference, cross-check, combine or manipulate it) easily and cheaply with standard commercial software; and store information in vast quantities almost indefinitely on cheap, miniature and portable digital devices, or in the 'cloud', independent of any particular device.

Viewed in historical perspective, then, we might say that the 'information environment' started off local and intimate, when humans communicated mainly by voice in small kinship groups, and remained that way for a long time until they learned to communicate in a transmissible and semi-permanent medium. It then, by degrees as physical transportation links grew, became global, albeit confined to those who were literate and, latterly, those with access to mass-communications media. Since then, it has rapidly become possible for anybody to talk to anybody else, in principle, as much as they would want. Meanwhile, in parallel, war changed too in similar ways, finding new means, filling new niches, and focusing on new points of pressure in accordance with society's changing ways of storing value.

This is why policy-makers and strategists are now so much more concerned with managing the perception of conflict than they have traditionally been and are occasionally coming across, perhaps unwittingly, as arch postmodernists. The problem is laid out in Britain's National Security Strategy, which warns of the 'future character of conflict' in terms that are really quite Virilio-esque:

> we must expect intense scrutiny of our operations by a more transparent society, informed by the speed and range of modern global communications. Our enemies will continue to attack our physical and electronic lines of communication. And the growth of communications technology will increase our enemies' ability to influence, not only all those on the battlefield, but also our own society directly. We must therefore win the battle for information, as well as the battle on the ground.[42]

In the 1960s Marshall McLuhan discerned the emergence of what he called a 'global village' as a result of the rise of global communications, a public sphere in which everyone was linked to everyone. War in this situation would, he argued, take the form of a 'war of icons', in which the belligerents would seek to defeat their rivals by the erosion of their 'collective countenance' with 'electric persuasion ... dunking entire populations in new imagery'. He also spoke of a trend towards 'more and more power with less and less hardware' being a characteristic of the new age.[43] This was prescient for the time.

Information and revolution

What has become clear, though, is the extent to which informationalisation has contributed to the decline of the external state-on-state mode of war, dominated by relatively small numbers of organised forces, and the rise of a more internally focused warfare featuring a plethora of moderately organised and loosely affiliated non-state groups. Connectivity has proven to be an invaluable tool of social mobilisation, for good or for ill. As the Spanish sociologist Manuel Castells put it, 'Cyberspace has become a global electronic agora where the diversity of human disaffection explodes in a cacophony of accents'.[44] Populism, activism, social movements and revolutions are certainly nothing new—they have been the stuff of politics for as long as it has made sense to speak of political order. Moreover, 'electronic populism', 'hacktivism', and 'networked social movements', it must be recalled, are simply variants of these much older concepts.[45]

It remains unclear whether what is new about them is really important, though there are no few claims that what is occurring now is profoundly transformative of political order:

> We are at an extraordinary moment in human history: never before has the possibility of true democracy been so close to realisation. As the cost of publishing and duplication has dropped to near zero, a truly free press, and a truly informed public becomes a reality. A new Information Enlightenment is dawning where knowledge flows freely, beyond national boundaries. Technology is breaking down traditional social barriers of status, class, power, wealth and geography, replacing them with an ethos of collaboration and transparency.[46]

This seems, for the time being, both over-exuberant, since the effect of these forms of electronic civil disobedience is almost certainly less than is often asserted, and also too optimistic, since the moves by defenders of the status quo to counter them have been extensive and just as innovative. It cannot be denied, though, that the field is in play and no one truly can know the result. We live in interesting times. This is most obviously so in the case of the wave of revolts against repressive regimes in the Middle East which, since starting in late 2010, have toppled from power President Zine el Abidine Ben Ali in Tunisia, Hosni Mubarak in Egypt (and subsequently his elected successor President Mohammed Morsi of the Egyptian Muslim Brotherhood), and Muammar Gaddafi in Libya.

There is great controversy over the degree to which social media has driven these so-called 'Twitter Revolutions'. On the one side, enthusiasts of social media see in the new technology a liberalising force with literally revolutionary potential.[47] Activists speak effusively of how social media allows them to organise protests, document and publicise security force crackdowns, and seek moral and material support for their causes globally. On the other side, there are sceptics who warn of the dark potential of the technology to strengthen the control of authoritarian states, firstly through the provision to their populations of cheap but distracting entertainments and, secondly, by giving the state extensive new means of detecting anti-regime speech (or thought-crime).[48]

No good historian would attempt to render judgment on how, ultimately, the balance of power between people and states may be realigned by digital connectivity. Still, it is possible to discern the essential dynamic that is at work, which is the shift in the way in which information is communicated, stored and analysed.

THE NEW AGE OF ANXIETY

It comes back to the nature of the information environment, or the paradigm of communication, which is undergoing a change from one where a few privileged speakers (governments, corporations and owners of major media outlets) could to a large extent control what appeared in the public sphere, to one of 'mass self-communication' where many people can speak to many others relatively easily and cheaply about whatever they want. To quote Castells again:

> In a world marked by the rise of mass self-communication, social movements and insurgent politics have the chance to enter the public space from multiple sources. By using both horizontal communication networks and mainstream media to convey their images and messages, they increase their chances of enacting social and political change—even if they start from a subordinate position in institutional power, financial resources, or symbolic legitimacy.[49]

The issue of transparency clearly looms large for those arguing that we are now witnessing a profound change in governance. The fundamental proposition is that connectivity increases transparency massively. As noted in the previous chapter with William Hague's speech to the 2011 London Cyberspace Conference, governments acknowledge the truth of this point. The publication of a massive cache of sensitive American government documents by Wikileaks in the spring of 2010 and the revelations about the National Security Agency's PRISM programme in 2013 would make denial ridiculous.

The issue is certainly confounding governments, but does this transparency actually make us more or less secure, or more or less free, and to what extent are freedom and security now in tension? On the one side we find those such as Carne Ross, a former British diplomat who quit over the dissimulation of government communications in the lead-up to the Iraq War, who argues that it is simply beyond normal politics to bring either security or freedom. 'The evidence is accumultaing', he writes, 'that inherited bodies and values are less and less able to arbitrate the forces now swirling around us.'[50] Even worse, claim others such as Rop Gonggrijp, a Dutch hacker who said in a keynote address to the annual conference of the Berlin-based Chaos Computer Club:

> Most of today's politicians realize that nobody in their ministry or any of their expensive consultants can tell them what is going on anymore. They have a steering wheel in their hands without a clue what—if anything—it is connected to. Our leaders are reassuring us that the ship will certainly survive the coming storm. But on closer inspection they are either quietly pocketing the silverware or discreetly making their way to the lifeboats.[51]

It would be nice to dismiss such statements out of hand. It cannot be gainsaid, however, that governments have been seriously wrong-footed by connectivity, whatever the ultimate effect on international relations, and are struggling to reorient themselves. Their efforts to articulate the threats that they fear to justify their intensive surveillance and security efforts have not resonated with a large fraction of the public. They certainly have not outlined a coherent strategy that balances necessary measures to protect society with believable checks and balances against their potential abuse. And having declared after 11 September 2001 that the terrorists would not be allowed to change our way of life it seems to many that they are doing just that.

They also, however, really are confronted with the problem of some networked social movements that have cottoned on to the power of connectivity to multiply their violent capacity. As has been richly described in the literature, al-Qaeda is a superb example of an organisation turning itself into what Mark Duffield has called a 'non-territorial network enterprise' which has no territory but stretches around the world in geographically isolated but digitally interconnected groups which share a common cause driven by a shared sense of outrage.[52] Naturally, the literature has dwelled lengthily on what the terrorism analyst Marc Sageman describes as 'leaderless jihad'.[53]

What is worse, though, is that there is really nothing special about al-Qaeda in this respect—many other movements use some or all of the same techniques, notably resource mobilization via propaganda and propaganda by deed, a 'flattened' organisational hierarchy, decentralization of command and control, and self-organisation, which all depend on networks.

A handful of such groups, such as the environmental group Earth Liberation Front (ELF), use violence (though not to the same extent as al-Qaeda) and are intent on radically changing Western civilization, which the ELF regard as intrinsically hostile to and destructive of the Earth's environment. With remarkably few changes in word choice, the ELF's communiqué in response to the development of genetically modified organisms by several major corporations and universities could read like a suicide bomber's 'martyrdom' video:

> In pursuance of justice, freedom, and equal consideration for all innocent life across the board, segments of this global revolutionary movement are no longer limiting their revolutionary potential by adhering to a flawed, inconsistent 'non–violent' ideology ... Where it is necessary, we will no longer hesitate to pick up the gun to implement justice, and provide the needed protection for our planet that decades of legal battles, pleading, protest, and economic sabotage have failed so drastically to achieve.[54]

Others simply use networks to enhance their ability to organise various forms of protest including demonstrations that may end, deliberately or accidentally, in violent street battles. A strong element of the 'smart mob' has long been apparent in the global anti-capitalist movement, for instance, which came into prominence with the 1999 'Battle for Seattle' in which networked activists used mobile phones, websites and laptop computers to deploy 'swarming tactics' in protest against a World Trade Organisation meeting in the city.[55]

Moreover, these movements are avowedly global. The umbrella group 'We are Everywhere', for instance, describes itself as:

> the rise of an unprecedented global rebellion—a rebellion which is in constant flux, which swaps ideas and tactics across oceans, shares strategies between cultures and continents, gathers in swarms and dissolves, only to swarm again elsewhere.[56]

Similarly, the 'Occupy' movement (or movements), which captured world attention in 2011 by forming encampments in New York, London and other cities around the world, explicitly drew a connection between itself and the revolutions in the Middle East. In its own words, Occupy Wall Street is a 'leaderless resistance movement ... using the revolutionary Arab Spring tactic to achieve our ends'.[57] There is no way that governments and security forces would not be drawn to such groups. As one recent study of the 'cybered' world concluded:

> The United States is now fully a deeply internally interconnected large complex socio-technical system embedded for its quality of life in an even bigger, more complex, turbulent, and dynamically surprising global socio-technical system. National responses will need to be much beyond simply securing the borders and hoping to reach a breakthrough before the main competitor does.[58]

In this case, the 'main competitor' was conceived as another state, specifically China, but the obvious reality is that the sources of danger to the 'socio-technical system' simply do not consist only, or perhaps even primarily, of states. Non-state actors have also come under much scrutiny, causing much aggravation to them, particularly as the vast majority pursue their goal of systemic change non-violently. As was concluded in a recent study of the attention of security forces directed against environmentalist groups, 'green is the new red':

> We have sacrificed too much in the name of fighting terrorism, and the enemy keeps growing. Since September eleventh the word has been stretched and pulled and hemmed and cuffed and torn and mended to fit a growing body of political whims.[59]

The trouble for such groups is that governments understand very well that the difference between violent and non-violent groups is actually not all that great. At some point, serious revolutionaries encountering real resistance come up against a hard choice of whether to escalate to bloodshed or not. To illustrate, in 1964, while on trial by the Apartheid regime in South Africa for sabotage, Nelson Mandela explained the remorseless logic of contested change:

> I, and the others who started the organization [Umkhonto we Sizwe, the armed wing of the African National Congress], felt that without violence there would be no way open to the African people to succeed in their struggle against the principle of white supremacy. All lawful modes of expressing opposition to this principle had been closed by legislation, and we were placed in a position in which we had either to accept a permanent state of inferiority, or to defy the government. We chose to defy the law.[60]

Once the decision is taken to go beyond the law, claimed Mandela, there are four violent options in ascending order of severity—sabotage, guerrilla warfare, terrorism and open revolution. The 'global justice' movement, as it sometimes terms itself, has been suspended on the cusp of political violence for at least a decade (notwithstanding the flirtation with violence—typically property damage and intimidation—practiced by some sub-groups). This is not to castigate the movement, whose cause, frankly, has much to commend it. Amongst its friends are Nobel Prize winners such as the economist Joseph Stiglitz, who described it as being rooted in a:

> widespread feeling that something is wrong with our economic system, and the political system as well, because rather than correcting our economic system, it reinforced the failures. The gap between what our economic and political system is supposed to do ... and what it actually does became too large to be ignored. Governments around the world were not addressing the economic problems, and so the feeling of unfairness became a feeling of betrayal. Universal values of freedom and fairness had been sacrificed to the greed of a few.[61]

Stiglitz remarked that it was not surprising that in Tunisia and Egypt, where there was no political process, the result was revolution. But in democracies there was still belief that the 'electoral process *might* work'.[62]

It behoves us to ask, what if it does not? It is not as though the leaders of such movements are unaware of the pregnancy of the moment and blithe to the possibility of adopting tactics that go beyond the law. As Starhawk, a prominent long-time activist and canny strategic thinker, wrote in 2000: 'We're at a crucial point right now. We can evolve further into an unpaid militant mercenary army, travelling to actions that get more violent, smaller, more isolated, and less effective or....'[63]

'Or' indeed—that is the tricky part. What happens when and if it becomes apparent that there will be no change to the status quo? What if the grievances outlined by Stiglitz are not alleviated but get worse? Quite obviously, the issue is extremely politically awkward. A healthy society accommodates a degree of subversion because it is a main source of new ideas that keep it fresh and fair. Consider that just over 100 years ago, on 4 June 1913, the English suffragette activist Emily Wilding Davison was killed stepping in front of the King's horse on Derby Day in arguably the first 'propaganda of the deed' event designed explicitly to harness the power of the moving image.[64] *The Times* editorialised on it the following day, arguing that it would only harm the cause of women's suffrage:

> Reckless fanaticism is not regarded by [the public] as a qualification for the franchise ... The bulk of the suffragist party, and the abler of its leaders, are doubtless conscious of this truth. They seem, however, to be quite unable to lay the spirit which some of them have helped to raise, and to prevent the perpetration of crimes, the utter inanity of which as a means of political propaganda is even more striking than their wickedness.[65]

But Davison had clearly come to the conclusion that militancy would prove efficacious. Whether or not a movement goes beyond the law depends less on the objective righteousness of its cause than it does on a strategic calculation of the political landscape at the time. Again, to quote Starhawk:

> We often argue tactics on the grounds of morality—is it right or wrong, violent or non-violent ... We might do better to ask, 'Do these particular tactics support our goals and objectives?'[66]

Her conclusion, based not on any personal belief in the immorality of violence, was that violent tactics would be counterproductive now because the system is already reeling toward collapse and to go beyond the law would merely serve to shore up its crumbling legitimacy. Given recent analyses suggesting that the ongoing financial crisis in Europe might lead to 'some form of authoritarian or military government' it is not an implausible supposition.[67]

Hopefully, we are a long way from any such eventuality. Without doubt, however, it can be seen that connectivity enables movements to mobilise rapidly in forms that are highly fluid and hard to defeat. This does not change the fact that revolutionary groups need to do more than disrupt and attack the status quo—they must also paint a convincing picture of a better future. It is significant, however, that as opposed to Islamism, which in the West appeals to a minority within a minority, many of these movements are thriving on a widespread and deepening perception that the current order is unjust.

It is also apparent that, as Jaron Lanier worried might happen, a new elite is emerging—in large part amongst the most disaffected youth segment of the population—which derives its power from a greater than normal ability to delve between the layers of cyberspace: 'hacktivists' who are experimenting with new ways and means of inflicting pain and grief and destroying value.[68] Strictly speaking, this is not altogether a new development. In fact, the first politically motivated hack occurred in October 1989 on the eve of the launch of the *Galileo* space-probe, when NASA staff logged onto their computers to find this message on their screens:

Worms Against Nuclear Killers Wank

> Your System Has Been Officially WANKed. You talk of times of peace for all, and then prepare for war.[69]

The worm then appeared to start deleting all the files on the infected systems. In actuality, the worm was not deleting files; it was merely pretending to in order to cause heart palpitations amongst NASA's network administrators. *Galileo* had attracted protest from the anti-nuclear movement because its space-bound electrical systems were powered by the radioactive decay of 24 kilograms of plutonium, which in the event of a crash might have caused an Earth-bound ecological disaster. The WANK-worm was sophisticated, with a basic ability to learn, explore infected computers and propagate by copying itself through any open network connections; but it was also very simple in attack profile, exploiting the tendency of lazy computer users to use their username as a password.

Political hacking has grown quite a bit more sophisticated since then. In August 2012 Saudi Aramco, the national oil company of Saudi Arabia, was subject to a cyberattack that knocked out 30,000 computers—two thirds of the company total. A group calling itself the 'Cutting Sword of Justice' claimed credit for the attack, justifying it as a response to the Saudi regime's support of other Middle Eastern governments resisting the Arab Spring.[70]

It needs to be acknowledged, however, that the two most damaging hacks of recent times—Bradley Manning's leak of hundreds of thousands of American government documents in 2010 and Edward Snowden's similar leaks in 2013—were accomplished through nothing more technically sophisticated than a low level insider copying data to a transportable medium and just walking out of the building. The facts do not speak to the state's overweening control as much as they do to its naïveté and unpreparedness. As Bruce Sterling put it:

It did not occur to [Manning's] superiors that a bored soldier in a poorly secured computer system would download hundreds of thousands of diplomatic cables. Because, well, why? They're very boring. Soldiers never read them. The malefactor has no use for them. They're not particularly secret. They've got nothing much to do with his war. He knows his way around the machinery, but Bradley Manning is not any kind of black hat programming genius.[71]

How does the state respond when the 'enemy' is, in effect, a stupid kid? Declare war on stupid kids? This is not to diminish the potential harm that they can do. It is simply to acknowledge that the problem is that connectivity equips one's own stupid kids with the potential to do great harm. It lends the security conundrum a perniciousness that makes one wonder if those who argue that it is beyond solving within the present state-oriented frame are right.

A case in point is the massive attention paid to the Internet collective known as 'Anonymous', whose attacks in the main have been of the relatively simple denial of service type, though some of its attacks on organisations such as the reputable data security company HBGary suggest that it has the capability to cause harm.[72] It is, however, very difficult to judge its consequence as a strategic actor. Anonymous describes itself in terms redolent of teenage nihilism, observable also in its grinning Guy Fawkes mask iconography:

> Anonymous represents the collective whole of the Internet ... As individuals, they can be intelligent, rational, emotional and empathetic. As a mass, a group, they are devoid of humanity and mercy. Never before in the history of humanity has there once been such a morass, a terrible network of the peer-pressure that forces people to become one, become evil. Welcome to the soulless mass of blunt immorality known only as the Internet.[73]

Anonymous clearly makes it very easy for individuals to engage in high-impact but low-cost/low-effort activism. The obvious parallel is sometimes drawn between it and the nineteenth- and early-twentieth-century anarchists with whom many members seem to consciously identify. But the connection, while not as egregious as the comparison of cyber and nuclear attacks, cannot be drawn very far. Between the Revolt of the Paris Commune in 1871 and the Bolshevik Revolution of 1917, anarchist terror's victims included, among others, Russia's Tsar Alexander II (1881), France's President Nicolas Carnot (1894), Empress Elisabeth of Austria (1898), King Umberto of Italy (1900), American President William McKinley (1901), King Carlos I of Portugal (1908), Spanish Prime Minister Jose Canalejas (1912), Greece's King George I (1913) and Austro-Hungarian Archduke Ferdinand.

By comparison, Anonymous's efforts amount essentially to a series of more or less tiresome pranks. Will more disciplined revolutionaries be able to employ the dumb mass of other cheap 'clicktivists' or 'hacktivists' as *ad hoc* shock troops in the way that nineteenth-century anarchists were used by others? At present it is hard to see, but the championing of the transparency agenda of Wikileaks may represent the beginnings of a coherent ideological identity; it remains to be seen, however, whether this will outweigh the inherent capriciousness of the group.

In sum, there is a revolutionary zeitgeist to our time and yet it is one that feels rather ersatz—like cyber war, somehow its potential power is enervated by the murkiness of its political purpose, which has failed as yet to gel around a specific cause. When Mandela embarked upon a course of sabotage, terrorism and guerrilla war it was in the belief that there was no other choice between that and slavery. The Bolsheviks rose to power in Russia in 1917 on the slogan 'Bread, Land, Peace', which resonated with the peasantry because they were literally starving and actually landless and had just suffered nearly two million dead in war with Germany. Fortunately, Western society is under less existential pressures today—student loan debt and underemployment notwithstanding, the people are not starving nor are hundreds of thousands of lives being snuffed out in trench warfare.

History, however, never stands in one place for too long.

CONCLUSION

Like it or not we live in interesting times. They are times of danger and uncertainty; but they are also more open to the creative energy of men than any other time in history.

Robert F. Kennedy, 'Day of Affirmation Speech', University of Cape Town
South Africa (6 June 1966)

Connectivity has important implications for the practice of war but it does not substantially alter its nature as much as is commonly supposed.

It has not by any means erased chance as a key factor in war. To be sure, information systems have brought clarity and sped decision cycles in some aspects of warfare but always where it gives with one hand it takes with the other. It is not that the sophistication of sensors and information systems has not leapt forward; the problem is that obtaining perfect knowledge of one's enemy depends on having a stupid enemy unable to keep pace with relevant countermeasures. Such enemies are in short supply.

And connectivity has not by any means made up for the deficit of passion that has plagued the shambolic and half-hearted coalition efforts in Iraq and particularly Afghanistan. In fact, it has repeatedly showed up the gap between rhetoric and reality in the strategic narratives of these campaigns. Amongst the casualties and costs must be counted not only many thousands of dead and injured and a colossal sum of money but also NATO, which has been very badly damaged—a sad and ironic fact, for the Afghan campaign was launched in large part on the premise that it was vital to preserving the Alliance's relevance in the twenty first century.

Nor has connectivity created, through cyberwar, a decisive new form of warfare that cleverly gets around the problem of escalation that has held back major war for decades. It does, however, look set to enable the United States to replace the protracted, thankless, and invertebrate expeditionary campaigns of the war on terror with a perpetual, *sub rosa*, light-footprint global drone war instead.

Overall, in terms of the balance of power among states it does not appear to change very much. If anything it shores up the existing distribution of conventional military power rather than undermining it. The evidence is clear from the Stuxnet attacks as well as the Israeli use of cyberattack against Syrian air defences in 2007 that Western powers have thought hard about cyberattack and are pretty good at it. Our best guide to the likely significance of cyber weapons are the examples of air power, to which it bears many similarities, as well as electronic warfare. Both have been enormously important aspects of combined arms warfare for a century. Neither has a record of independent war-winning capability.

Things fall apart, in new ways and old

This is not to say, however, that the effects of connectivity on strategic affairs more broadly are not significant. It is to say, rather, that the major effects have been felt outside of the nation-state.

First, there has been a large increase in the number and type of potential strategic actors as more and more people and organisations find ways of using cyberspace to mobilize for causes that would likely have failed to find a constituency in a less densely networked age. Second, the ability of violent movements to organise in wispy networked forms that are difficult to defeat with the kinetic blows of a conventional military campaign has been sharply enhanced. Third, it has become much more difficult for states to keep secrets as some of their own employees have fervently embraced a burgeoning new ideology of radical transparency, not to mention the efforts of foreign and domestic hackers.[1] Fourth, it has become very difficult for liberal democratic states to generate and to sustain coherent and compelling narratives in support of their military activities.

Taken together, these trends create a significant potential for disruption of the status quo. In fact, it is hard to see what states can do about it. The first two arguably provide a rationale for things such as the PRISM surveillance and communications meta-data analysis programme. But the third allowed a low-level contract-employee of the US National Security Agency to reveal the whole thing to the world, not least the home population. And the fourth has become a problem of such magnitude primarily because the rapidity with which events—causes and effects—propagate in our densely connected world shows up the faulty premises, flawed assumptions, and wishful thinking of bad strategies more swiftly than before. This should not be seen as a bad thing a priori.

After all, the status quo throughout much of the world is not good. Much attention has been paid, naturally, to the massive outpourings of disaffection and anger in the various revolutions of the 'Arab Spring' and the subsequent volcanic turmoil of the Middle East. The problem, though, is not simply or specifically one of the effect of connectedness as a sort of supercharger of terrorism, nor is the mood of dissent one which exists only in non-Western populations.[2] It is rather a more general and widespread problem of tensions and disjuncture across multiple dimensions of the global cultural economy.[3] It is all too apparent to citizens nowadays, for instance, how failures in the subprime mortgage market of the United States led to a global financial crisis in 2008 that continues to plague the world economy, not least in the knock-on effect it had upon the stability of the Eurozone which is currently teetering on the brink of collapse.[4] Or, even more literally, how a primarily West African outbreak of haemorrhagic fever could spread over the course of 2014 into an international public health crisis that at present defies containment.[5] No one thinks it odd that the anti-capitalist 2011 Occupy Wall Street movement should proclaim itself a 'leaderless resistance movement' using the tactics of the anti-regime Arab Spring movements to achieve its ends because we have grown accustomed to the sheer interconnectedness of things.[6]

In 1968, the established German journalist Ulrike Meinhof wrote an essay entitled 'From Protest to Resistance' in which she laid out this solipsistic epigram on dissent and violence:

> Protest is when I say I don't like this. Resistance is when I put an end to what I don't like. Protest is when I say I refuse to go along with this any more. Resistance is when I make sure everybody else stops going along too.[7]

In 1970 she would cofound the Red Army Faction, popularly known as the Baader-Meinhof Group, which up until 1977 when its leaders committed suicide in prison conducted attacks that killed forty-seven people, including seventeen 'urban guerrillas'.[8] How might today's protesters react if the grievances that animate them are not resolved? It is important not to overstate the case, but history does show it is quite possible to go from middle class protestor to outlaw 'vanguard of the resistance' in fairly short order.

Moreover, in the parts of the world where material and political conditions really are intolerable it is worth remembering that the insurgencies that have vexed and flummoxed conventional military powers for the last decade have not deployed any weapons of exceptional novelty or power. The AK-47 'Kalashnikov' assault rifle was developed at the end of the Second World War and (with its variants) remains the popular choice of insurgents to this day.[9] The Improvised Explosive Device (IED) is as old as explosives. In fact, the 'car bomb' actually predates the car.[10]

'Hybrid' opponents such as Hezbollah, which analysts have found noteworthy amongst irregular forces for their high discipline, tactical acuity and relatively sophisticated armament, as evidenced by the hard fight they gave the Israel Defence Forces in Lebanon in 2006, are different only to a degree.[11] The main thing the Lebanon War showed was that irregular opponents require only fairly marginal military capability in order to force the regular forces engaged with them to use every element of high intensity combined arms warfare for their own protection.

Finally, the machete, statistically still amongst the deadliest weapons in human hands, is a practically un-improvable technology. The agricultural implement-cum-weapon of war is a recurrent theme in the classic novel *Things Fall Apart* by the Nigerian author Chinua Achebe:

> 'I have heard', said Okonkwo. 'But I have also heard that Abame people were weak and foolish. Why did they not fight back? Had they no guns and machetes? We would be cowards to compare ourselves with the men of Abame. Their fathers had never dared to stand before our ancestors. We must fight these men and drive them from the land.'[12]

A thoughtful exploration of the clash between colonialism and traditional culture, the book deserves to be read more widely by students of insurgency and counterinsurgency. It is supremely doubtful that Michael Adebolajo and Michael Adebowale, both British-born Muslim converts of Nigerian descent, who in May 2013 hacked to death the off-duty British Army drummer Lee Rigby outside Woolwich Barracks in London, had ever read Achebe. Nonetheless, the words above would not seem odd coming from their mouths. Their actual testimony, captured on the mobile phone of a random passerby (we have all in a sense become 'citizen journalists'), was this:

> I apologise that women had to witness this today but in our lands women have to see the same. You people will never be safe. Remove your governments. They don't care about you. You think David Cameron is going to get caught in the street when we start busting our guns? Do you think politicians are going to die? No, it's going to be the average guy, like you and your children. So get rid of them. Tell them to bring our troops back. Leave our lands and you will live in peace.[13]

Our world may be densely digitally connected in a way that allows ideas to flash around the world in seconds producing reactions in minutes and hours in places far removed from their origin. But the way in which brute reality is shaped remains brutally simple: bombs, guns and kitchen knives in the street.

Ripples of rage

The point is that time-tested means of violence that are easy to obtain and not massively difficult to operate are still quite effective. In fact, changes in warfare are rarely caused by uniquely military technologies—that is to say specific weapons and weapons systems. The most profound readjustments of military practice have been those that are driven by broader developments in society, as the burgeoning of connectivity is.

The speech by United States Senator Robert F. Kennedy, brother of the slain President John F. Kennedy, and an icon of American progressivism in his own right, quoted at the beginning of this chapter overtly echoed the dominant social and political ideals of the postwar 'Baby Boom' generation that was just then coming into adulthood. Kennedy extolled the power of youth to overcome the 'cruelties and obstacles of this swiftly changing planet' and decried the 'obsolete dogmas and outworn slogans' of the old elite while declaring it to be a 'revolutionary world' that we lived in. It was, in effect, a prose version of Bob Dylan's 1964 protest anthem *The Times They Are a-Changin'*.

The world had become so open to the 'creative energy of men' because the post-1945 growth of migration, liberalisation of trade, and communications technology was making it smaller. While he did not use the term that I have in this book, quite clearly it was the increasing connections between people that Kennedy found noteworthy:

> Each time a man stands up for an ideal, or acts to improve the lot of others, or strikes out against injustice, he sends forth a tiny ripple of hope, and crossing each other from a million different centres of energy and daring those ripples build a current which can sweep down the mightiest walls of oppression and resistance.

That would be the bright side of connectivity; and there is a dark side too. According to Manuel Castells, there are three major features of networks, each of which significantly empowers violent non-state groups, regardless of the weapons they are able to wield. First, there is flexibility:

> the ability to reconfigure according to changing environments and retain their goals while changing their components, sometimes bypassing blocking points of communication channels to find new connections.[14]

As a result they are able to deliver results in the form of attacks that require a minimum of command and control. The 9/11 attacks remain an exemplary case in point: though not without some central planning and support, the operation was still conducted relatively independently and extremely economically. Similarly, the 7/7 bombings in London 2005 were largely independently conceived, planned and conducted. The November 2008 attacks in Mumbai, which killed at least 173 people, wounded more than 300, and shut down a major world city for three days, are perhaps the most relevant example of what death, destruction and disruption can be achieved with a combination of low-cost civilian systems and highly motivated personnel using basic infantry tactics and weapons.

Second, there is scalability, 'the ability to expand or shrink with little disruption' as some businesses are said to have, meaning that they are able to respond quickly to increased pressure (either upward on demand or downward on supply). Historically, insurgent groups have not been very scalable—that is why Mao Zedong's contribution to insurgency theory and practice is so often characterised as involving the slow, cautious, methodical building up of parallel political structures and military capabilities.[15] Al-Qaeda is a distinctly different sort of entity: it has inherent scalability, like a 'brand' as terrorism expert Audrey Kurth Cronin has explained:

> Al Qaeda's most potent sources of strength are its powerful image and carefully crafted narrative ... This message is capturing the attention of young Muslims in many states, including in relatively privileged settings in the West, where clichés about terrorism arising out of deprivation or personal grievance may ring hollow.[16]

Third, there is survivability, which is the ability of the network, since it has no single centre, to reconstitute itself after an attack. In July 2011, after a decade of efforts to destroy it, in which several generations of its leaders were killed including, finally, Osama Bin Laden, the *Washington Post* announced that American counterterrorism officials believed al-Qaeda was on the brink of collapse. Even then not everyone was convinced.[17] Either way, clearly the organisation had shown enormous powers of resilience.

In summary, in a tactical sense, what connectedness does is help those who seek to disrupt the system to make more and more use of materials made available by the society they are attacking. It relieves them of the necessity of defending core production assets, leaving them free to focus on offence rather than defence. It also relieves them of the logistics burden of moving supplies long distances. Instead, they have only to move ideas—which can be digitized and moved instantly via information and communications technology as ripples of rage.

CONCLUSION

Retribalisation?

Inevitably, this will produce a counteraction, the contours of which we can perhaps already discern. Governments of rich countries, for instance, are reinforcing their borders with physical barriers and detection systems, as well as naval patrols, border guards, police and soldiers, primarily to prevent illegal migration from poorer places.[18] The forces driving this trend are widely apprehended, in Europe for example:

> Everyone pays grudging homage to the American model of cultural diversity, but European governments of all persuasions are dour about its advantages and alert to its dangers: cities eroded by poverty and profit; the cantonisation of social space; urban and rural societies doubly fractured by ethnicity and class; most forms of negotiation dragged along the runnels of identity politics. And if governments incline to the gloomy view, so do many citizens.[19]

It seems fitting to conclude by reflecting on a remark of Marshall McLuhan, who was amongst the first to recognise, or at any rate to popularise, the arrival of the information age. 'Today we appear to be poised between two ages—one of detribalisation and one of retribalisation'.[20] His point was more than a little obscure and has been the subject of much debate. But he seems to have meant that whereas industrial society was homogenised the better to service its mechanistic needs, an information society could return to a more natural heterogeneous condition. In fact, a decade before McLuhan the sociologist Hannah Arendt already perceived a dark side to the information age, warning that in a world in which 'every man feels the shock of events which take place at the other end of the globe ... [t]echnology, having provided the unity of the world, can just as easily destroy it'.[21] Now we can see that happening.

In a short lecture at the 2010 Salt Lake *Ignite* conference on 'Superempowerment, Networked Tribes and the End to Business as We Know It', the young speaker, filled with the 'creative energy of men', enjoined his listeners:

> You can't just idly sit back and decide that somebody else is going to solve your problems; that somebody else is going to come save you; that somebody else is going to be the champion that you've been waiting for. It's all up to you. The alternative is sitting in darkness, stumbling around victimized by boom and bust cycles. It's imperative that you take action. You decide the problems that you want to solve. You decide the world that you want to make. You can keep calm and just hope that things get better. Or you can make the effort to get excited and make the world that you want. Find your tribe. Decide what you believe. Rally them around you.[22]

As calls to arms go this was very mild stuff—there is no question that it was a call for non-violent activism in pursuit of changes, which most people would

185

regard as positive. Yet the subtext was that the existing authority, the government, is unable or uninterested in changing the status quo because it is enslaved to corporate interests, which are the real enemy. It trumpets a grievance, 'victimization by boom and bust', which resonates with youth, particularly urban, educated and middle class youth whose life prospects have been hit hard by the global economic crisis. It implies an 'in-group' and an 'out-group' and it ends with a rousing and passionate call to make the world what you want it to be.

There is no call to violence, nor is any implied; however, a world of do-it-yourself revolution is open to all types. Consider this one, another young man filled with destructive energy:

> I am extremely proud of my ethnic group, Norwegians which is a Northern-Germanic tribe. Furthermore, I seek to serve Norwegian AND European interests in everything I do ... It is essential that we fight for Europe, consolidate cross borders, and do our best to acknowledge that this is a European struggle ... ANY Christian European, anywhere in the world, can become a Justiciar Knight for the Knights Templar. As a Justiciar Knight you have been given the mandate to execute category A and B traitors by the war crimes tribunal known as PCCTS, Knights Templar ... We will not win this war unless we work together...[23]

Anders Breivik raided a youth camp of the Norwegian Labour Party on 22 July 2011, shooting and killing sixty-nine people, most of them teenagers, after killing seven others with a bomb in Oslo. He decided what he believed and what made him angry, which he explained in laborious detail in a 1500-page-long manifesto. He chose his 'tribe'—one that was defined almost entirely by his solitary online activities. And he went out to make the world what he wanted it to be. The attackers who murdered the staff of the Charlie Hebdo magazine in Paris in January 2015, the thousands of young Muslims born in the West now flocking to the banner of Islamic State, the pro-Russian volunteers fighting to carve out the Donetsk People's Republic from Ukraine are all pursuing the same tribal impulse.

Ultimately, connectivity may be much for the good of humanity, unleashing waves of industrious creativity. But the balance between hope and rage is, at present, a fine one to judge. In 1948 George Orwell's vision of future tyranny in *Nineteen Eighty-Four* was the all-seeing, all-hearing Big Brother. One wonders if he were writing today what tyranny he would fear the most: would it be Big Brother or the wild connectedness of his fellow men?

NOTES

INTRODUCTION

1. John Naisbitt, *Megatrends: Ten New Directions Transforming our Lives* (New York: Warner Books, 1984).

2. The RMA spawned a vast literature amongst which William Owens' *Lifting the Fog of War* (London: Johns Hopkins University Press, 2000) stands out as the most important of the genre.

3. Rupert Smith's *The Utility of Force: The Art of War in the Modern World* (London: Allen Lane, 2005) captured the problem at hand most penetratingly. Other important works that covered similar ground, however, include Thomas X. Hammes, *The Sling and the Stone: On War in the 21st Century* (St Paul, MN: Zenith Press, 2004) and Frank Hoffman, *Conflict in the 21st Century: The Rise of Hybrid Wars* (Arlington, VA: Potomac Institute for Policy Studies, 2007).

4. John Mackinlay's *The Insurgent Archipelago* (London: Hurst, 2009) is a landmark in this literature, although the basic ideas have been greatly developed in either parallel or in extension in the work of, *inter alia*, Manuel Castells, *Networks of Outrage and Hope: Social Movements in the Internet Age* (Cambridge: Polity, 2012), Neville Bolt, *The Violent Image: Insurgent Propaganda and the New Revolutionaries* (London: Hurst, 2012), and Carston F. Roennfeldt, 'Productive War: A Reconceptualisation of War', *Journal of Strategic Studies*, Vol. 34, No. 1 (2011).

5. David Betz and Tim Stevens, *Cyberspace and the State: Toward a Strategy for Cyberpower* (London: International Institute for Strategic Studies, 2011).

6. 'High-touch' is originally from Naisbitt's, *Megatrends* but has now established itself firmly in the lexicon of commerce to describe a business characterized by a very close relationship with its customers and clients—specifically one that is not completely confined to a computer screen.

7. UK *National Security Strategy: A Strong Britain in an Age of Uncertainty* (London: The Stationery Office, 2010).

8. John Ralson Saul, *The Collapse of Globalism and the Reinvention of the World* (London: Atlantic Books, 2005), p. 3.

9. Susanne Huttner, 'The Internet Economy: Towards a Better Future', *OECD Observer*, No. 268 (June 2008).

10. Neville Bolt, 'The Leak Before the Storm: What Wikileaks Tells us About Modern Communication', *RUSI Journal*, Vol. 155, No. 4 (August/September 2010), p. 50.

11. Neville Bolt, 'Unsettling Networks', *RUSI Journal*, Vol. 154, No. 5 (October 2009), p. 35.

12. Matt Ridley, *The Rational Optimist: How Prosperity Evolves* (London: Fourth Estate, 2010).

13. Zygmunt Bauman, *Liquid Times: Living in an Age of Uncertainty* (Cambridge: Polity, 2007), p. 6.

14. On the theme of surprise and its effect on an enemy see Edward Luttwak, *Strategy: The Logic of War and Peace* (Cambridge, MA: Harvard University Press, 2001), p. 13.

15. On the politics of the war as well as its campaigns Geoffrey Parker's *The Thirty Years War* (London: Routledge, 1984) remains the go-to resource.

16. The concept of 'postmodern system' I take from Robert Cooper, *The Breaking of Nations: Order and Chaos in the 21ˢᵗ Century* (London: Atlantic Books, 2003), p. 28.

17. Tony Corn, 'Clausewitz in Wonderland', *Policy Review, Hoover Institution* (1 September 2006).

18. Victor Davis Hanson, *Why the West has Won: Carnage and Culture from Salamis to Vietnam* (London: Faber and Faber, 2001), p. 445.

19. On the 'expert problem' in particular some cogent thoughts are to be found in Nassim Nicholas Taleb, *The Black Swan: The Impact of the Highly Improbable* (London: Penguin, 2007), pp. 145–160.

20. Paul Hirst, *Space and Power: Politics, War, and Architecture* (Cambridge: Polity, 2005), p. 4.

21. Michael Howard, 'When are Wars Decisive?', *Survival*, Vol. 41, No. 1 (Spring 1999), p. 128.

22. Colin Gray, *Fighting Talk: Forty Maxims on War, Peace, and Strategy* (Dulles, VA: Potomac Books, 2009), p. 147.

23. Bertrand Russell, *Power: A New Social Analysis* (London: Routledge, 2004 [1938]), p. 23.

24. See Robert Dahl, 'The Concept of Power', *Behavioural Science*, Vol. 2, No. 3 (July 1957), pp. 201–215.

25. Michel Foucault, *Discipline and Punish: The Birth of the Prison* (New York: Vintage Books, 1979), p. 194.

26. The work of Carsten F. Roennfeldt is most helpful in this respect. See 'Productive

War: A Re-Conceptualisation of War', *Journal of Strategic Studies*, Vol. 34, No. 1 (2011), pp. 39–62.

27. See M.L.R. Smith, 'Politics and Passion: The Neglected Mainspring of War', *Infinity Journal*, Vol. 4, No. 2 (Fall 2014), pp. 32–6.

28. John Robb, *Brave New War: The Next Stage of Terrorism and the End of Globalization* (London: Wiley, 2007).

29. David Fisher, *Morality and War* (Oxford: Oxford University Press, 2011), p. 23.

30. Bauman, *Liquid Times*, p. 1.

31. Carl Von Clausewitz (Michael Howard and Peter Paret, trans. and eds.), *On War* (New York: Knopf, 1993), p. 216.

1. ANTINOMIES OF WAR

1. Carl von Clausewitz (Michael Howard and Peter Paret, trans and eds), *On War* (New York: Alfred A. Knopf, Everyman's Library, 1993), p. 101.

2. *Ibid.*

3. Alan Beyerchen, 'Clausewitz, Nonlinearity and the Unpredictability of War', *International Security*, Vol. 17, No. 3 (Winter: 1992), pp. 59–90.

4. See Colin Gray, *Strategy and History: Essays on Theory and Practice* (Abingdon, Oxon: Routledge, 2006), p. 82; also Antulio J. Echevarria who draws a distinction between war's 'objective' (unchanging) and 'subjective' (ever changing) natures in *Globalization and the Nature of War* (Carlisle, PA: Strategic Studies Institute, US Army War College, 2003).

5. Any number of battles might be plucked from history for comparison. These three were those chosen by John Keegan in his classic work *Face of Battle* (London: Penguin, 1978). Richard Holmes' *Acts of War: The Behaviour of Men in Battle* (New York: The Free Press, 1985) is another key work in this genre.

6. Clausewitz, *On War*, p. 86.

7. Lawrence Freedman, *Transformation of Strategic Affairs* (London: International Institute for Strategic Studies, Adelphi Papers, 2006), p. 9.

8. Helmuth Von Moltke, 'On Strategy' (1871) in Daniel J. Hughes (ed.), *Moltke On the Art of War: Selected Writings* (New York: Ballantine Books, 1993), p. 45.

9. Clausewitz, *On War*, p. 138.

10. Erwin Rommel, *Infantry Attacks* (Novato, CA: Presidio Press, 1990); also Martin Blumenson's chapter 'Rommel' in Corelli Barnett (ed.), *Hitler's Generals* (London: Weidenfeld and Nicolson, 1989).

11. Sun Tzu, *The Art of War* in Thomas Cleary (trans.), *Classics of Strategy and Counsel* (Boston: Shambhala Publications, 2000), p. 85.

12. Quoted in Appendix B of Loch Johnson, *Strategic Intelligence* (Westport, CT: Praeger Security International, 2007), p. 214.

13. T.E. Lawrence, 'The Science of Guerrilla Warfare' in *Encyclopaedia Britannica*,

14th ed. (New York: Encyclopaedia Britannica, 1929) reprinted in Thomas Mahnken and Joe Maiolo (eds), *Strategic Studies: A Reader* (Abingdon, Oxon: Routledge, 2008), pp. 244–51.

14. See Kalevi J. Holsti, *The State, War, and the State of War* (Cambridge: Cambridge University Press, 1996) and for an extended treatment on guerrilla war in history, Max Boot, *Invisible Armies: An Epic History of Guerrilla Warfare from Ancient Times to the Present* (New York: Liveright, 2013).

15. Victor Davis Hanson, *Why the West has Won: Carnage and Culture From Salamis to Vietnam* (London: Faber and Faber, 2001), pp. 21–24 & *passim*.

16. *Ibid.*, pp. 32–39. Christopher Coker argues along similar lines in *Waging War Without Warriors* (London: Lynne Reinner Publishers, 2002); as do John Keegan in *A History of Warfare* (London: Knopf, 1993) and Paul Bracken in *Fire in the East: The Rise of Asian Military Power and the Second Nuclear Age* (New York: HarperCollins, 1993).

17. Patrick Porter, *Military Orientalism: Eastern War Through Western Eyes* (London: Hurst, 2009), p. 19.

18. For a careful untangling of these terms and critique of their contribution to the understanding of war and strategy, see M.L.R Smith, 'Guerrillas in the Mist: Reassessing Strategy and Low-Intensity Warfare', *Review of International Studies*, Vol. 29 (2003), pp. 19–37.

19. United Nations Charter (San Francisco, CA: 26 June 1945), http://www.un.org/en/documents/charter/intro.shtml

20. See Larry H. Addington, *The Patterns of War Through the Eighteenth Century* (Bloomington, IN: Indiana University Press, 1990) and *The Patterns of War Since the Eighteenth Century* (Bloomington, IN: Indiana University Press, 1994).

21. Stathis Kalyvas, *The Logic of Violence in Civil War* (Cambridge: Cambridge University Press, 2006).

22. See Richard English, *Irish Freedom: The History of Nationalism in Ireland* (London: Macmillan, 2006).

23. J.F. Baddeley's *The Russian Conquest of the Caucasus* (London: Longmans, Green & Company, 1908) is still amongst the best treatments of the subject. A more recent work taking the story through the end of the twentieth century is Sebastian Smith's *Allah's Mountains: The Battle for Chechnya* (London: I.B. Tauris, 2001).

24. See Ahron Bregman, *Israel's Wars: A History Since 1947* (London: Routledge, 2000). Arguably, though, the conflict really originates with the Zionist movement and the migration of diaspora Jews back to Palestine in the latter half of the nineteenth century. In which case Martin Gilbert's larger *Israel: A History* (London: Black Swan, 1998) is a better survey.

25. Liddell-Hart's criticisms of Clausewitz featured in much of his writing but were especially pointed in *The Ghost of Napoleon* (New Haven, CT: Yale University Press, 1934).

26. Jon Tetsuro Sumida critically assesses Liddell-Hart's critique of Clausewitz effectively in *Decoding Clausewitz: A New Approach to On War* (Lawrence, KS: Kansas University Press, 2008), pp. 25–35.

27. See Christopher Daase, 'Clausewitz and Small Wars' in Hew Strachan and Andreas Herberg-Rothe (eds.), *Clausewitz in the Twenty-First Century* (Oxford: Oxford University Press, 2007), pp. 182–205; also, Stuart Kinross, 'Clausewitz and Low-Intensity Conflict', *Journal of Strategic Studies*, Vol. 27, No. 1 (2004), pp. 35–58.

28. Clausewitz, p. 581.

29. This is not to say that Marx and Engels copied Clausewitz or were necessarily inspired by him directly. Byron Dexter described Engels as a 'devoted student' of Clausewitz in 'Clausewitz and Soviet Strategy', *Foreign Affairs*, Vol. 29, No. 1 (October 1950), p. 43. Azar Gat, on the other hand, argues that the similarity is explained by the common rootedness of both Marxism and Clausewitz's thinking in the German philosopher Georg Hegel's concepts, particularly historical dialecticism. See 'Clausewitz and the Marxists: Yet Another Look', *Journal of Contemporary History*, Vol. 27, No. 2 (April 1992), pp. 363–382.

30. Friedrich Engels, *Revolution and Counter-Revolution in Germany* (1852), chap. 17.

31. Mary Kaldor, *New and Old Wars* (Cambridge: Polity Press, 1999), p. 3.

32. An excellent example is Mats Berdal, 'The New Wars Thesis Revisited', in Hew Strachan and Sibylle Scheipers (eds), *The Changing Character of War* (Oxford: Oxford University Press, 2011), pp. 109–133.

33. Martin Van Creveld, *The Transformation of War* (New York: The Free Press, 1991), p. 1.

34. Robert Kaplan, *The Coming Anarchy* (New York: Vintage Books, 2000), p. 8.

35. Michael Howard, *The Invention of Peace: Reflections on War and International Order* (London: Profile, 2001), chap. 2.

36. See Jay Winter, 'Reflections on War and Barbarism' in George Kassimeris (ed.), *The Barbarisation of Warfare* (London: Hurst, 2006), pp. 254–265.

37. Quoted in Peter Bergen, *The Osama Bin Laden I Knew: An Oral History of Al Qaeda's Leader* (New York: Simon and Schuster, 2006), p. 322.

38. Amin Maalouf, *In the Name of Identity: Violence and the Need to Belong* (New York: Penguin Books, 2000). See also Faisal Devji, *The Terrorist in Search of Humanity: Militant Islam and Global Politics* (London: Hurst, 2009).

39. Dominique Moisi, *The Geopolitics of Emotion: How Cultures of Fear, Humiliation, and Hope are Reshaping the World* (New York: Random House, 2009); Tzvetan Todorov, *The Fear of Barbarians: Beyond the Clash of Civilisations* (Cambridge: Polity, 2010), esp. pp. 86–95; also see Christopher Coker, 'A Low, Dishonest Decade', *RUSI Journal*, Vol. 156, No. 4 (August/September 2011), pp. 18–24.

40. Peter Neumann, *Old and New Terrorism* (Cambridge: Polity, 2009); Mark Duffield, 'War as a Network Enterprise: The New Security Terrain and its Implications', *Cultural Values*, Vol. 6, Nos 1&2 (2002); John Mackinlay, *The Insurgent*

Archipelago: From Mao to Bin Laden (London: Hurst, 2009); and, Neville Bolt, *The Violent Image: Insurgent Propaganda and the New Revolutionaries* (London: Hurst, 2012).

41. Mats Berdal and David Malone (eds), *Greed and Grievance: Economic Agendas in Civil Wars* (London: Lynne Reinner, 2000). For a neo-mediaevalist thesis on the new wars see Herfried Munkler, *The New Wars* (Cambridge: Polity, 2005).

42. Andreas Osiander, 'Sovereignty, International Relations, and the Westphalian Myth', *International Organisation*, Vol. 55, No. 2 (Spring 2001), pp. 251–287.

43. See Michael Howard, *War in European History*, Updated Edition (Oxford: Oxford University Press, 2001), especially chs 2 and 4. The relationship between armies and their parent societies in this period is covered well by Andre Corvisier, *Armies and Societies in Europe, 1494–1789* (Bloomington, IN: Indiana University Press, 1979). Also still useful is Theodore Ropp, *War in the Modern World*, New Revised Edition (London: Collier Macmillan, 1962), ch. 1.

44. Philip Windsor (Mats Berdal and Spyros Economides, eds), *Strategic Thinking: An Introduction and Farewell* (London: Lynne Reinner, 2002), p. 18.

45. Von Moltke, 'War and Peace' in Hughes, *Moltke on the Art of War*, p. 23.

46. Clausewitz, *On War*, p. 89.

47. Mark Zacher, 'The Decaying Pillars of the Westphalian Temple: Implications for International Order and Governance', in James N. Rosenau and Ernst-Otto Czempiel (eds), *Governance Without Government: Order and Change in World Politics* (Cambridge: Cambridge University Press, 1992), pp. 58–101.

48. Francis Deng et al, *Sovereignty as Responsibility: Conflict Management in Africa* (Washington, DC: Brookings Institution Press, 1996).

49. International Commission on Intervention and State Sovereignty, *The Responsibility to Protect* (Ottawa: International Development Research Centre, 2001).

50. Philip Cerny, *Rethinking World Politics: A Theory of Transnational Neopluralism* (Oxford: Oxford University Press, 2010), p. 166.

51. Robert Cooper, in *The Breaking of Nations: Order and Chaos in the Twenty-First Century* (New York: Grove Press, 2004), refers to the emergence of the 'post-modern state' (exemplified by the European Union), which exists alongside two other systems: the 'pre-modern', typified by chaotic disorder', and the 'modern', where nation states continue to compete in a traditional manner.

52. Hew Strachan, 'The Lost Meaning of Strategy', *Survival*, Vol. 47, No. 3, (2005), p. 49.

53. This is a key theme in the literature on 'fourth generation warfare'. See T.X. Hammes, 'War Evolves into the Fourth Generation', *Contemporary Security Policy*, Vol. 26, No. 2 (2005). It was also the major thesis of Van Creveld's *Transformation of War*; see also Van Creveld, 'It Will Continue to Conquer and Spread', *Contemporary Security Policy*, Vol. 26, No. 2 (2005), pp. 229–32.

54. See P.W. Singer, *Corporate Warriors: The Rise of Privatised Military Industry* (Ithaca, NY: Cornell University Press, 2003).

55. Howard, *The Invention of Peace*, pp. 95–96.

56. *Inter alia*, Philip Gordon in *Winning the Right War: The Path to Security for America and the World* (New York: Henry Holt & Co, 2007).

57. Secretary of Defense Robert M. Gates Speech (West Point, NY: 25 February 2011). For a discussion of the speech, see David Ucko, 'Gates on COIN: What was Really Said', *Kings of War* (27 February 2011).

58. Karl-Heinz Frieser's account of 1940's Battle of France is the best recent treatment of the development of Blitzkrieg by Germany—the first country to integrate the new technologies in an appropriate military formation with an effective combined arms doctrine. See *The Blitzkrieg Legend: The Campaign in the West, 1940* (Annapolis, MD: Naval Institute Press, 2005).

59. General Sir David Richards, 'Future Conflict and Its Prevention: People and the Information Age', speech at the International Institute for Strategic Studies (18 January 2010).

60. *Ibid.*

61. Donald Rumsfeld, 'New Realities in the Media Age', Council on Foreign Relations speech (New York: 17 February 2006).

62. Robert Gates, Landon Lecture, Kansas State University (Manhattan, KS: 26 November 2007).

63. On 'mediatisation', see Andrew Hoskins and Ben O'Loughlin, *War and Media: The Emergence of Diffused War* (Cambridge: Polity Press, 2010), in particular pp. 4–5; also David Betz, 'The Virtual Dimension of Contemporary Insurgency and Counterinsurgency', *Small Wars and Insurgencies*, Vol. 19, No. 4 (2008), pp. 513–43; see also Thomas Rid and Marc Hecker, *War 2.0: Irregular Warfare in the Information Age* (London: Praeger, 2009).

64. Much of this is driven by the exigencies of the campaign in Afghanistan where it is felt that NATO is performing poorly relative to the Taliban. See, for example, Simon Klingert, 'Losing the War on Perception', *Foreign Policy* (13 September 2011). The issue, however, is put into historical perspective by Dominic Tierney and Dominic Johnson in *Failing to Win: Perceptions of Victory and Defeat in International Politics* (Cambridge, MA: Harvard University Press, 2006).

65. The intercepted letter was released by the United States Office of the Director of National Intelligence, Letter from al-Zawahiri to al-Zarqawi (2005).

66. Rupert Smith, *The Utility of Force: The Art of War in the Modern World* (London: Allen Lane, 2005), pp. 286, 289.

67. H.R. McMaster, 'Foreword' in G.J. David Jr. and T.R. McKeldin III, *Ideas as Weapons: Influence and Perception in Modern Warfare* (Dulles, VA: Potomac Books, 2009).

68. Asa Briggs and Peter Burke, *A Social History of the Media: From Gutenberg to the Internet* (Cambridge: Polity, 2010), p. 70.

69. The terms are from Andrew Bacevich, 'The Petraeus Doctrine', *The Atlantic* (Octo-

ber 2008). Gian Gentile is seen as the poster-child for the conservatives while John Nagl is said to epitomize the crusaders. See John A. Nagl, 'Let's Win the Wars We're In', *Joint Force Quarterly*, Issue 52, 1st Quarter (2009), 20–26; and Gian P. Gentile, 'Let's Build an Army to Win All Wars', *Joint Force Quarterly*, Issue 52, 1st Quarter 2009), 27–33.

70. Charles C. Krulak, 'The Strategic Corporal: Leadership in the Three Block War', *Marines Magazine* (January 1999).

71. Frank G. Hoffman, *Conflict in the Twenty-First Century: The Rise of Hybrid Wars* (Washington DC: Potomac Institute, 2007), p. 29.

72. Michael Evans, 'From Kadesh to Kandahar: Military Theory and the Future of War', *Naval War College Review*, Vol. LVI, No. 3 (Summer 2003), p. 136.

73. On the end of history see Francis Fukuyama, *The End of History and the Last Man* (The Free Press, 1992); on advances in military capability see William Owens, *Lifting the Fog of War* (Baltimore: Johns Hopkins University Press, 2000).

2. THE CONTEXT OF CONTEMPORARY WAR

1. US Army Capstone Concept, *Operational Adaptation: Operating Under Conditions of Uncertainty and Complexity in an Era of Persistent Conflict*, TRADOC Pam 525–3–0 (21 December 2009).

2. Developments, Concepts, and Doctrine Centre, *Strategic Trends Programme: Future Character of Conflict* (London: United Kingdom Ministry of Defence, 2010), pp. 21–25.

3. Hew Strachan, 'The Changing Character of War', Europaeum Lecture delivered at the Graduate Institute of International Relations, Geneva (9 November 2006), 2.

4. James Adams, *The Next World War* (New York: Simon and Schuster, 1998), p. 93.

5. See 'Class, Status, Party', in Hans Gerth and C. Wright Mills (eds), *From Max Weber: Essays in Sociology* (London: Routledge and Kegan Paul, 1948), p. 180.

6. Manuel Castells, *The Rise of the Network Society, The Information Age: Economy, Society, and Culture*, Vol. 1, Second Edition (London: Wiley-Blackwell, 2010), p. 215.

7. One might imagine, for example, that he would have found fascinating David Lande's *The Unbound Prometheus: Technological Change and Industrial Development in Western Europe from 1750 to the Present* (Cambridge: Cambridge University Press, 1969).

8. Again, if one might be forgiven for speculating about what Clausewitz's reading habits would be if he were writing '*On War for Century 21*', works such as these which each try to explain aspects of today's network society would appear on his shelf: Marshall McLuhan, *Understanding Media* (McGraw Hill, 1964); Peter Drucker, *The Age of Discontinuity* (HarperCollins, 1969); Daniel Bell, *The Coming of Post-Industrial Society* (Harper, 1974); Yoneji Masuda, *The Information Society*

as Post-Industrial Society (World Future Society, 1981); and most recently Manuel Castells' *The Information Age: Economy, Society and Culture*, Vols. 1–3, (Oxford: Blackwell, 2010).

9. Carl Von Clausewitz (Michael Howard and Peter Paret, trans and eds), *On War* (New York: Alfred A. Knopf, Everyman's Library, 1993), p. 718.

10. See Hew Strachan, *Clausewitz's On War: A Biography* (New York: Grove Press, 2007); also 'In Our Time: Clausewitz', BBC Radio 4 (17 May 2012).

11. Norman Angell, *The Great Illusion* (London: William Heinemann, 1909), p. 222.

12. Philip Bobbitt, *The Shield of Achilles: War, Peace, and the Course of History* (New York: Alfred A. Knopf, 2002).

13. Amongst his keenest and most compelling defenders John Mueller stands out. See *Retreat from Doomsday: The Obsolescence of Major War* (New York: Basic Books, 1989).

14. Christopher Layne provides a solid critique in 'Kant or Cant: The Myth of the Democratic Peace', *International Security*, Vol. 19, No. 2 (Autumn, 1994), pp. 5–49. A popular derivative theory holds that no two countries with McDonalds outlets have ever gone to war with each other. See, Mark Rice-Oxley, 'War and McPeace: Russia and the McDonalds Theory of War', *Guardian* (6 September 2008).

15. Ralph Peters, 'The Counterrevolution in Military Affairs', *The Weekly Standard*, Vol. 11, No. 20 (6 February 2006).

16. The *pro et contra* debate between Zbigniew Brzezinski and John Mearsheimer, 'Clash of the Titans', *Foreign Policy* (5 January 2005) covers much of the rhetorical ground on either side of the argument.

17. Steven Pinker, *The Better Angels of our Nature* (London: Penguin, 2011).

18. Lawrence Freedman, *The Evolution of Nuclear Strategy* (London: St Martin's Press, 1989).

19. Robert Jervis, *The Meaning of the Nuclear Revolution* (Ithaca, NY: Cornell University Press, 1989).

20. The West Point Military Academy's History Department lists Thucydides in its 'Top 10 Military Classics' amongst which just three others are from the twentieth century, and only one of those post-1945. See, Thomas E. Ricks, 'Reading Lists: The West Point History Dept. Selects its Top 10 Military Classics', *The Best Defense* (19 September 2012). Of course, such lists are exceedingly common and highly subjective; nonetheless, they are indicative of certain conservatism in the field.

21. Michael Howard, 'The Use and Abuse of Military History', *RUSI Journal*, Vol. 138, No. 1 (February 1993), p. 29.

22. Richard Ned Lebow, *Why Nations Fight* (Cambridge: Cambridge University Press, 2010), p. 191.

23. Chantale Mouffe, *The Return of the Political* (London: Verso, 1993), p. 1.

24. Alex J. Bellamy, 'The Great Beyond: Rethinking Military Responses to New Wars and Complex Emergencies', *Defence Studies*, Vol. 2, No. 1 (2002), p. 25.

25. The best account of the thinking that led to both campaigns is found in Lawrence Freedman, *A Choice of Enemies: America Confronts the Middle East* (New York: Public Affairs, 2008), pp. 373–422.

26. Jessica Stern, 'The Protean Enemy', *Foreign Affairs*, Vol. 82, No. 4 (July/April 2003).

27. C.E. Callwell, *Small Wars: Their Principles and Practice*, Third Edition (Abingdon, Oxon: Purnell Book Services, 1976 [1906]), p. 27.

28. See Christopher Coker, *War in an Age of Risk* (Cambridge: Polity, 2009).

29. Robert M. Gates, 'A Balanced Strategy: Reprogramming the Pentagon for a New Age', *Foreign Affairs*, Vol. 88, No. 1 (January/February 2009).

30. See Ron Suskind, *The One Percent Doctrine: Deep Inside America's Pursuit of its Enemies Since 9/11* (New York: Simon and Schuster, 2007).

31. Madeleine Albright, *Madam Secretary: A Memoir* (New York: Harper Collins, 2003), p. 182.

32. Colin Powell, *My American Journey: An Autobiography* (New York: Random House, 2005), p. 609.

33. Colin Powell, 'US Forces: Challenges Ahead', *Foreign Affairs*, Vol. 71, No. 5 (Winter 1992/1993).

34. Condoleezza Rice, 'Promoting the National Interest', *Foreign Affairs*, Vol. 79, No. 1 (January/February 2000), p. 53.

35. See Steven Metz, *Iraq and the Evolution of American Strategy* (Dulles, VA: Potomac Books, 2008). More generally, James Mann's, *Rise of the Vulcans: A History of Bush's War Cabinet* (New York: Penguin, 2004), provides an excellent intellectual history of the key players and their ideas at the time.

36. President George W. Bush, Graduation Speech at the US Military Academy (West Point, NY: 1 June 2002).

37. Thomas P.M. Barnett, *The Pentagon's New Map: War and Peace in the Twenty-First Century* (New York: Berkley Books, 2004), p. 56.

38. *Ibid*, p. 320.

39. Robert Kaplan, *Imperial Grunts: The American Military on the Ground* (New York: Random House, 2005), p. 3

40. See David Betz, 'Counterinsurgency, Victorian Style', *Survival*, Vol. 54, No. 4 (2012), pp. 161–182.

41. Mark Duffield, 'War as a Network Enterprise: The New Security Terrain and its Implications', *The Journal for Cultural Research*, Vol. 6, Nos. 1 & 2 (January–April 2006), pp. 153–166.

42. Mackinlay, p. 190

43. Jeremy Black, *War and the New Disorder in the 21st Century* (New York: Continuum, 2004), pp. 163–164.

44. Powell, 'US Forces: Challenges Ahead'.
45. Robert J. Lieber, *The American Era: Power and Strategy for the Twenty-First Century* (Cambridge: Cambridge University Press, 2005), p. 40.
46. See *The 9/11 Commission Report* (Washington, DC: National Commission on Terrorist Attacks on the United States, 2004), ch. 8 for details of what was known and not known prior to the event and ch. 11 on the reasons why these were not acted upon. See also Lawrence Freedman, *A Choice of Enemies: America Confronts the Middle East* (New York: Public Affairs, 2008), pp. 383–385.
47. 'Anonymous' (Michael Scheuer), *Imperial Hubris: Why the West is Losing the War on Terror* (Washington, DC: Brassey's, 2004), p. ix.
48. President George W. Bush, *State of the Union Address* (Washington, DC: United States Congress, 29 January 2002).
49. See Fred Charles Ikle, *Annihilation from Within: The Ultimate Threat to Nations* (New York: Columbia University Press, 2005), p. 59.
50. Fred Charles Ikle, *Every War Must End*, Second Revised Edition (New York: Columbia University Press, 2005), p. xvii.
51. Michael Howard, 'A Long War', *Survival*, Vol. 48, No. 4 (2006), p. 11.
52. Sayyid Qutb, *Milestones* (New Delhi: Abdul Naeem for the Islamic Book Service, 2007 [1964]), p. 75.
53. See the section on Qutb in the essay on Ayman Al-Zawahiri's ideological influences in Gilles Kepel and Jean-Pierre Mililli (eds), *Al Qaeda in its Own Words* (Cambridge, MA: Harvard University Press, 2008), pp. 149–150
54. Francis Fukuyama, *The End of History and the Last Man* (The Free Press, 1992), p. 237.
55. Osama bin Laden, 'Tactical Recommendations (Excerpts)' in Kepel and Milelli (eds), *Al Qaeda in its Own Words*, pp. 63–64.
56. Ikle, *Annihilation from Within*, p. 65.
57. Bush, *State of the Union Address* (2002).
58. The distinctions between deterrence, pre-emption and prevention are discussed by Lawrence Freedman in 'Prevention, Not Preemption', *Washington Quarterly*, Vol. 26, No. 2 (Spring 2003), pp. 105–114.
59. For an overview on these developments see Tim Blanning, *The Pursuit of Glory: Europe, 1648–1815* (London: Penguin, 2007).
60. Thomas Carlyle, 'The Signs of the Times' (1829) in *Critical and Miscellaneous Essays by Thomas Carlyle* (Boston: Dana Estes and Charles F. Lauriat, 1884), p. 464.
61. *Ibid.*, p. 465.
62. *Ibid.*, p. 466.
63. R.J. Forbes, 'Power to 1850' in C. Singer (ed.), *A History of Technology, Vol. 4: The Industrial Revolution, 1750–1850* (Oxford: Oxford University Press, 1958), p. 148.
64. Ray Kurzweil, *The Singularity is Near: When Humans Transcend Biology* (London: Duckworth, 2005), p. 10–14.

65. H.G. Wells, *The Work, Wealth, and Happiness of Mankind* (Garden City, NY: Doubleday, Doran and Company, 1931), ch. 3.

66. R.D. Laing, *The Politics of Experience* (London: Harmondsworth, 1967).

67. Zbigniew Brzezinksi, *Between Two Ages: America's Role in the Technotronic Era* (New York: Viking, 1970), p. 52.

68. Robert Hassan, *The Information Society* (Cambridge: Polity, 2008), p. 13.

69. Carlyle, 'The Signs of the Times', p. 466.

70. Thucydides (Rex Warner trans.), *History of the Peloponnesian War* (London: Penguin, 1954), p. 48.

71. John Maynard Keynes, *The Economic Consequences of the Peace* (New York: Harcourt, Brace, and Howe, 1920), pp. 12–13.

72. Clay Shirky, *Cognitive Surplus: Creativity and Generosity in a Connected Age*, (New York: Penguin Press, 2010), p. 17.

73. Stephen Castles and Mark J. Miller, *The Age of Migration: International Population Movements in the Modern World*, Fourth Edition (New York: Palgrave, 2009), p. 3.

74. See James H. Mittelman, *Hyperconflict: Globalization and Insecurity* (Stanford: Stanford University Press, 2010), p. 2

75. On great men in history, see Thomas Carlyle, *On Heroes, Hero Worship and the Heroic in History* (London: Chapman and Hall, 1840), p. 3. On the 'spirit of the age' and 'world-historical individuals' see Georg Hegel (Ruben Alvarado, trans.), *Lectures on the Philosophy of History* (Aalten, Netherlands: Wordbridge, 2011 [1837]), pp. 27–30.

76. Kevin Kelly, *What Technology Wants* (New York: Penguin, 2010), pp. 11–12.

77. Karl Marx and Friedrich Engels, *Manifesto of the Communist Party* (New York: New York Labor News Co., 1908), p. 35.

3. WAR WITHOUT CHANCE: SOMETHING BETTER THAN WAR

1. Joshua Davis, 'If we run out of batteries, this war is screwed', *Wired* (21 June 2003).

2. The three essays are collected and translated with an introduction by Paul Patton in Jean Baudrillard, *The Gulf War Did Not Take Place* (Bloomington, IN: Indiana University Press, 1995).

3. Baudrillard, *The Gulf War*, p. 67.

4. James Der Derian, *Virtuous War: Mapping the Military-Industrial-Media-Entertainment Network* (Boulder, CO: Westview Press, 2001), p. 210. Robert Cooper's *The Breaking of Nations: Order and Chaos in the Twenty-First Century*, 2nd ed. (London: Atlantic Books, 2007) also robustly posits the idea that international affairs are permeated by postmodernism.

5. Daniel Pipes, 'The Gulf War Did Not Take Place' (review) *Middle East Quarterly*, Vol. 3, No. 2 (March 1996).

6. Baudrillard, *The Gulf War*, p. 74.

7. *Ibid.*, p. 43.

8. On the 'modern system', see: See Stephen Biddle, *Military Power: Explaining Victory and Defeat in Modern Battle* (Princeton, NJ: Princeton University Press, 2004), p. 3. On Saddam Hussein's ill-judgment, see, John Mueller, 'The Perfect Enemy: Assessing the Gulf War', *Security Studies*, Vol. 5, No. 1 (Autumn 1995), pp. 77–117.

9. Marc Cerasini, *The Future of War: The Face of Twenty-First Century Warfare* (Indianapolis, IN: Alpha Books, 2003), p. 32.

10. John Collins, *Desert Shield and Desert Storm: Implications for US Force Requirements* (Washington, DC: Congressional Research Service, 1991), p. 1.

11. Quoted in George C. Herring, 'America and Vietnam: The Unending War', *Foreign Affairs*, Vol. 70, No. 5 (Winter 1991/1992).

12. Jeffrey Record, *Hollow Victory* (Washington, DC: Brassey's, 1993).

13. Quoted in Chris Hables Gray, *Postmodern War: The New Politics of Conflict* (London: Guilford Press, 1997), p. 48.

14. Quoted in Andrew Bacevich, *American Empire: The Realities and Consequences of US Diplomacy* (Cambridge, MA: Harvard University Press, 2002), p. 62.

15. Biddle, *Military Power*, p. 133.

16. See Thomas K. Adams, *The Army After Next: The First Postindustrial Army* (Stanford, CA: Stanford University Press, 2008), espially chs 3, 4 and 5, which tell the story of the American military's RMA-inspired 'transformation' efforts from the end of the administration of the forty-first president George H.W. Bush to the administration of the forty-third, George W. Bush.

17. Kenneth Pollack, *Arabs at War: Military Effectiveness, 1948–1991* (Lincoln, NE: Nebraska University Press, 2004).

18. Lawrence Freedman, *A Choice of Enemies: America Confronts the Middle East* (New York: Public Affairs, 2008), p. 236–7.

19. Lawrence Freedman and Efraim Karsh, *The Gulf Conflict, 1990–1991: Diplomacy and War in the New World Order* (Princeton, NJ: Princeton University Press, 1993), p. 391.

20. See Biddle, *Military Power*, pp. 132–5 and ch. 7 *passim*. There are many accounts of the Gulf War. Lawrence Freedman and Efraim Karsh, *The Gulf Conflict, 1990–1991: Diplomacy and War in the New World Order* (Princeton, NJ: Princeton University Press, 1993) stands out for the quality of its treatment of the political and strategic dynamics of the war. US News and World Report, *Triumph Without Victory* (New York: Random House, 1992) was one of the first published and captured well (as the title suggests) the ambiguity of the war's outcome in the larger sense. In terms of military science, the actual conduct of war, perhaps the biggest and longest lasting controversy has been over the relative contribution of air power and land power to Iraq's defeat. In *Military Power* and his earlier article 'Victory Misunderstood: What the Gulf War Tells us about the Future of Conflict', *Inter-*

national Security, Vol. 21, No. 2 (Fall 1997), pp. 139–179, Stephen Biddle emphasises the salience of land forces. Thomas Mahnken and Barry Watts, on the other hand, in 'What the Gulf War Can (and Cannot) Tell Us about the Future Of Warfare', *International Security*, Vol. 22, No. 2 (Autumn 1997), pp. 151–162, caution that air power's role in 'shaping the operational and strategic setting in which engagements like 73 Easting occurred' must be considered more prominently. The 'air power debate' is too vast and vociferous to be dealt with in a footnote. For readers interested in the contribution to it of the Gulf War, however, the best empirically-grounded analysis is Eliot Cohen *et al*, *Gulf War Air Power Survey* (Washington, DC: United States Government Printing Office, 1993) and the shorter article by him, 'The Mystique of US Air Power', *Foreign Affairs*, Vol. 73, No. 1 (January/February, 1994), pp. 109–124, in which he draws some larger lessons.

21. Freedman and Karsh, *The Gulf Conflict*, p. 409.
22. Biddle, *Military Power*, p. 133.
23. Baudrillard, *The Gulf War*, p. 85.
24. Tommy Franks, *American Soldier* (New York: Regan Books), p. 169.
25. Elinor Sloan, *The Revolution in Military Affairs: Implications for Canada and NATO* (Montreal: McGill and Queen's University Press, 2002).
26. Sun Tzu (trans. S.B. Griffith), *The Art of War*, (London: Oxford University Press, 1971), p. 84.
27. Quoted in James Holland, *Together We Stand: Turning the Tide in the West: North Africa, 1942–1943* (London: Harper Collins, 2005), p. 24.
28. *Conduct of the Persian Gulf War, Final Report to Congress* (Washington, DC: Department of Defence, 1992), p. 678.
29. Franks, *American Soldier*, p. 175.
30. David S. Alberts, John J. Garstka, Richard E. Hayes and David A. Signori, *Understanding Information Age Warfare* (Washington, DC: Command and Control Research Program, Department of Defence, 2001), p. 37.
31. William Owens, *Lifting the Fog of War* (London: Johns Hopkins University Press, 2000), p. 15.
32. Paul Kennedy, *The Rise and Fall of the Great Powers: Economic Change and Military Conflict from 1500 to 2000* (London: Fontana Press, 1989), p. 672.
33. For example, see Michael Mazarr, Jeffrey Shaffer and Benjamin Ederington, *The Military Technical Revolution: A Structural Framework* (Washington, DC: Centre for Strategic and International Studies, 1993), p. 58.
34. Carl Von Clausewitz (Michael Howard and Peter Paret, trans and eds), *On War* (New York: Alfred A. Knopf, Everyman's Library, 1993), p. 117.
35. *Ibid.*, p. 95.
36. Bernard W. Rogers, 'Follow-On Forces Attack: Myths and Realities', *NATO Review*, Vol. 32, No. 6 (December 1984), p. 2.

37. *Ibid.* Also see, Group Captain S.J. Coy, 'Depth Firepower: The Violent, Enabling Element' in Brian Holden Reid (ed.), *The Science of War: Back to First Principles* (London: Routledge, 1993), pp. 131–148.

38. Dima Adamsky, *The Culture of Military Innovation: The Impact of Cultural Factors on the Revolution in Military Affairs in Russia, the US, and Israel* (Stanford, CA: Stanford University Press, 2010), pp. 2–4 and ch. 2.

39. Richard Simpkin, *Race to the Swift: Thoughts on Twenty First Century Warfare* (London: Brasseys, 1985), p. 303.

40. *Ibid.*, p. 169.

41. *Ibid.*, p. 172.

42. *Ibid.*, p. 174.

43. As the title of one monograph of the British Strategic and Combat Studies Institute edited by David Potts suggested, this was the 'big issue'. See *The Big Issue: Command and Combat in the Information Age* (Washington, DC: Department of Defense, Command and Control Research Programme, 2003).

44. On technology in American strategic culture see Thomas Mahnken, *United States Strategic Culture* (Washington, DC: Defence Threat Reduction Agency, Advanced Systems and Concepts Office, 2006), pp. 11–12.

45. Andrew F. Krepinevich, 'Cavalry to Computer: The Pattern of Military Revolutions', *The National Interest*, No. 37 (Fall 1994), p. 30.

46. Colin Gray, *Recognising and Understanding Revolutionary Change in Warfare: The Sovereignty of Context* (Carlisle, PA: US Army War College, Strategic Studies Institute, 2006), p. 6. On the distinct intellectual climate of the ONA vis-à-vis the larger American defence establishment see Adamsky, pp. 69–74.

47. Owens, *Lifting the Fog of War*, p. 118.

48. Rupert Smith, *The Utility of Force: The Art of War in the Modern World* (London: Allen Lane, 2005), p. 333.

49. On the larger picture of the failings of UNOSOM II, see Theo Farrell, 'Sliding into War: The Somalia Imbroglio and US Army Peace Operations Doctrine', *International Peacekeeping*, Vol. 2, No. 2 (1995), p. 211. Mark Bowden's *Black Hawk Down* (London: Bantam, 1999) provides a minute-by-minute account of the 3 October mission to capture Aideed. The Somali death toll can only be guessed at. Bowden reckons it at 500 dead and 1000 wounded.

50. Bowden, *Black Hawk Down*, p. 30.

51. The full text of the address may be found in Bing West and Ray Smith, *The March Up: Taking Baghdad with the First Marine Division* (London: Pimlico, 2003), p. 1.

52. Bowden, *Black Hawk Down*, p. 74.

53. *Ibid.*, p. 111.

54. *Ibid.*, p. 125.

55. Quoted in Farrell, 'Sliding into War', p. 211.

56. Smith, *The Utility of Force*, p. 292.

57. *Ibid.*, pp. 299 & 333.

58. Wesley Clark, *Waging Modern War* (New York: Public Affairs, 2001), p. 417.

59. Good accounts of the ambush are to be found in Anatol Lieven, *Chechnya: Tombstone of Russian Power* (New Haven, CT: Yale University Press, 1998), pp. 108–113 and Sebastian Smith, *Allah's Mountains: The Battle for Chechnya* (London: I.B. Tauris, 1998), pp. 159–162.

60. Benjamin Lambeth, 'Russia's Wounded Military', *Foreign Affairs*, Vol. 74, No. 2 (March/April 1995), pp. 86–98.

61. The case of the Chechen commander Shamil Basayev is illustrative of Chechen brutality, daring, and inflexible determination. See Raymond C. Finch, 'A Face of Future Battle: Chechen Fighter Shamil Basayev' *Military Review*, Vol. LXXVII, No. 3 (May/June 1997), pp. 33–41.

62. Quoted in Carlotta Gall and Thomas de Waal, *Chechnya: A Small Victorious War* (London: Pan, 1997), p. 157.

63. David Betz, *Civil-Military Relations in Russia and Eastern Europe* (London: Routledge, 2004), pp. 95–96.

64. The quote is from the pro-Western liberal former Prime Minister Yegor Gaidar and may be found in Gall and de Waal, *Chechnya*, p. 165.

4. OVERESTIMATE YOURSELF, UNDERESTIMATE YOUR ENEMY, NEVER KNOW VICTORY

1. Sebastian Smith, *Allah's Mountains: The Battle for Chechnya* (London: I.B.Tauris, 1998), pp. 157–158.

2. The retaking of Grozny is described grippingly by Smith in *Allah's Mountains*, pp. 240–258.

3. Martin Van Creveld, *The Sword and the Olive: A Critical History of the Israeli Defence Force* (New York: Public Affairs, 1998), p. 306.

4. Ian Bickerton, *The Arab-Israeli Conflict, A History* (London: Reaktion Books, 2009), p. 183.

5. Keith E. Bonn and Anthony E. Baker, *Guide to Military Operations Other Than War: Tactics, Techniques, and Procedures for Stability and Support Operations, Domestic and International* (Mechanicsburg, PA: Stackpole Books, 2000), p. 2.

6. Quoted in Christopher Bellamy, *Knights in White Armour: The New Art of War and Peace* (London: Hutchinson, 1996), pp. 144–145.

7. Gordon R. Sullivan and James M. Dubik, *Land Warfare in the 21ˢᵗ Century* (Carlisle, PA: US Army War College, Strategic Studies Institute, 1993), p. xiii.

8. See Frederick Kagan, *Finding the Target: The Transformation of American Military Policy* (New York: Encounter Books, 2006), pp. 159–175.

9. John Warden, 'Employing Air Power in the Twenty-First Century' in Richard H. Shultz, Jr and Robert L. Pfaltzgraff, Jr (eds), *The Future of Air Power in the After-*

math of the Gulf War (Maxwell Air Force Base, Alabama: Air University Press, 1992), pp. 78 & 81.

10. Both Short and Keegan are quoted in Daniel L. Byman and Matthew C. Waxman, 'Kosovo and the Great Air Power Debate', *International Security*, Vol. 24, No. 4 (Spring 2000), p. 5.

11. John Arquila, David Ronfeldt, and Michele Zanini's 'Networks, Netwar, and Information Age Terrorism in Zalmay M. Khalilzad and John P. White, *Strategic Appraisal: The Changing Role of Information in Warfare* (Santa Monica, CA: Rand, 1999), pp. 75–112, stands out as a particularly prescient example.

12. Thomas X. Hammes, 'War Evolves into the Fourth Generation', *Contemporary Security Policy*, Vol. 26, No. 2 (2005), pp. 189–221.

13. Lawrence Freedman, 'War Evolves into the Fourth Generation: A Comment on Thomas X. Hammes', *Contemporary Security Policy*, Vol. 26, No. 2 (2005), pp. 254–263.

14. William S. Lind *et al*, 'The Changing Face of War: Into the Fourth Generation', *Marine Corps Gazette*, Vol. 73, No. 10 (October 1989), pp. 22–26.

15. In general, on the issue of Marine Corps thinking in this period the key resource is Terry Terriff, 'Of Romans and Dragons: Preparing the US Marine Corps for Future Warfare', *Contemporary Security Policy*, Vol. 28, No. 1 (2007), pp. 143–162.

16. General Charles Krulak interview with Jim Lehrer, *PBS Newshour* (25 June 1999).

17. Stephen Graham, *Cities Under Siege: The New Military Urbanism* (London: Verso, 2010), pp. 1–2.

18. For a useful discussion of the strengths and weaknesses of the concept, see Walter Dorn and Michael Varey, 'Fatally Flawed: The Rise and Demise of the "Three-Block War" Concept in Canada', *International Journal*, Vol. 63, No. 4 (Autumn 2008), pp. 967–978.

19. Joseph Nye and William Owens, 'America's Information Edge', *Foreign Affairs*, Vol. 75, No. 2 (March–April 1996), p. 20.

20. *Ibid.*, p. 20.

21. *Ibid.*, p. 20.

22. Joseph Nye, *Soft Power: The Means to Success in World Politics* (New York: Public Affairs, 2004), p. ix.

23. Alvin and Heidi Toffler, *War and Anti-War: Making Sense of Today's Global Chaos* (New York: Warner Books, 1993), pp. 79–80.

24. *Ibid.*, pp. 73–93.

25. John Arquilla and David Ronfeldt, 'Cyberwar is Coming!', in Arquilla and Ronfeldt (eds), *In Athena's Camp: Preparing for Conflict in the Information Age* (Santa Monica, CA: RAND, 1997), pp. 22–23.

26. *Ibid.*, pp. 34–37.

27. *Ibid.*, p. 27.

28. Robert Leonhard, *The Principles of War for the Information Age* (Novato, CA: Presidio Press, 1998), p. 19.

29. From the introduction by Admiral William Owens to Martin Libicki and Stuart Johnson (eds), *Dominant Battlespace Knowledge* (Washington, DC: National Defence University, 1995), pp. ii-iii.

30. Ben Bernanke, Remarks of the Chairman of the United States Federal Reserve on 'The Great Moderation' (Washington, DC: Eastern Economic Association, 20 February 2004).

31. Thomas Friedman, *The World is Flat: A Brief History of the Twenty First Century* (New York: Farrar, Straus and Giroux, 2005), p. 8.

32. James Hazlett, 'Just-in-Time Warfare', in Libicki and Johnson (eds), *Dominant Battlespace Knowledge*, pp. 54–55.

33. From Owens' introduction in Libicki and Johnson (eds), *Dominant Battlespace Knowledge*, pp. v-viii. A pithy example of such criticism is to be found in Christopher Ankersen and Losel Tethong, 'Rapid Decisive Ops are Risky Business', *US Naval Institute Proceedings*, Vol. 129, No. 10 (2003), pp. 52–55.

34. Owens, *Lifting the Fog of War*, p. 236.

35. Harlan Ullman and James Wade, *Shock and Awe: Achieving Rapid Dominance* (Washington, DC: National Defence University, 1996), p. 9.

36. *Ibid.*, p. 36.

37. *Ibid.*, p. 9

38. Colin Gray, *The American Revolution in Military Affairs: An Interim Assessment* (Camberley, UK: Strategic and Combat Studies Institute Occasional 28, 1997), p. iii.

39. Michael O'Hanlon, *Technological Change and the Future of Warfare* (Washington, DC: Brookings Institution, 2000), pp. 194–195.

40. John Antal, 'Battleshock XXI', in Robert Bateman (ed.), *Digital War: The Twenty-First Century Battlefield* (New York: iBooks, 1999), p. 58.

41. Lawrence Freedman, *The Revolution in Strategic Affairs* (London: International Institute for Strategic Studies, Adelphi 318, 1998), p. 10.

42. Arthur K. Cebrowski and John J. Garstka, 'Network Centric Warfare: Its Origin and Future', *Proceedings of the US Naval Institute*, Vol. 124, No. 1 (January 1998), pp. 28–35.

43. See Lawrence Freedman, *Official History of the Falklands Campaign: Vol. II, War and Diplomacy* (Abingdon, Oxon: Routledge, 2005), esp. chs 32 on the landings at San Carlos and 33 on the subsequent Argentine efforts to shut them down in what came to be called 'Bomb Alley'. The problems of fusing of Argentine bombs are discussed in Stephen Badsey, Rob Harris, Mark Grove *et al*, *The Falklands Conflict Twenty Years On: Lessons for the Future* (London: Frank Cass, 2007), p. 7.

44. David Alberts, John Garstka and Frederick Stein, *Network Centric Warfare: Developing and Leveraging Information Superiority* (Washington, DC: Department of Defence, Command and Control Research Programme, 2003), pp. 175–176.

45. David Alberts, John Garstka, Richard Hayes and David Signori, *Understanding Information Age Warfare* (Washington, DC: Department of Defence, Command and Control Research Programme, 2003), pp. 212–215.
46. Alberts *et al, Network Centric Warfare*, p. 175.
47. From a handout provided to the author at ISAF Headquarters (Kabul, Afghanistan: August 2010).
48. Tommy Franks, *American Soldier* (New York: Regan Books), p. 135.
49. *Ibid.*, p. 400.
50. Quoted in Richard Sanders, 'The Myth of Shock and Awe: Why the Iraqi Invasion was a Disaster', *Daily Telegraph* (19 March 2013).
51. President George W. Bush, Remarks at the Citadel (Charleston, SC: 11 December 2001).
52. Stephen Biddle, *Afghanistan and the Future of Warfare* (Carlisle, PA: United States Army War College, Strategic Studies Institute, 2002). Also see Anthony Cordesman, *The Lessons of Afghanistan: Warfighting, Intelligence, and Force Transformation* (Washington, DC: Centre for Strategic and International Studies, 2002) for another early critical assessment.
53. Biddle, *Afghanistan and the Future of Warfare*, p. 54.
54. Bob Woodward, *Plan of Attack* (London: Pocket Books, 2004), p. 41.
55. Senator Carl Levin, opening remarks of the Senate Armed Services Committee hearing on 'Lessons Learned from Operation Iraqi Freedom' (Washington, DC: 7 September 2003).
56. Victor Davis Hanson, 'Don Rumsfeld, A Radical for Our Time', National Review Online (5 May 2003), reprinted in Victor Davis Hanson, *Between War and Peace: Lessons from Afghanistan to Iraq* (New York: Random House, 2004), pp. 219–20.
57. Quoted in Linda Kozaryn, 'Regime's Collapse Evident, but Hard Fighting Ahead, Cheney Says', *Armed Forces Press Service* (9 April 2003).
58. Max Boot, 'The New American Way of War', *Foreign Affairs*, Vol. 89, No. 4 (July/August 2003).
59. *Ibid.*
60. Bing West, *The March Up: Taking Baghdad with the First Marine Division* (London: Pimlico, 2003), pp. 40–42.
61. Evan Wright, *Generation Kill: Living Dangerously on the Road to Baghdad with the Ultraviolent Marines of Bravo Company* (London: Bantam Press 2004), p. 180.
62. West, *The March Up*, p. 254.
63. Ralph Peters, 'Shock, Awe and Overconfidence', *Washington Post* (25 March 2003).
64. Quoted in Sanders, 'The Myth of "Shock and Awe"'.
65. See Williamson Murray and Robert Scales, *The Iraq War: A Military History* (Cambridge, MA: Belknap Press of Harvard University Press, 2003), pp. 103 & 147.
66. *Ibid.*, p. 176.
67. Randa Habib, 'Saddam Fled Just Before Bombing', Agence France Presse (6 Novem-

ber 2003). The story also figures in Yossef Bodansky's *The Secret History of the Iraq War* (New York: Regan Books, 2004), p. 235.

68. Cebrowski and Garstka, 'Network Centric Warfare'.

69. Victor Davis Hanson, 'Postbellum Thoughts', *National Interest Review Online* (9 May 2003), reprinted in Victor Davis Hanson, *Between War and Peace: Lessons from Afghanistan to Iraq* (New York: Random House, 2004), p. 227.

70. Carl von Clausewitz (Michael Howard and Peter Paret, trans and eds), *On War* (New York: Alfred A. Knopf, Everyman's Library, 1993), p. 102.

71. Interview with General James Mattis, Commander US Joint Forces Command, *Defence News* (23 May 2010).

72. Robert Warburton, *Eighteen Years on the Khyber, 1879–1898* (London: John Murray, 1900), pp. 80–81.

73. See David Loyn, *Butcher and Bolt: Two Hundred Years of Foreign Engagement in Afghanistan* (London: Windmill Books, 2008), p. 269; also Tim Bird and Alex Marshall, *Afghanistan: How the West Lost its Way* (London: Yale University Press, 2011), especially ch. 3.

74. Andrew Marshall in Zalmay Khalilzad and John White (eds), *The Changing Role of Information in Warfare* (Santa Monica, CA: RAND, 1999), pp. 4–5 & 6.

75. In the speech in which Bush announced this he did not actually say 'Mission Accomplished'. His slightly more cautious speech was simply given under a banner with those words raised by the exuberant crew of the USS Abraham Lincoln aircraft carrier on the deck of which the speech was delivered. The story of how the insurgency in Iraq was 'created' while the administration avoided saying the word 'insurgency' is told in Thomas Ricks, *Fiasco: The American Military Adventure in Iraq* (London: Allen Lane, 2006).

5. WAR WITHOUT PASSION: SOMETHING OTHER THAN WAR

1. Statement by Sir John Chilcot, Chairman of the Iraq Inquiry (London: 30 July 2009).

2. 55 per cent of Britons agreed with that statement in 2010 according to a poll reported by Tom Clark, 'Iraq War "Delivered Little but Bloodshed", say Britons in Ten Year Anniversary Poll', *Guardian* (15 February 2013).

3. Rupert Smith, *The Utility of Force: The Art of War in the Modern World* (London: Allen Lane, 2006), p. 270.

4. *Ibid.*, p. 1.

5. *Ibid.*, p. 3.

6. *Ibid.*, p. 1.

7. Adam Elkus, 'Only the West has Seen the End of War', *Infinity Journal* (August 2012).

8. Colin Gray, *Another Bloody Century: Future Warfare* (London: Weidenfeld and Nicolson, 2005), p. 382.

9. There is considerable agreement that the future of major war in Asia, particularly, is far from over. See, for example, Bill Emmott, *Rivals: How the Power Struggle Between China, India and Japan Will Shape Our Next Decade* (London: Allen Lane, 2008); also Paul Bracken, *Fire in the East: The Rise of Asian Military Power and the Second Nuclear Age* (New York: HarperCollins, 1999).

10. To be fair to him, Smith (in *The Utility of Force*, pp. 155–6) does argue that the 'deep roots' of 'war amongst the people' as the antithesis of industrial war go back to the irregular campaigns of the Napoleonic-era Peninsular War in Spain, the birthplace of the 'guerrilla' (Spanish for 'small war'); but he sticks to a language of 'paradigm' and 'counter-paradigm', which is unnecessary and confusing. Adam Roberts' review of *The Utility of Force*, entitled 'Theatre of Blood', *Independent* (11 November 2005), p. 24, notes several of these criticisms.

11. Smith, *The Utility of Force*, p. 3.

12. Azar Gat, *War in Human Civilisation* (Oxford: Oxford University Press, 2006).

13. Smith, *The Utility of Force*, p. 270.

14. Eliot Cohen, 'The End of War as We Know It' (review), *Washington Post* (21 January 2007).

15. Polybius, *The Rise of the Roman Empire* (London: Penguin Classics, 1979), p. 274; Livy, *The War with Hannibal: The History of Rome from its Foundation* (London: Penguin Classics, 1965), p. 149. An overall assessment is J.F. Lazenby, *Hannibal's War: A Military History of the Second Punic War* (Norman, OK: Oklahoma University Press, 1978).

16. Quoted in Livy, *The War with Hannibal*, p. 51.

17. Although the Anglo-Canadian press baron Lord Beaverbrook, who had a tight grip on the British media and much influence on politics through his ownership of the *Daily Express* and *Evening Standard* newspapers, seems unconsciously to have thought along these lines. He entitled his small book on the life and teachings of Jesus, *The Divine Propagandist* (London: Heinemann, 1962). It takes one to know one, a wag might say.

18. See Jane Burbank and Frederick Cooper, *Empires in World History: Power and the Politics of Difference* (Princeton, NJ: Princeton University Press, 2010), p. 17.

19. Diarmaid MacCulloch, *Christianity: The First Three Thousand Years* (London: Penguin, 2009), pp. 165–166.

20. *Ibid*, pp. 9 & 159. Leave aside the informational content, the religious dogma, and consider the Bible simply as a communications 'device'. The peculiar thing about it is that it takes the form of a codex—a book, in other words—whereas the norm in the ancient world was the scroll. As such, it had certain small but important advantages. While no more durable than scrolls, nor able to hold more information, books present information in a considerably more mobile and 'user-friendly' way. As opposed to a scroll, where cross-referencing different parts of a text requires laborious and space consuming unrolling, with a book you just flip back and forth

from chapter to chapter—from gospel to prophecy and back to gospel again. Specific passages and words can be referenced much more accurately, which in turn was useful to early Christian code writing. A book is also more uniform and simply easier to produce. The qualities of the codex as a form and its relation to Christian expansion are discussed extensively in David Trobisch, *The First Edition of the New Testament* (Oxford: Oxford University Press, 2000), pp. 69–77.

21. Jean-Francois Lyotard, *The Postmodern Condition: A Report on Knowledge* (Manchester: Manchester University Press, 2001), p. xxiv.

22. *The National Security Strategy of the United States of America* (Washington, DC: The White House, September 2002).

23. See Michael Howard, 'A Long War', *Survival*, Vol. 48., No. 4 (Winter 2006–2007), pp. 7–14.

24. For example, see Steve Metz, *Iraq and the Evolution of American Strategy* (Washington, DC: Potomac Books, 2008), p. 93. It must be said, however, that some find the term reasonably accurate and suitable. See Howard, 'A Long War', pp. 9–10.

25. Andrew Bacevich, *The New American Militarism: How Americans are Seduced by War* (Oxford: Oxford University Press, 2005), p. 203.

26. See James Kitfield, 'A Hollow Military Again', *National Journal* (12 June 2013). Dana Priest and William Arkin, *Top Secret America: The Rise of the New American Security State* (London: Little Brown, 2011), details the massive post-9/11 growth of the defence and intelligence sectors in the United States.

27. Naomi Klein, *The Shock Doctrine: The Rise of Disaster Capitalism* (London: Allen Lane, 2007), pp. 323–382.

28. Noam Chomsky, 'Who are the Global Terrorists?', in Ken Booth and Tim Dunne (eds), *Worlds in Collision: Terror and the Future of Global Conflict* (Houndmills, Basingstoke: Palgrave Macmillan, 2002), pp. 128–137.

29. Lev Grossman, 'Why the 911 Conspiracy Theories Won't go Away', *Time* (3 September 2006).

30. President George W. Bush, Remarks at a rally in support of the Senate candidacy of Elizabeth Dole (Charlotte, NC: 24 October 2002).

31. Benjamin Barber, 'Democracy and Terror in the Age of Jihad vs. McWorld', in Booth and Dunne (eds), *Worlds in Collision*, pp. 245–262.

32. Philip Seib, *The Global Journalist: News and Conscience in a World of Conflict* (Oxford: Rowman and Littlefield, 2002), p. 12.

33. Robert Kaplan, *The Coming Anarchy: Shattering the Dreams of the Post Cold War* (New York: Vintage Books, 2001), pp. 172–173.

34. Rwanda is the most important example of this. See Alan Kuperman, 'Rwanda in Retrospect', *Foreign Affairs*, Vol. 79, No. 1 (January–February 2000), pp. 94–118.

35. Colin McInnes, *Spectator-Sport War: The West and Contemporary Conflict* (London: Lynne Reiner, 2002), p. 2.

36. Edward Luttwak, 'Toward Postheroic Warfare', *Foreign Affairs*, Vol. 74, No. 3 (May–June 1995), p. 122.

37. *Ibid.*, p. 110.

38. Alexis de Tocqueville's reflections on the relationship of the individual and the state in America are still illuminating. See (Henry Reeve, trans.) *Democracy in America*, Vol. 2 (Pennsylvania State University Electronic Classics, 2002 [1840]), pp. 573–580. On firepower in American military culture see Robert Scales, *Firepower in Limited War* (Novato, CA: Presidio Press, 1995), pp. 3–22; David Johnson's *Fast Tanks and Heavy Bombers: Innovation in the US Army, 1917–1945* (London: Cornell University Press, 1998) is also an invaluable study of American military culture and thinking.

39. A 'war of choice' as opposed to a 'war of necessity' is not about national survival but some lesser (sometimes very much lesser) interest. Importantly, they are also wars conducted not just in lieu of doing nothing but when an alternative means of achieving the declared interest is perceived, rightly or wrongly, by a wide fraction of society to be a viable option. See Richard Haass, *War of Necessity, War of Choice: A Memoir of Two Iraq Wars* (New York: Simon and Schuster, 2009), pp. 9–11 & *passim*.

40. Andrew Mack, 'Why Big Nations Lose Small Wars', in Klaus Knorr (ed.), *Power, Strategy, and Security: A World Politics Reader* (Princeton, NJ: Princeton University Press, 1975), pp. 126–151. Ivan Arreguin-Toft further developed the theory in *How the Weak Win Wars: A Theory of Asymmetric Conflict* (Cambridge: Cambridge University Press, 2005).

41. See Gil Merom, *How Democracies Lose Small Wars: State, Society, and the Failures of France in Algeria, Israel in Lebanon, and the United States in Vietnam* (Cambridge: Cambridge University Press, 2003).

42. Edward Luttwak, 'Give War a Chance', *Foreign Affairs*, Vol. 78, No. 4 (July/August 1999), pp. 36–44.

43. From a 1996 interview by Barrie Dunsmore in 'Live from the Battlefield', in Pippa Norris (ed.), *Politics and the Press: The News Media and Their Influences* (London: Lynne Reiner, 1997), p. 261.

44. W.H. Auden, 'September 1, 1939', in *Another Time* (London: Random House, 1940), with thanks for inspiration to Christopher Coker's assessment of the 2000s as 'A Low, Dishonest Decade', *RUSI Journal*, Vol. 156, No. 4 (August/September 2011), pp. 18–24.

45. Carl Von Clausewitz (Michael Howard and Peter Paret trans and eds) *On War* (New York: Alfred A. Knopf, Everyman's Library, 1993), p. 101.

46. Norman H. Gibbs, 'Clausewitz and the Moral Forces in War', *Naval War College Review*, Vol. XXVII, No. 4 (January/February 1975), p. 15.

47. William Shakespeare, *Henry V*, Act III.

48. Georges Sorel (T.E. Hulme, trans.), *Reflections on Violence* (London: George Allen & Unwin, 1915), p. 27.

49. Christopher Coker, 'The Unhappy Warrior', *RUSI Journal*, Vol. 150, No. 6 (December 2005), p. 13.

50. *Ibid.*, p. 16.

51. Smith, *The Utility of Force*, p. 9.

52. Quoted in *Ibid.*, p. 240.

53. *Ibid.*, p. 240.

54. See Julian Reid, 'Foucault on Clausewitz: Conceptualising the relationship Between War and Power', *Alternatives: Global, Local, Political*, Vol. 28, No. 1 (January/February 2003), pp. 1–28.

55. Smith, *The Utility of Force*, p. 243.

56. For illustration of which see James Gow, *Triumph of the Lack of Will: International Diplomacy and the Yugoslav War* (London: Hurst, 1997); also, Christopher Dandeker, 'The End of War? The Strategic Context of International Missions in the Twenty First Century', in Magnus Christiansson (ed.), *Eight Essays in Contemporary War Studies* (Stockholm: Military Academy Karlberg, Acta Politica II, 2007), pp. 19–49.

57. Clausewitz, *On War*, p. 111. Marc Lynch in his *Voices of the New Arab Public: Iraq, Al-Jazeera, and Middle East Politics Today* (New York: Columbia University Press, 2006), also focuses on this idea describing a purpose of his book as being to capture the 'symbolic battle, the interaction between strategy and rhetoric, between legitimacy and power' (p. 59).

58. Jean Baudrillard, *The Gulf War did not Take Place* (Bloomington, IN: Indiana University Press, 1995), p. 62.

59. Smith, *The Utility of Force*, p. 403.

60. Sorel, *Reflections on Violance*, p. 29.

61. Nicholas O'Shaughnessy, *Politics and Propaganda: Weapons of Mass Seduction* (Manchester: Manchester University Press, 2004), p. 90.

62. On the construction of the idea of victory, see Dominic Tierney and Dominic Johnson, *Failing to Win: Perceptions of Victory and Defeat in International Politics* (Cambridge, MA: Harvard University Press, 2006).

6. THEATRE OF WAR

1. George Orwell, *Shooting an Elephant and Other Essays* (London: Penguin, 2003), pp. 36–37.

2. Ernesto Londono, 'Iraq, Afghan Wars Will Cost $4 to $6 Trillion, Harvard Study Says', *Washington Post* (28 March 2013).

3. Frank Ledwidge counts the cost for Afghanistan forensically in *Investment in Blood: The Real Cost of Britain's Afghan War* (London: Yale University Press, 2013). He does not add up the Iraq and Afghan costs.

4. For detail see Lawrence Freedman, *A Choice of Enemies: America Confronts the Middle East* (New York: Public Affairs, 2008), pp. 397–422.

5. Quoted in Tommy Franks, *American Soldier* (New York: Regan Books, 2004), p. 528.

6. Sarah Sands, 'Sir Richard Dannatt: A Very Honest General', *Daily Mail* (12 October 2006).

7. See James Fallows, 'Blind into Baghdad', *Atlantic Monthly*, Vol. 293, No. 1 (January/February 2004).

8. The much-quoted United Nations *Arab Human Development Report: Creating Opportunities for Future Generations* (New York: United Nations Development Programme, Regional Bureau for Arab States, 2002) encouraged such thinking in so far as it painted a picture of Arab governments as unable to accept the rule of law and fair elections, equality of the sexes, and other basic freedoms, and unable to foster innovative economies. See also on this point Freedman, *A Choice of Enemies*, p. 431.

9. Vice President Dick Cheney, speech to the Veterans of Foreign Wars national convention, full text in *The Guardian* (27 August 2002).

10. Fouad Ajami, *The Foreigner's Gift: The Americans, the Arabs, and the Iraqis in Iraq* (New York: Simon and Schuster, 2006), p. 5.

11. Rajiv Chandrasekaran, *Imperial Life in the Emerald City: Inside Baghdad's Green Zone* (London: Bloomsbury, 2006), pp. 3–4.

12. Kanan Makiya, 'The Arab Spring Started in Iraq', *New York Times* (6 April 2013).

13. Francesca Panetta et al, 'Faces of War: Hear the Stories Behind the Iconic Images of Iraq Conflict', *Guardian* (15 March 2013).

14. Quoted in Bob Woodward, *Plan of Attack* (London: Pocket Books, 2004), p. 150.

15. Dan Ariely, *Predictably Irrational: The Hidden Forces that Shape our Decisions* (New York: Harper Collins, 2008), pp. 137–138.

16. This title refers to the words British Prime Minister Harold Macmillan used to describe Britain's role in 'civilising and guiding the immature giant', that is, the United States. Quoted in Patrick Porter, 'Last Charge of the Knights: Iraq, Afghanistan, and the Special Relationship', *International Affairs*, Vol. 86, No. 2 (2010), p. 359.

17. For a further discussion, see Thomas Waldman, *War, Clausewitz, and the Trinity* (Farnham, Surrey: Ashgate, 2013), pp. 6–7.

18. James A. Baker III *et al*, *The Iraq Study Group Report* (Washington, DC: United States Institute for Peace, 2006), p. 27.

19. *Ibid.*, p. 28

20. President George W. Bush, 'The New Strategy in Iraq', Primetime Address to the Nation (10 January 2007).

21. Thomas E. Ricks, *The Gamble: General Petraeus and the Untold Story of the American Surge in Iraq, 2006–2008* (London: Allen Lane, 2008), p. 123.

22. 'Outrage at "Old Europe" Remarks', BBC (23 January 2003).

23. Ewan MacAskill *et al*, 'US May Go It Alone as Blair is Caught in a Diplomatic Deadlock', *Guardian* (12 March 2003).

24. As described in Chandrasekaran, *Imperial Life*, p. 78.

25. Quoted in Thomas E. Ricks, *Fiasco: The American Military Adventure in Iraq* (London: Allen Lane, 2006), p. 163.

26. Nigel Aylwin-Foster, 'Changing the Army for Counterinsurgency Operations', *Military Review*, Vol. 85, No. 6 (November/December 2005), p. 3. The essay was originally published as a Seaford Paper of the United Kingdom's Defence Academy.

27. *Ibid.*, p. 4.

28. Kevin C.M. Benson, 'OIF Phase IV: A Planner's Reply to Brigadier Aylwin-Foster', *Military Review*, Vol. 86, No. 2 (March/April 2006).

29. Aylwin-Foster, 'Changing the Army', p. 7.

30. Donald B. Vought, 'Preparing for the Wrong War?', *Military Review*, Vol. LVII, No. 6 (May 1977), pp. 28–29; see also, Paul Herbert, 'Deciding What Has To Be Done: General William E. Dupuy and the 1976 Edition of FM 100–5, Operations', *Leavenworth Papers, 16* (Fort Leavenworth, KS: Combat Studies Institute, July 1988).

31. C.E. Callwell, *Small Wars* (Lincoln, NE: University of Nebraska Press, 1996 [1906]); Robert Thompson, *Defeating Communist Insurgency* (St Petersburg, FL: Hailer Publishing, 2005); Frank Kitson, *Low-Intensity Operations* (London: Faber and Faber, 1972).

32. See Thomas R. Mockaitis, *British Counterinsurgency, 1919–60* (New York: St. Martin's Press, 1990), p. 146; also Robert Cassidy, 'The British Army and Counterinsurgency: The Salience of Military Culture', *Military Review*, Vol. LXXXV, No. 3 (May/June 2005), pp. 53–59.

33. Statement of Major General Robert Scales, USA (ret.), 'Army Transformation: Implications for the Future', Testimony before the House Armed Services Committee (15 July 2004).

34. Patrick Devenny and Robert Mclean, 'The Battle for Basra', *The American Spectator* (11 January 2005).

35. 'UK Troops Recount Burning Tank Escape', *Reuters* (22 September 2005).

36. Quoted in 'British Troops Complete Withdrawal from Basra Base', *PBS Newshour* (3 September 2007).

37. Quoted by Mona Mahmoud, Maggie O'Kane and Ian Black in 'UK has Left Behind Murder and Chaos, says Basra Police Chief', *Guardian* (17 December 2007); see also David Betz and Anthony Cormack, 'Iraq, Afghanistan and British Strategy', *Orbis*, Vol. 53, No. 2 (2009), pp. 319–336.

38. Frank Hoffman, *Changing Tires on the Fly: The Marines and Post-Conflict Stability Ops* (Philadelphia, PA: Foreign Policy Research Institute, 2006).

39. Freedman, *A Choice of Enemies*, p. 441.

40. Quoted in Bing West, *The Strongest Tribe: War, Politics, and the Endgame in Iraq* (New York: Random House, 2008), p. 50.

41. Marc Lynch, *Voices of the New Arab Public: Iraq, Al-Jazeera, and Middle East Politics Today* (New York: Columbia University Press, 2006), p. 6.

42. A point also emphasised in David Kilcullen, *The Accidental Guerrilla: Fighting Small Wars in the Midst of a Big One* (London: Hurst, 2009), pp. 58–59.

43. *FM 3–24 Counterinsurgency* (Washington DC: Headquarters, Department of the Army, December 2006).

44. David Ucko, *The New Counterinsurgency Era: Transforming the US Military for Modern Wars* (Washington DC: Georgetown University Press, 2009).

45. Fred Kaplan, *The Insurgents: David Petraeus and the Plot to Change the American Way of War* (New York: Simon and Schuster, 2013), p. 164.

46. On the 'brain trust', see Ricks, *The Gamble*, pp. 133–148.

47. *FM 3–24*, pp. 1–26–1–28. Kaplan gives an interesting blow-by-blow account of the development of the 'paradoxes' and some of the colourful criticism aimed at them in *The Insurgents*, pp. 149–151 & 217–22.

48. Ricks, *The Gamble*, p. 15.

49. It should be noted that historians also contest the actual degree of British counterinsurgency competence full stop. See, Douglas Porch, *Counterinsurgency: Exposing the Myths of the New Way of War* (Cambridge: Cambridge University Press, 2013).

50. Richard Iron, 'The Charge of the Knights', *RUSI Journal*, Vol. 158, No. 1 (2013), pp. 54–62; also Stephen Grey, 'Retreat from Basra—Learning the Lessons', *Sunday Times* (20 September 2009).

51. See, for instance, the account of the adjustments to the manual occasioned by the objections of the military intelligence community to the chapter on intelligence in Kaplan, *The Insurgents*, pp. 213–216. It should be pointed out, too, that the French counterinsurgent David Galula's book *Counterinsurgency Warfare: Theory and Practice* (New York: Frederick A. Praeger, 1964) was also a main influence on the field manual. John Nagl mentions this explicitly in the foreword to the civilian version of the manual, *Counterinsurgency* (Chicago, IL: Chicago University Press, 2007), p. xix.

52. See John Kiszely, 'Learning About Counterinsurgency', *RUSI Journal*, Vol. 151, No. 6 (2006), pp. 16–21; also Frank Ledwidge, *Losing Small Wars: British Military Failure in Iraq and Afghanistan* (London: Yale University Press, 2011); and David Betz and Anthony Cormack, 'Iraq, Afghanistan and British Strategy'.

53. Kilcullen, *The Accidental Guerrilla*, pp. 184–185.

54. Christopher Lamb and Evan Munsing, 'Secret Weapon: High-Value Target Teams as an Organisational Innovation', *Strategic Perspectives* 4, (Washington, DC: Centre for Strategic Research, Institute for National Strategic Studies, National Defence University, March 2011), pp. 19–20.

55. As quoted in William Prochnau, *Once Upon a Distant War: David Halberstam, Neil Sheehan, Peter Arnett—Young Correspondents and their Early Vietnam Battles* (New York: Vintage Books, 1995), p. 162.

56. Academic research on the efficacy of such systems is still scant. Deirdre Collins and Rafal Rohozinski's *Shifting Fire: Information Effects in Counterinsurgency and Stabilisation Operations—A Workshop Report* (Carlisle, PA: US Army War College, 2006), was one of the first to look at the issue systematically. Bing West's account of the US campaign in Iraq, *The Strongest Tribe: War, Politics, and the Endgame in Iraq* (New York: Random House, 2008), also touched on the issue noting that the Pentagon dragged its feet on the development and deployment of these systems (pp. 369–370). An unclassified US Army Centre for Lessons Learned newsletter entitled 'Biometrics in Support of Information Dominance', No. 09–35 (May 2009), is also a useful source of data.

57. Lamb and Munsing, 'Secret Weapon', p. 5.

58. 'Interview: General David Petraeus', PBS Frontline: 'Kill/Capture' (14 June 2011).

59. General Sir Richard Dannatt, speech to the Royal United Services Institute Land Warfare Conference (London: 12 June 2008).

60. Callwell, *Small Wars*, pp. 75–76.

61. William F. Owen, 'Killing Your Way to Control', *British Army Review*, No. 151 (Spring 2011), pp. 34–37.

62. Saul David's *Victoria's Wars* (London: Penguin, 2007) provides an engaging account of this period.

63. This subject is addressed throughout Chapter VI (and also on p. 90) in Callwell, *Small Wars*.

64. Mark Urban, *Task Force Black: The Explosive True Story of the SAS and the Secret War in Iraq* (London: Little, Brown, 2010), p. xvi.

65. David Galula, *Counterinsurgency Warfare: Theory and Practice* (London: Praeger, 1964), p. 73.

66. Aylwin-Foster, 'Changing the Army', pp. 5–6.

67. *Ibid.*, p. 6.

68. Callwell, *Small Wars*, p. 91.

69. *Ibid.*, pp. 147–148.

70. William Langewiesche, 'Letter from Baghdad: Life in The Wilds of a City Without Trust', *The Atlantic* (1 January 2005).

71. Andrew Garfield, *Succeeding in Phase IV: British Perspectives on the US Effort to Stabilise and Reconstruct Iraq* (Philadelphia, PA: Foreign Policy Research Institute, 2006), p. 13.

72. Iron, 'The Charge of the Knights', p. 55.

73. Eitan Shamir, *Transforming Command: The Pursuit of Mission Command in the US, British and Israeli Armies* (Stanford, CA: Stanford University Press, 2011), p. 68.

74. Martin Van Creveld, *The Changing Face of War: Lessons of Combat from the Marne to Iraq* (New York: Ballantine Books, 2006), p. 234.

75. Stephen Grey, 'Cracking on in Helmand', *Prospect* (27 August 2009), and Anthony King, 'Why We're Getting it Wrong in Afghanistan', *Prospect* (4 September 2009).

76. Betz and Cormack, 'Iraq, Afghanistan and British Strategy', p. 336; and Iron, 'The Charge of the Knights', p. 55.

7. STRATEGIC NARRATIVE AND STRATEGIC INCOHERENCE

1. Porter, 'Last Change of the Knights: Iraq, Afghanistan, and the Special Relationship', *International Affairs*, Vol. 86, No. 2 (2010), p. 357.
2. Lawrence Freedman, 'the Special Relationship—Then and Now', *Foreign Policy*, Vol. 85, No. 3 (2006), p. 73. The latest National Security Strategy, *A Strong Britain in an Age of Uncertainty* (London: The Stationery Office, 2010) twice reiterates the position of the United States as Britain's 'key ally'.
3. John Cantwell, *Exit Wounds: One Australian's War on Terror* (Melbourne: Melbourne University Press, 2012), p. 13.
4. 'London Bomber: Text in Full', *BBC News* (1 September 2005). On 22 May 2013 outside Woolwich Barracks in London two British-born Muslim converts brutally murdered a British soldier, stabbing him to death in the middle of a busy daytime street. Recorded on the mobile phone of a passerby, one of the attackers justified the attack in exactly the same terms. See Gordon Rayner and Steven Swinford, 'Woolwich Attack: Terrorist Proclaimed "an Eye for an Eye" After Attack', *Daily Telegraph* (22 May 2013).
5. Carl Von Clausewitz (Michael Howard and Peter Paret trans and eds) *On War* (New York: Alfred A. Knopf, Everyman's Library, 1993), p. 100.
6. Michael Howard, 'A Long War', *Survival*, Vol. 48, No. 4 (2006), pp. 11–12.
7. This is a main theme in the account of Ronald E. Neumann, American ambassador in Afghanistan from 2005 through 2007, of the war in *The Other War: Winning and Losing In Afghanistan* (Washington, DC: Potomac Boos, 2009), p. 105 and *passim*. See also Antonio Giustozzi, *Koran, Kalashnikov, and Laptop: The Neo-Taliban Insurgency in Afghanistan* (London: Hurst, 2007), pp. 163–166.
8. Tim Bird and Alex Marshall, *Afghanistan: How the West Lost its Way* (London: Yale University Press, 2011), pp. 249–250.
9. Interviews conducted by the author in ISAF HQ Kabul, Afghanistan in August 2010.
10. Rick Hillier, *A Soldier First: Bullets, Bureaucrats, and the Politics of War* (Toronto: HarperCollins, 2009).
11. Terry Terriff, 'Fear and Loathing in NATO', *Perspectives on European Politics and Society*, Vol. 5, No. 3 (September 2004), p. 432.
12. See Lawrence Freedman, *The Politics of British Defence, 1979–1998* (Houndmills, Basingstoke: Macmillan, 1999), p. 35; and Freedman, *A Choice of Enemies: America Confronts the Middle East* (New York: Public Affairs, 2008), p. 404.
13. Joseph Fletcher, Heather Bastedo, and Jennifer Hove, 'Losing Heart: Declining Support and the Political Marketing of the Afghanistan Mission', *Canadian Journal of Political Science*, Vol. 142, No. 4 (December 2009), pp. 912–913.

14. Colonel Bernd Horn, *No Lack of Courage: Operation Medusa, Afghanistan* (Toronto: Dundurn Press, 2010).

15. Janice Gross Stein and Eugene Lang, *The Unexpected War: Canada in Afghanistan* (Toronto: Viking, 2007), p. 244.

16. Quoted and discussed in Fletcher *et al*, 'Losing Heart', pp. 914–915.

17. *Ibid.*, p. 931.

18. *Independent Panel on Canada's Future Role in Afghanistan*, 'The Manley Report' (Ottawa: Her Majesty the Queen in Right of Canada, represented by the Minister of Public Works and Government Services, 2008), p. 3.

19. *Ibid.*, p. 32.

20. President Barack Obama, remarks to the Veterans of Foreign Wars Annual Conference (Phoenix, AZ: 17 August 2009).

21. See Hillier, *A Solider First*, chap. 21.

22. *Ibid.*

23. *Ibid.*

24. Rupert Smith, *The Utility of Force: The Art of War in the Modern World* (London: Allen Lane, 2006), pp. 284–285.

25. Julian Corbett, quoted in C.E. Callwell, *Military Operations and Maritime Preponderance* (London: William Blackwell and Sons, 1905), p. 179.

26. Julian Corbett, *Some Principles of Maritime Strategy* (Annapolis, MD: Naval Institute Press, 1988), p. 57.

27. Frances Cairncross, *The Death of Distance: How the Communications Revolution is Changing Our Lives* (Cambridge, MA: Harvard Business School Press, 2001).

28. Joseph Matthews, *Reporting the Wars* (Minneapolis, MN: 1957).

29. See Thomas Pakenham, *The Boer War*, Illustrated Edition (London: Weidenfeld and Nicolson, 1979), particularly the illustrations from *L'Assiette au Beurre* on pp. 250–1, 286, 288; also David Betz, 'Counterinsurgency: Victorian Style', *Survival*, Vol. 54, No. 4 (2012), pp. 161–182.

30. Pakenham, *The Boer War*, p. 215, especially the illustration of a postcard produced by an enterprising publisher featuring Baden-Powell in a triumphant pose with the words 'Well done, Gallant Little Mafeking. The Empire is Proud of You'.

31. However, it should be pointed out that opinion was somewhat schizophrenic. Parts of the British press were critical of the leniency of commanders, particularly Field Marshal Frederick Roberts's amnesty policy (which allowed Boer combatants to return to their homes after surrendering). See Alexander Downes, 'Draining the Sea By Filling the Graves', *Civil Wars*, Vol. 9, No. 4 (2007), p. 432 and Thomas Pakenham, *The Boer War* [original unillustrated edition] (London: Weidenfeld and Nicolson, 1979), p. 549.

32. Thomas Rid, *War and Media Operations: The US Military and the Press from Vietnam to Iraq* (Abingdon: Taylor & Francis, 2007), p. 9

33. Peter Maass, 'The Toppling: How the Media Inflated a Minor Moment in a Long War', *The New Yorker* (10 January 2011); also Sean Aday, Sean Cluverius, and Ste-

ven Livingston, 'As Goes the Statue, So Goes the War: The Emergence of the Victory Frame in Television Coverage of the Iraq War', *Journal of Broadcasting and Electronic Media*, Vol. 49, No. 3 (2005), pp. 314–331.

34. Quoted in Greg Mitchell, *So Wrong for so Long: How the Press, The Pundits—and the President—Failed on Iraq* (London: Union Square Press, 2008), pp. 119–120.

35. Bernard Trainor quoted in Rid, *War and Media Operations*, p. 61.

36. James Gleick, *The Information, A Theory, A Flood* (London: Harper Collins, 2011), pp. 402–403.

37. Neville Bolt, 'The Leak Before the Storm: What Wikileaks Tells us About Modern Communication', *RUSI Journal*, Vol. 155, No. 4 (August/September 2010), p. 49.

38. General Sir David Richards, 'Future Conflict and Its Prevention: People and the Information Age', speech at the International Institute for Strategic Studies (18 January 2010).

39. Quoted in Thomas Ricks, *The Gamble: General Petraeus and the Untold Story of the American Surge in Iraq, 2006–2008* (London: Allen Lane, 2009), p. 250.

40. Quoted in David Betz, 'Communications Breakdown: Strategic Communications and Defeat in Afghanistan', *Orbis*, Vol. 55, No. 4 (Fall 2011), p. 619.

41. Philip Taylor, *Munitions of the Mind: A History of Propaganda from the Ancient World to the Present Day*, 3rd Edition (Manchester: Manchester University Press, 2003), p. 323.

42. Walter Lippmann, *Public Opinion* (Minnneapolis, MI: Filiquarian Publishing, 2007 [1972]), p. 288.

43. Nicholas O'Shaughnessy, *Politics and Propaganda: Weapons of Mass Seduction* (Manchester: Manchester University Press, 2004), chap. 3.

44. Lippmann, *Public Opinion*, p. 184.

45. Jacques Ellul (Konrad Kellen and John Lerner, trans), *Propaganda: The Formation of Men's Attitudes* (New York: Vintage Books, 1973), p. 11.

46. *Ibid.*, chap. 1 *passim*.

47. David Betz, 'The Virtual Dimension of Contemporary Insurgency and Counterinsurgency', *Small Wars and Insurgencies*, Vol. 19, No. 4 (December 2008), pp. 522–525.

48. Carsten Roennfeldt, 'Productive War: A Reconceptualistaion of War', *Journal of Strategic Studies*, Vol. 34, No. 1 (2011), pp. 39–62.

49. Andrew Marr, 'Digital Cameras have Dispelled the Fog of War', *Daily Telegraph* (12 May 2004).

8. WAR WITHOUT REASON: SOMETHING JUST SHORT OF WAR

1. From Robert Hedin (ed.), *The Zeppelin Reader: Stories, Poems, and Songs from the Age of the Airships* (Iowa City, IA: Iowa University Press, 1998), p. 36.

2. See Michael Clarke, 'The United Kingdom's Strategic Moment' and Geoffrey Till,

'British Strategy After Afghanistan', in Michael Codner and Michael Clarke (eds), *A Question of Security: The British Defence Review in an Age of Austerity* (London: I.B. Tauris for the Royal United Services Institute, 2011), pp. 7–19 & 131–51.

3. *A Strong Britain in an Age of Uncertainty: The National Security Strategy* (London: The Stationery Office, 2010), p. 3.

4. *United States National Security Strategy* (Washington, DC: The White House, 2010), p. 27.

5. *Ibid.*, p. 1.

6. *The Economist* (1 July 2010).

7. The catchline from the David Cronenburg (dir.) film, *The Fly* (1986).

8. Anna Mulrine, 'CIA Chief Leon Panetta: The Next Pearl Harbour Could be a Cyberattack', *Christian Science Monitor* (9 June 2011).

9. Qiao Liang and Wang Xiangsiu, *Unrestricted Warfare* (United States Foreign Broadcast Information Service English translation) (Beijing: PLA Literature and Arts Publishing House, February 1999), p. 129.

10. *Ibid.*, p. 117.

11. In business, a 'pure play' is a company that specialises in a single product or product type. For example, *Coca Cola*, which retails only beverages.

12. Tim Ross, 'Osborne promises no further cuts to soldier numbers—and more funding for cyber warfare', *Daily Telegraph* (23 June 2013).

13. 'Remarks by Deputy Secretary Carter at the Centre for a New American Security on Defence Priorities in an Era of Constrained Budgets' (Washington DC: 12 June 2013).

14. The clash of modernity has long been of interest in the arts and humanities, for instance. Robert Hughes' much regarded *The Shock of the New: The Hundred-Year History of Modern Art, Its Rise, Its Dazzling Achievement, Its Downfall*, 2nd Edition (New York: McGraw Hill, 1991), opens with a quote from the French scholar, Charles Peguy, writing in 1913 that 'the world has changed less since the time of Jesus Christ than it has in the last thirty years' (p. 9). Another reminder that we have been here before.

15. Canadian Broadcasting Corporation, 'Marshall McLuhan in Conversation with Norman Mailer', *The Way It Is*, broadcast 26 November 1967.

16. Charles Mackay, *Memoirs of Extraordinary Popular Delusions and the Madness of Crowds*, 2nd Edition (London: Robson, Levey, and Franklyn, 1852), p. 7.

17. See Walter B. Gallie, 'Essentially Contested Concepts', *Proceedings of the Aristotelian Society*, new series, Vol. 56 (1956), pp. 167–198. On the contestedness of cyberspace specifically, see David Betz and Tim Stevens, 'Analogical Reasoning and Cyber Security', *Security Dialogue*, Vol. 44, No. 2 (2013), pp. 147–164.

18. White House, *Cyberspace Policy Review: Assuring a Trusted and Resilient Information and Communications Infrastructure* (Washington, DC: United States Government Printing Office, 2009), p. iii.

19. Cabinet Office, *Cyber Security Strategy of the United Kingdom: Safety, Security, and Resilience in Cyberspace* (Norwich: The Stationery Office, 2009), p. 7.

20. Betz and Stevens, 'Analogical Reasoning', pp. 149–54.

21. Ron Deibert, 'The Growing Dark Side of Cyberspace (...and What to do About It), *Penn State Journal of Law and International Affairs*, Vol. 1, No. 2 (November 2012), p. 271.

22. William Gibson, interviewed in the documentary film Mark Neale (dir.), *No Maps for these Territories* (Mark Neale Productions, 2000).

23. Bruce Sterling, *The Hacker Crackdown* (New York: Bantam, 1994), p. 10.

24. Martin Libicki, *Conquest in Cyberspace: National Security and Information Warfare*, (New York: Cambridge University Press, 2007), pp. 236–240; also by the same author, *Cyberdeterrence and Cyberwar* (Santa Monica, CA: RAND Corporation, 2009), pp. 12–13.

25. Betz and Stevens, 'Analogical Reasoning', p. 149. 'Fly, fight, and win... in air, space, and cyberspace' is the tagline of the United States Air Force's *Air and Space Power Journal*.

26. Dale Hayden, 'Air Mindedness', *Air and Space Power Journal*, Vol. 22, No. 4 (2008), p. 44.

27. BBC, *The Virtual Revolution*, Episode 2 'The Enemy of the State?', aired on BBC 2 (6 February 2010).

28. Ivan S. Bloch (W.T. Stead, trans.), *Modern Weapons and Modern War* (London: Grant Richards, 1900), p. xxiv.

29. *Ibid.*, p. 337.

30. Jonathan House, *Combined Arms Warfare in the Twentieth Century* (Lawrence, KS: Kansas University Press, 2001).

31. Gerald Gilbert, *The Evolution of Tactics* (London: Hugh Rees, 1907), pp. 183–4.

32. J.F.C. Fuller, *Armament and History: A Study of the Influence of Armament on History from the Dawn of Classical Warfare to the Second World War* (New York: Da Capo Press, 1998 [1945]), p. 31.

33. The best assessment of Fuller is to be found in Brian Holden Reid's *J.F.C. Fuller: Military Thinker* (New York: St. Martin's Press, 1987). Colin Gray spiritedly disputes this particular passage of Fuller's in *Perspectives on Strategy* (Oxford: Oxford University Press, 2013), pp. 153–4.

34. Brian Holden Reid, *Studies in British Military Thought: Debates with Fuller and Liddell-Hart* (Lincoln, NB: Nebraska University Press, 1998), p. 16.

35. J.F.C. Fuller, *The Reformation of War* (London: Hutchinson, 1923), p. 148.

36. Basil Liddell-Hart, *Paris, Or the Future of War* (London: Faber and Faber, 1925), pp. 42–3. This passage appears to be heavily cribbed from a similar one in Fuller's *Reformation of War*: 'picture, if you can, what the result [of a mass aerial bombardment] will be: London for several days will be one vast raving Bedlam... the enemy will dictate his terms, which will be grasped at like a straw by a drowning man.

Thus may a war be fought in forty-eight hours and the losses of the winning side may be actually nil!' (p. 150).

37. Liddell-Hart, *Paris*, pp. 46–7.

38. See Brian Bond, *Liddell-Hart: A Study of his Military Thought* (London: Cassell, 1977), pp. 54–7.

39. Stanley Baldwin MP, House of Commons Debate, Hansard, Vol. 270 (10 November 1932), cols, 632–8.

40. See Tami Davis-Biddle, 'British and American Approaches to Strategic Bombing: Their Origins and Implementation in the World War II Combined Bomber Offensive', in John Gooch (ed.), *Airpower: Theory and Practice* (London: Frank Cass, 1995), pp. 121–2. Overall, in four raids over six days 148 Flying Fortress bombers were lost while German fighter strength actually increased.

41. Quoted in Davis-Biddle, 'British and American Approaches', p. 92.

42. *Ibid.*, p. 104.

43. Winston Churchill MP, House of Commons Debate, *Hansard* (13 May 1940), col. 1502.

44. Baldwin, *ibid.*, col. 633.

45. *The UK Cyber Security Strategy: Protecting and Promoting the UK in a Digital World* (London: Cabinet Office, November 2011), p. 7.

46. Jim Garamone, 'Lynn Calls for Collaboration in Establishing Cyber security', *Armed Forces Press Service* (1 October 2009).

47. Baldwin, House of Commons Debate, *Hansard* (13 May 1940), col. 637.

48. Michael Sherry, *The Rise of American Air Power* (New Haven, CT: Yale University Press, 1987), p. 41.

49. William Hague MP, Chair's Statement, London Conference on Cyberspace (2 November 2011).

50. Not to mention the imaginations of science fiction writers. George Orwell's dystopian 1949 novel *Nineteen Eighty-Four*, republished in *The Complete Novels of George Orwell* (London: Penguin, 2009), and Aldous Huxley's *Brave New World* (London: Chatto and Windus, 1932), were frequently invoked in the press after the PRISM revelations. See, for example, Jennifer Daley-Nicholson, 'Do we Live in George Orwell's 1984, Aldous Huxley's Brave New World—or 2013?', *News Limited Network* (12 June 2013).

51. Quoted in Sherry, *Rise of American Air Power*, p. 30.

52. Eliot Cohen, 'The Mystique of US Air Power', *Foreign Affairs*, Vol. 73, No. 1 (January/February 1994), p. 109.

53. See Sun Tzu (Samuel B. Griffin, trans.), *The Art of War* (Oxford: Clarendon, 1963), p. 84. Readers of Sun Tzu may note that the relevant passage is translated variously (I make no claim to have the linguistic ability to judge the meaning in the original) by others. One translates it as, 'In all fighting, the direct method may be used for joining battle, but indirect methods will be needed in order to secure vic-

tory', Lionel Giles (trans.), in T.R. Philips (ed.), *Roots of Strategy* (Mechanicsburg, PA: Stackpole Books, 1985), p. 31. Another says, 'In battle, confrontation is done directly, victory is gained by surprise', Thomas Cleary, in *Classics of Strategy and Counsel*, Vol. 1 (Boston, MA: Shambhala Publications, 2001), p. 99.

54. Robert Leonhard, *The Principles of War for the Information Age* (Novato, CA: Presidio, Press, 1998), p. 73.

55. James Bamford, 'The Secret War', *Wired* (12 June 2013).

56. Basil-Liddell Hart, *Thoughts on War* (London: Faber and Faber, 1944), p. 20.

57. Glenn Fleishman, 'Cartoon Captures Spirit of the Internet', *New York Times* (14 December 2000).

58. For a wider discussion on the 'attribution problem' see Thomas Rid, *Cyber War Will Not Take Place* (London: Hurst, 2013), chap. 7.

59. Carl Von Clausewitz (Michael Howard and Peter Paret, trans and eds), *On War* (New York: Alfred A. Knopf, Everyman's Library, 1993), p. 83.

60. See John Stone, 'Cyberwar Will Take Place!', *Journal of Strategic Studies*, Vol. 36, No. 1 (2013), pp. 101–18.

61. After the Zen kōan of Hakuin Ekaku, 'You know the sound of two hands clapping. What is the sound of one hand?'

62. Benjamin Lambeth, 'Airpower, Spacepower, and Cyberpower', *Joint Force Quarterly*, Iss. 60, 1st Quarter (2011), p. 51.

63. James Gavin, *War and Peace in the Space Age* (London: Hutchinson, 1959), p. 236.

64. Basil Liddell-Hart (ed.), *The Rommel Papers* (New York: Harcourt Brace, 1953), pp. 284–286.

65. *Ibid.*, p. 476.

66. Thomas Rid and Peter McBurney, 'Cyber Weapons', *RUSI Journal*, Vol. 157, No. 1 (February/March 2012), pp. 6–13.

67. David Fulgham, David Wall and Amy Butler, 'Cyber Combat's First Shot', *Aviation Week and Space Technology*, Vol. 167, No. 21 (26 November 2007), p. 28.

68. Alfred Price, *The History of US Electronic Warfare*, First Edition (Arlington, VA: Association of Old Crows, 1984), pp. 1–2.

69. Alex Butterworth, *The World That Never Was: A True Story of Dreamers, Schemers, Anarchists, and Secret Agents* (New York: Vintage Books, 2010), p. 18.

70. Nicholas Rankin, *Churchill's Wizards: The British Genius for Deception, 1914–1945* (London: Faber and Faber, 2008), p. xiii.

71. See Don Gordon, *Electronic Warfare: Element of Strategy and Multiplier of Combat Power* (New York: Pergamon Press, 1981), p. 67.

72. John Arquila and David Ronfeldt, 'Cyberwar is Coming!', in Arquila and Ronfeldt (eds.), *In Athena's Camp: Preparing for Conflict in the Information Age* (Santa Monica, CA: RAND, 1997), p. 23.

73. This is a key theme in Eliot Cohen and John Gooch's *Military Misfortunes: The Anatomy of Failure in War* (New York: The Free Press, 1990).

74. James Adams, *The Next World War: Computers are the Weapons and the Frontline is Everywhere* (New York: Simon and Schuster, 1998), pp. 30 & 58.

75. Oddly, Adams paints Clausewitz and Liddell-Hart as like-minded confreres and does not recognise the connection between his own ideals and those of the latter, and their distinctness from those of Clausewitz. See *ibid.*, p. 120.

76. *Ibid.*, p. 16.

77. 'The Company that Spooked the World', *The Economist* (4 August 2012).

78. Clausewitz, *On War*, p. 111.

79. Rid, *Cyber War*, p. 1.

80. As discussed by Stone, 'Cyberwar is Coming', and David Betz and Tim Stevens, *Cyberspace and the State* (London: Routledge for The International Institute for Strategic Studies, 2011), p. 94.

81. Thomas Schelling, *Arms and Influence* (New Haven, CT: Yale University Press, 1966), p. 2.

82. Richard A. Clarke, *Cyber War: The Next Threat to National Security and What to do About It* (New York: Harper Collins, 2010), p. 149.

83. *Ibid.*, p. 68.

84. Clausewitz, *On War*, p. 101.

85. Martin Libicki, 'Sub Rosa Cyberwar', in C. Czossek and Kenneth Geers (eds), *The Virtual Battlefield: Perspectives on Cyber Warfare* (Amsterdam, NL: IOS Press, 2009), p. 58; see also Libicki, 'The Spectre of Non-Obvious Warfare', *Strategic Studies Quarterly*, Vol. 6, No. 3 (Fall 2012), pp. 88–101.

86. Liang and Xiangsiu, *Unrestricted Warfare*, pp. 212–16.

87. David Sanger, *Confront and Conceal: Obama's Secret Wars and Surprising Use of American Power* (New York: Crown Publishers, 2012), p. 244

88. *Ibid.*, p. 90.

89. See Ian Buruma and Avishai Margalit, *Occidentalism: A Short History of Anti-Westernism* (London: Atlantic Books, 2004).

90. Michael Axworthy, *Empire of the Mind: A History of Iran* (London: Hurst, 2007), pp. 288–9.

91. Quoted in Sanger, *Confront and Conceal*, p. 227.

92. Yaakov Katz, 'Stuxnet Virus Set Back Iran's Program By Two Years', *Jerusalem Post* (15 December 2010).

93. Ivanka Barzbka, 'Are Cyber-Weapons Effective?', *RUSI Journal*, Vol. 158, No. 2 (2013), p. 54.

94. On the early years of air warfare, see: Lee Kennett, *The First Air War, 1914–1918* (New York: The Free Press, 1991); Edward Fischer, *The Development of Military Night Aviation to 1919* (Maxwell Air Force Base, AL: Air University Press, 1998); and, John Morrow, *The Great War in the Air: Military Aviation from 1909 to 1921* (Washington, DC: Smithsonian Institution Press, 1993).

95. In Rick Archbold, *Hindenburg: An Illustrated History* (London: weidenfeld and Nicolson, 1994), p. 40.

96. In chap. 8, 'Information Systems Security', in Joint Security Commission, *Redefining Security* (Washington, DC: 28 February 1994).

9. THE NEW AGE OF ANXIETY

1. Interviewed in Fred Freed and Len Giovannitti, *The Decision to Drop the Bomb* (NBC News with Encycloapedia Britannica Films, 1965).
2. Quoted in Joshua Davis, 'Hackers Take Down the Most Connected Country in Europe', *Wired* (21 August 2007).
3. See J.R. Beniger, *The Control Revolution: Technological and Economic Origins of the Information Society* (Cambridge, MA: Harvard University Press, 1986); also, Krishan Kumar, *From Post-Industrial to Post-Modern Society: New Theories of the Contemporary World* (Oxford: Blackwell, 1995), pp. 15–22.
4. John Perry Barlow, *Declaration of the Independence of Cyberspace* (Davos, Switzerland: 8 February 1996).
5. John Perry Barlow, lecture to the European Graduate School (Saas-Fee, Switzerland: 29 May 2006).
6. David Betz and Tim Stevens, *Cyberspace and the State: Towards a Strategy for Cyberpower* (London: Routledge for the International Institute for Strategic Studies, 2011), pp. 138–9.
7. Fred Turner; *From Counterculture to Cyberculture: Stewart Brand, the Whole Earth Network, and the Rise of Digital Utopianism* (London: Chicago University Press, 2006), p. 240.
8. Jaron Lanier, *You Are Not a Gadget* (London: Penguin, 2010), p. 64.
9. There has been a flood of texts on this issue recently, mostly concerned with the ills of the economic system. See Richard Duncan, *The New Depression: The Breakdown of the Paper Economy* (Chichester: John Wiley and Sons, 2012) and David Stockman, *The Great Deformation: The Corruption of Capitalism in America* (New York: Public Affairs, 2013). More generally, Slavoj Žižek, *Living in the End Times* (London: Verso, 2010).
10. John Kenneth Galbraith, *The Age of Uncertainty: A History of Economic Ideas and their Consequences* (London: Houghton Mifflin, 1977).
11. Joshua Cooper Ramo, *The Age of the Unthinkable: Why the New World Disorder Constantly Surprises Us and What We Can Do About It* (London: Little Brown, 2009), p. 171.
12. Philip Bobbitt, *The Shield of Achilles: War, Peace, and the Course of History* (London: Penguin, 2008), p. 806.
13. *Ibid.*, p. 797.
14. Bruce Sterling, *The Hacker Crackdown* (New York: Bantam, 1994), p. 19.
15. Steven Levy, *Hackers: Heroes of the Revolution* (New York: Dell, 1984), p. 1.
16. George Orwell, 'You and the Atom Bomb', *Tribune* (19 October 1945).

17. United States Department of Defence, *Quadrennial Defence Review Report* (Washington, DC: February 2010), p. 8.

18. United States Department of Defence, *National Defence Strategy* (Washington, DC: 2008), p. 16.

19. Walter Russell Mead, *God and Gold: Britain, America, and the Making of the Modern World* (London: Atlantic Books, 2007), p. 173.

20. Tim Berners-Lee quoted in H. Peter Alesso and George Smith, *Patterns of Discovery* (Hoboken, NJ: John Wiley and Sons, 2008), p. 122.

21. *A Strong Britain in an Age of Uncertainty: The National Security Strategy* (London: The Stationery Office, 2010), p. 21.

22. Susan Buck, *The Global Commons: An Introduction* (Washington, DC: Island Press, 1998), pp. 5–6.

23. See Patrick Franzese, 'Sovereignty in Cyberspace: Can it Exist?, *Air Force Law Review*, Vol. 64 (2009), pp. 14–17.

24. Martin Libicki, *Conquest in Cyberspace: National Security and Information Warfare* (New York: Cambridge University Press, 2007), p. 6.

25. Clay Shirky, *Cognitive Surplus: Creativity and Generosity in a Connected Age* (London: Allen Lane, 2010), p. 37. See also Julie Cohen's highly regarded legal analysis in which she writes: 'Cyberspace is in and of the real world, and is so not (only) because real-space sovereigns decree it, or (only) because real-space sovereigns can exert power over real-space users, but also and more fundamentally because cyberspace users are situated in real-space. Cyberspace is not, and never could be the Kingdom of the Mind; minds are attached to bodies, and bodies exist in the space of the world.' Cohen, 'Cyberspace as/and Space', *Columbia Law Review*, Vol. 107 (2007), pp. 217–18.

26. John Arquila and David Ronfeldt, 'The Advent of War' in Arquila and Ronfeldt (eds), *In Athena's Camp: Preparing for Conflict in the Information Age* (Santa Monica, CA: RAND, 1997), p. 275.

27. *Quadrennial Defence Review*, p. 37.

28. *FM 3–24 Counterinsurgency* (Washington, DC: Headquarters, Department of the Army, December 2006), pp. 1–3.

29. See Neville Bolt and David Betz, *Propaganda of the Deed 2008: Understanding the Phenomenon*, Whitehall Paper (London: Royal United Services Institute, 2008).

30. Andrew Hoskins and Ben O'Loughlin, *Television and Terror* (Houndmills, Basingstoke: Palgrave Macmillan, 2009), p. 13.

31. Paul Virilio, *War and Cinema: The Logistics of Perception* (London: Verso, 1989), p. 7.

32. For discussion of this see Julian Reid, 'Foucault on Clausewitz: Conceptualising the Relationship of War and Power', *Alternatives: Global, Local, Political*, Vol. 28, No. 1 (January/February 2003), pp. 18–21.

33. General Sir David Richards, 'Future Conflict and Its Prevention: People and the Information Age', speech at the International Institute for Strategic Studies (London: 18 January 2010).

34. Denise Schmandt-Besserat, *Before Writing* (Austin, TX: University of Texas Press, 1998), pp. 158–161.

35. *Ibid*, p. 192.

36. Francis Fukuyama, *The Origins of Political Order: From Prehuman Times to the French Revolution* (London: Profile Books, 2011).

37. Carl Kaestle, 'The History of Literacy and the History of Readers', *Review of Research in Education*, Vol. 12 (1985), p. 19.

38. Asa Briggs and Peter Burke, *A Social History of the Media: From Gutenberg to the Internet* (Cambridge: Polity, 2010), p. 70.

39. Jurgen Habermas, *The Structural Transformation of the Public Sphere* (Cambridge, MA: MIT Press, 1991 [1962]).

40. The clip may be heard on the website of the United States National Park Service with an accompanying essay by Stephan Puille, 'Prince Bismarck and Count Moltke Before the Recording Horn: The Edison Phonograph in Europe, 1889–1890' (30 January 2012).

41. This idea is addressed in depth by Albert Borgmann in *Holding onto Reality: The Nature of Information at the Turn of the Millennium* (Chicago, IL: University of Chicago Press, 1999).

42. *A Strong Britain in an Age of Uncertainty*, p. 16.

43. Marshall McLuhan, *Understanding Media: The Extensions of Man* (Abingdon: Routledge, 2011 [1964]), p. 370.

44. Manuel Castells, *The Internet Galaxy: Reflections on the Internet, Business, and Society* (Oxford: Oxford University Press, 2001), p. 138.

45. See, respectively, *Theodore Roszak, The Cult of Information: The Folklore of Computers and the True Art of Thinking* (Cambridge: Lutterworth Press, 1986), Tim Jordan and Paul Taylor, *Hacktivism and Cyberwars: Rebels with a Cause?* (Abingdon: Routledge, 2004), and Manuel Castells, *Networks of Outrage and Hope: Social Movements in the Internet Age* (Cambridge: Polity, 2012).

46. Heather Brooke, *The Revolution will be Digitised: Dispatches from the Information War* (London: Windmill Books, 2012), p. ix.

47. Clay Shirky, 'The Political Power of Social Media', *Foreign Affairs*, Vol. 90, No. 1 (January/February 2011).

48. Evgeny Morozov, *The Net Delusion: How not to Liberate the World* (London: Allen lane, 2011).

49. Manuel Castells, *Communication Power* (Oxford: Oxford University Press, 2009), p. 302.

50. Carne Ross, *The Leaderless Revolution: How Ordinary People will Take Power and Change Politics in the Twenty First Century* (London: Simon and Schuster, 2011), p. 17.

51. Quoted in Brooke, *The Revolution will be Digitised*, p. 228.

52. Mark Duffield, 'War as a Network Enterprise: The New Security Terrain and its Implications', *Cultural Values*, Vol. 6, Nos 1 & 2 (2002), p. 158.

53. Marc Sageman, *Leaderless Jihad* (Philadelphia: University of Pennsylvania Press, 2008).

54. Quoted in Sean Parson, 'Understanding the Ideology of the Earth Liberation Front', *Green Theory & Praxis: The Journal of Ecopedagogy*, Vol. 4, No. 2 (2008).

55. Howard Rheingold, *Smart Mobs: The Next Social Revolution* (Cambridge, MA: Basic Books, 2002), pp. 160–2.

56. Notes from Nowhere (eds), *We are Everywhere: The Irresistible Rise of Global Anti-Capitalism* (London: Verso, 2003), p. 16.

57. From the Occupy Wall St webpage: http://occupywallst.org/ (last accessed 17 April 2015).

58. Chris Demchak, *Wars of Disruption and Resilience: Cybered Conflict, Power and National Security* (Athens, GA: University of Georgia Press, 2011), p. 289.

59. Will Potter, *Green is the New Red: An Insider's Account of a Social Movement Under Siege* (San Francisco, CA: City Lights Books, 2011), p. 250.

60. Nelson Mandela (20 April 1964), may be found on *The History Place, Great Speeches Collection*, http://www.historyplace.com/speeches/mandela.htm

61. Joseph Stiglitz, 'Introduction', in Anna Schifrin and Eamon Kircher-Allen (eds), *From Cairo to Wall Street* (New York: Perseus, 2012), p. 20.

62. *Ibid.* (emphasis in original), p. 20.

63. Starhawk, *Webs of Power: Notes from the Global Uprising* (Gabriola Island, British Columbia: New Catlyst Books, 2008), p. 60; for a different vision of this prospect which imagines such a mercenary force going from strength to strength see the near-future science fiction novel by Adam Roberts, *New Model Army* (London: Orion, 2010).

64. It is not clear whether Davison intended to kill herself or was attempting instead to pin a banner to the speeding horse. At any rate, she was a committed activist. See Vanessa Thorpe, 'Truth Behind the Death of Suffragette Emily Davison is Finally Revealed', *Observer* (26 May 2013).

65. 'A Memorable Derby', *The Times* (5 June 1913), p. 9.

66. Starhawk, *Webs of Power*, p. 150.

67. See UBS Investment Research, Global Economic Perspectives, 'Euro break-up: The Consequences' (6 September 2011).

68. The concept of force as 'bargaining power' is from Thomas C. Schelling, *Arms and Influence* (New Haven, CT: Yale University Press, 1966).

69. For an account of the attack see Sue Dreyfuss and Julian Assange, *Underground: Hacking, Madness, and Obsession on the Electronic Frontier* (Kew, Australia: Reed Books), chap. 1.

70. See Thomas Rid, *Cyber War Will not Take Place* (London: Hurst, 2013), chap. 4.

71. Bruce Sterling interview on Blast Shack about Wikileaks (22 December 2010).

72. For an overview, see Quinn Norton 'Anonymous 101: Introduction to the Lulz', *Wired* (8 November 2011).

73. From the *Encyclopedia Dramatica* entry on Anonymous, https://encyclopediadramatica.se/Anonymous/Original (last accessed 17 April 2015).

CONCLUSION

1. Micah Sifry, *Wikileaks and the Age of Transparency* (New Haven, CT: Yale University Press, 2011).

2. On which point, see John Robb, *Brave New War: The Next Stage of Terrorism and the End of Globalisation* (London: Wiley, 2007).

3. Arjun Appadurai, 'Disjuncture and Difference in the Global Cultural Economy', *Theory, Culture and Society*, Vol. 7, No. 2 (1990), pp. 295–310.

4. 'The Origins of the Financial Crisis', *The Economist* (7 September 2013).

5. Demise Roland, 'Ebola crisis 'unlikely to be under control within a year', says pharma boss', *The Telegraph* (22 October 2014).

6. From the Occupy Wall St webpage: http://occupywallst.org/ (last accessed 17 April 2015).

7. Ulrike Meinhof, 'From Protest to Resistance' (1968), reprinted in Karin Bauer (ed.), *Everybody Talks About the Weather, We Don't: The Writings of Ulrike Meinhof* (New York: Seven Stories Press, 2008), p. 239.

8. Stefan Aust, *The Baader Meinhof Complex* (London: The Bodley Head, 2008), p. 433. The last Red Army Faction continued to operate sporadically until the 1990s.

9. See C.J. Chivers, *The Gun: The Story of the AK 47* (London: Penguin, 2011).

10. Napoleon was nearly killed in the Rue Saint Nicaise in Paris by a cart bomb in 1800, while until recent years one of the most deadly terror attacks in American history was the exploding on Wall Street in Manhattan of a horse-drawn cart packed with dynamite and iron scraps that killed thirty-eight (April 2015)...external separation people and wounded nearly 150 others. See, Mike Davis, *Buda's Wagon: A Brief History of the Car Bomb* (New York: Verso Books, 2008), p. 5.

11. See Frank Hoffman, 'Lessons from Lebanon: Hezbollah and Hybrid Wars', *Foreign Policy Research Institute e-Note* (24 August 2006); also David E. Johnson, *Hard Fighting: Israel in Lebanon and Gaza* (Santa Monica, CA: RAND, 2011).

12. Chinua Achebe, *Things Fall Apart* (New York: Anchor Books, 1994 [1954]).

13. 'Woolwich Attack: The Terrorist's Rant', *Daily Telegraph* (23 May 2013).

14. Manuel Castells, *Communication Power* (Oxford: Oxford University Press, 2009), p. 23.

15. John Mackinlay, *The Insurgent Archipelago* (London: Hurst, 2009).

16. Audrey Kurth Cronin, *Ending Terrorism* (Abingdon: Routledge for the International Institute for Strategic Studies, 2008), p. 53.

17. Greg Miller, 'US Officials Believe Al Qaeda on Brink of Collapse', *Washington Post* (27 July 2011).

18. Matthew Carr, *Fortress Europe: Dispatches from a Gated Continent* (London: Hurst, 2012), p. 3.

19. Jeremy Harding, *Border Vigils: Keeping Migrants out of the Rich World* (London: Verso, 2012), p. 3.

20. Marshall McLuhan, *Understanding Media: The Extensions of Man* (London: Routledge, 2001 [1964]), p. 376.

21. Hannah Arendt, 'Karl Jaspers: Citizen of the World' (1958) republished in *Men in Dark Times* (New York: Harcourt Brace and World, 1968), p. 83.

22. Matthew Reinbold, 'Superempowerment, Networked Tribes and the End to Business as We Know It' Ignite 4, Salt Lake City (4 March 2010).

23. Anders Breivik, *A European Declaration of Independence* (London, 2011), p. 1159.

BIBLIOGRAPHY

Books

Adams, James, *The Next World War: Computers are the Weapons and the Frontline is Everywhere*, New York: Simon and Schuster, 1998.

Adams, Thomas, *The Army After Next: The First Postindustrial Army*, Stanford, CA: Stanford University Press, 2008.

Adamsky, Dina, *The Culture of Military Innovation: The Impact of Cultural Factors on the Revolution in Military Affairs in Russia, the US, and Israel*, Stanford, CA: Stanford University Press, 2010.

Addington, Larry, *The Patterns of War Through the Eighteenth Century*, Bloomington, IN: Indiana University Press, 1990.

——— *The Patterns of War Since the Eighteenth Century*, Bloomington, IN: Indiana University Press, 1994.

Ajami, Fouad, *The Foreigner's Gift: The Americans, the Arabs, and the Iraqis in Iraq*, New York: Simon and Schuster, 2006.

Alberts, David, John Garstka, Richard Hayes and David Signori, *Understanding Information Age Warfare*, Washington, DC: Command and Control Research Program, Department of Defense, 2001.

Alberts, David, John Garstka and Frederick Stein, *Network Centric Warfare: Developing and Leveraging Information Superiority*, Washington, DC: Department of Defense, Command and Control Research Programme, 2003.

Albright, Madeleine, *Madam Secretary: A Memoir*, New York: Harper Collins, 2003.

Angell, Norman, *The Great Illusion*, London: William Heinemann, 1909.

Anonymous [Michael Scheuer], *Imperial Hubris: Why the West is Losing the War on Terror*, Washington, DC: Brassey's, 2004.

Archbold, Rick, *Hindenburg: An Illustrated History*, London: Weidenfeld and Nicolson, 1994.

Ariely, Dan, *Predictably Irrational: The Hidden Forces that Shape Our Decisions*, New York: HarperCollins, 2008.

Arreguin-Toft, Ivan, *How the Weak Win Wars: A Theory of Asymmetric Conflict*, Cambridge: Cambridge University Press, 2005.

Auden, W.H., *Another Time*, London: Random House, 1940.

Axworthy, Michael, *Empire of the Mind: A History of Iran*, London: Hurst, 2007

Bacevich, Andrew, *American Empire: The Realities and Consequences of US Diplomacy*, Cambridge, MA: Harvard University Press, 2002.

——— *The New American Militarism: How Americans are Seduced by War*, Oxford: Oxford University Press, 2005.

Baddeley, J.F., *The Russian Conquest of the Caucasus*, London: Longmans, Green & Company, 1908.

Badsey, Stephen, Rob Havers and Mark Grove (eds), *The Falklands Conflict Twenty Years On: Lessons for the Future*, London: Frank Cass, 2007.

Baker, James, III and Lee Hamilton, *The Iraq Study Group Report: The Way Forward— A New Approach*, Washington, DC: United States Institute of Peace, 2006.

Barnett, Thomas, *The Pentagon's New Map: War and Peace in the Twenty-First Century*, New York: Berkley Books, 2004.

Baudrillard, Jean, *The Gulf War Did Not Take Place*, trans. Paul Patton, Bloomington, IN: Indiana University Press, 1995.

Beaverbrook, Lord [Max Aitken], *The Divine Propagandist*, London: Heinemann, 1962.

Bell, Daniel, *The Coming of Post-Industrial Society*, New York: Harper Colophon, 1974.

Bellamy, Christopher, *Knights in White Armour: The New Art of War and Peace*, London: Hutchinson, 1996.

Berdal, Mats and David Malone (eds), *Greed and Grievance: Economic Agendas in Civil Wars*, London: Lynne Reinner, 2000.

Bergen, Peter, *The Osama Bin Laden I Knew: An Oral History of Al Qaeda's Leader*, New York: Simon and Schuster, 2006.

Betz, David, *Civil-Military Relations in Russia and Eastern Europe*, London: Routledge, 2004.

Betz, David and Tim Stevens, *Cyberspace and the State*, London: Routledge for the International Institute for Strategic Studies, 2011.

Bickerton, Ian, *The Arab-Israeli Conflict, A History*, London: Reaktion Books, 2009.

Biddle, Stephen, *Afghanistan and the Future of Warfare*, Carlisle, PA: US Army War College, Strategic Studies Institute, 2002.

——— *Military Power: Explaining Victory and Defeat in Modern Battle*, Princeton, NJ: Princeton University Press, 2004.

Bird, Tim and Alex Marshall, *Afghanistan: How the West Lost Its Way*, London: Yale University Press, 2011.

Black, Jeremy, *War and the New Disorder in the Twenty-First Century*, New York: Continuum, 2004.

Blanning, Tim, *The Pursuit of Glory: The Five Revolutions That Made Modern Europe, 1646–1815*, London: Penguin, 2007.

Bloch, Ivan, *Modern Weapons and Modern War*, trans. W.T. Stead, London: Grant Richards, 1900.

Bobbitt, Philip, *The Shield of Achilles: War, Peace, and the Course of History*, New York: Alfred A. Knopf, 2002.

Bodansky, Yossef, *The Secret History of the Iraq War*, New York: Regan Books, 2004.

Bolt, Neville, *The Violent Image: Insurgent Propaganda and the New Revolutionaries*, London: Hurst, 2012.

Bond, Brian, *Liddell-Hart: A Study of His Military Thought*, London: Cassell, 1977.

Bonn, Keith and Anthony Baker, *Guide to Military Operations Other Than War: Tactics, Techniques, and Procedures for Stability and Support Operations, Domestic and International*, Mechanicsburg, PA: Stackpole Books, 2000.

Boot, Max, *Invisible Armies: An Epic History of Guerrilla Warfare from Ancient Times to the Present*, New York: Liveright, 2013.

Bowden, Mark, *Black Hawk Down*, London: Bantam, 1999.

Bracken, Paul, *Fire in the East: The Rise of Asian Military Power and the Second Nuclear Age*, New York: HarperCollins, 1999.

Bregman, Ahron, *Israel's Wars: A History Since 1947*, London: Routledge, 2000.

Brzezinski, Zbigniew, *Between Two Ages: America's Role in the Technotronic Era*, New York: Viking, 1970.

Burbank, Jane and Frederick Cooper, *Empires in World History: Power and the Politics of Difference*, Princeton, NJ: Princeton University Press, 2010.

Buruma, Ian and Avishai Margalit, *Occidentalism: A Short History of Anti-Westernism*, London: Atlantic Books, 2004.

Butterworth, Alex, *The World That Never Was: A True Story of Dreamers, Schemers, Anarchists, and Secret Agents*, New York: Vintage Books, 2010.

Callwell, C.E., *Small Wars: Their Principles and Practice*, 3rd. edn., Abingdon: Purnell Book Services, 1976 [1906].

——— *Small Wars*, Lincoln, NE: University of Nebraska Press, 1996 [1906].

Cantwell, John, *Exit Wounds: One Australian's War on Terror*, Melbourne: Melbourne University Press, 2012.

Carlyle, Thomas, *On Heroes, Hero Worship and the Heroic in History*, London: Chapman and Hall, 1840.

Carr, Matthew, *Fortress Europe: Dispatches from a Gated Continent*, London: Hurst, 2012.

Castells, Manuel, *Communication Power*, Oxford: Oxford University Press, 2009.

——— *The Rise of the Network Society, The Information Age: Economy, Society, and Culture*, vol. 1, 2nd. edn., London: Wiley-Blackwell, 2010.

——— *The Information Age: Economy, Society, and Culture*, 3 vols. 2nd. edn., London: Wiley-Blackwell, 2010.

Castles, Stephen and Mark Miller, *The Age of Migration: International Population Movements in the Modern World*, 4th. edn., New York: Palgrave, 2009.

Cerasini, Marc, *The Future of War: The Face of Twenty-First Century Warfare*, Indianapolis, IN: Alpha Books, 2003.

Cerny, Philip, *Rethinking World Politics: A Theory of Transnational Neopluralism*, Oxford: Oxford University Press, 2010.

Chandrasekaran, Rajiv, *Imperial Life in the Emerald City: Inside Baghdad's Green Zone*, London: Bloomsbury, 2006.

Clark, Wesley, *Waging Modern War*, New York: PublicAffairs, 2001.

Clarke, Richard and Robert Knake, *Cyber War: The Next Threat to National Security and What to Do About It*, New York: Ecco, 2010.

Clausewitz, Carl von, *On War* (eds Michael Howard, Peter Paret), New York: Alfred Knopf, 1993.

Cohen, Eliot and John Gooch, *Military Misfortunes: The Anatomy of Failure in War*, New York: The Free Press, 1990.

Coker, Christopher, *Waging War without Warriors*, London: Lynne Reinner Publishers, 2002.

—— *War in an Age of Risk*, Cambridge: Polity, 2009.

Collins, Deirdre and Rafal Rohozinski, *Shifting Fire: Information Effects in Counterinsurgency and Stabilization Operations—A Workshop Report*, Carlisle, PA: US Army War College, 2006.

Cooper, Robert, *The Breaking of Nations: Order and Chaos in the Twenty-First Century*, New York: Grove Press, 2004.

—— *The Breaking of Nations: Order and Chaos in the Twenty-First Century*, 2nd. edn., London: Atlantic Books, 2007.

Cordesman, Anthony, *The Lessons of Afghanistan: War Fighting, Intelligence, and Force Transformation*, Washington, DC: Center for Strategic and International Studies, 2002.

Corvisier, Andre, *Armies and Societies in Europe, 1494–1789*, Bloomington, IN: Indiana University Press, 1979.

David, Saul, *Victoria's Wars*, London: Penguin, 2007.

Deng, Francis, Sadikiel Kimaro, Terrence Lyons, Donald Rothchild and I. William Zartman, *Sovereignty as Responsibility: Conflict Management in Africa*, Washington, DC: Brookings Institution, 1996.

Der Derian, James, *Virtuous War: Mapping the Military-Industrial-Media-Entertainment Network*, Boulder, CO: Westview Press, 2001.

Devji, Faisal, *The Terrorist in Search of Humanity: Militant Islam and Global Politics*, London: Hurst, 2009.

Drucker, Peter, *The Age of Discontinuity*, London: HarperCollins, 1969.

Echevarria, Antulio, *Globalization and the Nature of War*, Carlisle, PA: Strategic Studies Institute, US Army War College, 2003.

Ellul, Jacques, *Propaganda: The Formation of Men's Attitudes*, trans. Konrad Kellen and John Lerner, New York: Vintage Books, 1973.

Emmott, Bill, *Rivals: How the Power Struggle Between China, India and Japan Will Shape Our Next Decade*, London: Allen Lane, 2008.

Engels, Friedrich, *Revolution and Counter-Revolution in Germany*, 1852.

English, Richard, *Irish Freedom: The History of Nationalism in Ireland*, London: Macmillan, 2006.

Fischer, Edward, *The Development of Military Night Aviation to 1919*, Maxwell Air Force Base, AL: Air University Press, 1998.

Fisher, David, *Morality and War*, Oxford: Oxford University Press, 2011.

Franks, Tommy, *American Soldier*, New York: Regan Books, 2004.

Freedman, Lawrence, *The Evolution of Nuclear Strategy*, London: St. Martin's Press, 1989.

――― *The Politics of British Defence, 1979–1988*, Houndmills, Basingstoke: Macmillan, 1999.

――― *Official History of the Falklands Campaign: Vol. II, War and Diplomacy*, Abingdon: Routledge, 2005.

――― *Transformation of Strategic Affairs*, Adelphi 318, London: International Institute for Strategic Studies, 2006.

――― *A Choice of Enemies: America Confronts the Middle East*, New York: PublicAffairs, 2008.

Freedman, Lawrence and Efraim Karsh, *The Gulf Conflict, 1990–1991: Diplomacy and War in the New World Order*, Princeton, NJ: Princeton University Press, 1993.

Friedman, Thomas, *The World is Flat: A Brief History of the Twenty-First Century*, New York: Farrar, Straus and Giroux, 2005.

Frieser, Karl-Heinz, *The Blitzkrieg Legend: The Campaign in the West, 1940*, Annapolis, MD: Naval Institute Press, 2005.

Fukuyama, Francis, *The End of History and the Last Man*, New York: The Free Press, 1992.

Fuller, J.F.C., *The Reformation of War*, London: Hutchinson, 1923.

――― *Armament and History: A Study of the Influence on Armament on History from the Dawn of Classical Warfare to the Second World War*, New York: Da Capo Press, 1998 [1945].

Gall, Carlotta and Thomas de Waal, *Chechnya: A Small Victorious War*, London: Pan, 1997.

Galula, David, *Counterinsurgency Warfare: Theory and Practice*, London: Praeger, 1964.

Garfield, Andrew, *Succeeding in Phase IV: British Perspectives on the US Effort to Stabilize and Reconstruct Iraq*, Philadelphia, PA: Foreign Policy Research Institute, 2006.

Gat, Azar, *War in Human Civilisation*, Oxford: Oxford University Press, 2006.

Gavin, James, *War and Peace in the Space Age*, London: Hutchinson, 1959.

Gilbert, Gerald, *The Evolution of Tactics*, London: Hugh Rees, 1907.

Gilbert, Martin, *Israel: A History*, London: Black Swan, 1998.

Giustozzi, Antonio, *Koran, Kalashnikov, and Laptop: The Neo-Taliban Insurgency in Afghanistan*, London: Hurst, 2007.

Gleick, James, *The Information: A History, A Theory, A Flood*, London: HarperCollins, 2011.

Gordon, Don, *Electronic Warfare: Element of Strategy and Multiplier of Combat Power*, New York: Pergamon Press, 1981.

Gordon, Philip, *Winning the Right War: The Path to Security for America and the World*, New York: Henry Holt & Co., 2007.

Gow, James, *Triumph of the Lack of Will: International Diplomacy and the Yugoslav War*, London: Hurst, 1997.

Graham, Stephen, *Cities Under Siege: The New Military Urbanism*, London: Verso, 2010.

Gray, Colin, *The American Revolution in Military Affairs: An Interim Assessment*, Occasional Paper 28, Camberley: Strategic and Combat Studies Institute, 1997.

——— *Another Bloody Century: Future Warfare*, London: Weidenfeld and Nicolson, 2005.

——— *Strategy and History: Essays on Theory and Practice*, Abingdon: Routledge, 2006.

——— *Recognising and Understanding Revolutionary Change in Warfare: The Sovereignty of Context*, Carlisle, PA: US Army War College, Strategic Studies Institute, 2006.

——— *Perspectives on Strategy*, Oxford: Oxford University Press, 2013.

Gray, Chris Hables, *Postmodern War: The New Politics of Conflict*, London: Guilford Press, 1997.

Harding, Jeremy, *Border Vigils: Keeping Migrants out of the Rich World*, London: Verso, 2012.

Haass, Richard, *War of Necessity, War of Choice: A Memoir of Two Iraq Wars*, New York: Simon and Schuster, 2009.

Hanson, Victor Davis, *Why the West has Won: Carnage and Culture from Salamis to Vietnam*, London: Faber and Faber, 2001.

Hassan, Robert, *The Information Society*, Cambridge: Polity, 2008.

Hedin, Robert (ed.), *The Zeppelin Reader: Stories, Poems, and Songs from the Age of the Airships*, Iowa City, IA: Iowa University Press, 1998.

Hegel, Georg, *Lectures on the Philosophy of History*, trans. Ruben Alvarado, Aalten: Wordbridge, 2011 [1837].

Hillier, Rick, *A Soldier First: Bullets, Bureaucrats, and the Politics of War*, Toronto: HarperCollins, 2009.

Hirst, Paul, *Space and Power: Politics, War, and Architecture*, Cambridge: Polity, 2005.

Hoffman, Frank, *Changing Tires on the Fly: The Marines and Post-Conflict Stability Ops*, Philadelphia, PA: Foreign Policy Research Institute, 2006.

––––– *Conflict in the Twenty-First Century: The Rise of Hybrid Wars*, Washington, DC: Potomac Institute, 2007.

Holland, James, *Together We Stand: Turning the Tide in the West: North Africa, 1942–1943*, London: HarperCollins, 2005.

Holmes, Richard, *Acts of War: The Behaviour of Men in Battle*, New York: The Free Press, 1985.

Holsti, Kalevi, *The State, War, and the State of War*, Cambridge: Cambridge University Press, 1996.

Horn, Bernd, *No Lack of Courage: Operation Medusa, Afghanistan*, Toronto: Dundurn Press, 2010.

Hoskins, Andrew and Ben O'Loughlin, *War and Media: The Emergence of Diffused War*, Cambridge: Polity Press, 2010.

House, Jonathan, *Combined Arms Warfare in the Twentieth Century*, Lawrence, KS: Kansas University Press, 2001.

Howard, Michael, *The Invention of Peace and the Reinvention of War*, London: Profile Books, 2001.

––––– *War in European History*, updated edn., Oxford: Oxford University Press, 2001.

Hughes, Robert, *The Shock of the New: The Hundred-Year History of Modern Art, Its Rise, Its Dazzling Achievement, Its Downfall*, 2nd. edn., New York: McGraw Hill, 1991.

Huxley, Aldous, *Brave New World*, London: Chatto and Windus, 1932.

Iklé, Fred Charles, *Every War Must End*, 2nd. revised edn., New York: Columbia University Press, 2005.

––––– *Annihilation from Within: The Ultimate Threat to Nations*, New York: Columbia University Press, 2006.

Jervis, Robert, *The Meaning of the Nuclear Revolution*, Ithaca, NY: Cornell University Press, 1989.

Johnson, David, *Fast Tanks and Heavy Bombers: Innovation in the US Army, 1917–1945*, London: Cornell University Press, 1998.

Johnson, Loch, *Strategic Intelligence*, Westport, CT: Praeger Security International, 2007.

Kagan, Frederick, *Finding the Target: The Transformation of American Military Policy*, New York: Encounter Books, 2006.

Kaldor, Mary, *New and Old Wars*, Cambridge: Polity Press, 1999.

Kalyvas, Stathis, *The Logic of Violence in Civil War*, Cambridge: Cambridge University Press, 2006.

Kaplan, Robert, *The Coming Anarchy: Shattering the Dreams of the Post Cold War*, New York: Vintage Books, 2000.

—— *The Insurgents: David Petraeus and the Plot to Change the American Way of War*, New York: Simon and Schuster, 2013.

Keaney, Thomas and Eliot Cohen, *Gulf War Air Power Survey*, Washington, DC: US Government Printing Office, 1993.

Keegan, John, *Face of Battle*, London: Penguin, 1978.

—— *A History of Warfare*, London: Knopf, 1993.

Kelly, Kevin, *What Technology Wants*, New York: Penguin, 2010.

Kennedy, Paul, *The Rise and Fall of the Great Powers: Economic Change and Military Conflict from 1500 to 2000*, London: Fontana Press, 1989.

Kennett, Lee, *The First Air War, 1914–1918*, New York: The Free Press, 1991.

Kepel, Gilles and Jean-Pierre Milleli (eds), *Al Qaeda in Its Own Words*, Cambridge, MA: Harvard University Press, 2008.

Keynes, John Maynard, *The Economic Consequences of the Peace*, New York: Harcourt, Brace, and Howe, 1920.

Kilcullen, David, *The Accidental Guerrilla: Fighting Small Wars in the Midst of a Big One*, London: Hurst, 2009.

Kitson, Frank, *Low-Intensity Operations*, London: Faber and Faber, 1972.

Klein, Naomi, *The Shock Doctrine: The Rise of Disaster Capitalism*, London: Allen Lane, 2007.

Kurzweil, Ray, *The Singularity Is Near: When Humans Transcend Biology*, London: Duckworth, 2005.

Laing, R.D., *The Politics of Experience*, London: Harmondsworth, 1967.

Lamb, Christopher and Evan Munsing, 'Secret Weapon: High-Value Target Teams as an Organizational Innovation', *Strategic Perspectives* 4, Washington, DC: Center for Strategic Research, Institute for National Strategic Studies, National Defense University, March 2011.

Landes, David, *The Unbound Prometheus: Technological Change and Industrial Development in Western Europe from 1750 to the Present*, Cambridge: Cambridge University Press, 1969.

Lazenby, J.F., *Hannibal's War: A Military History of the Second Punic War*, Norman, OK: Oklahoma University Press, 1978.

Lebow, Richard Ned, *Why Nations Fight*, Cambridge: Cambridge University Press, 2010.

Ledwidge, Frank, *Losing Small Wars: British Military Failure in Iraq and Afghanistan*, London: Yale University Press, 2011.

Leonhard, Robert, *The Principles of War for the Information Age*, Novato, CA: Presidio Press, 1998.

Liang, Qiao and Wang Xiangsiu, *Unrestricted Warfare*, trans. US Foreign Broadcast Information Service, Beijing: PLA Literature and Arts Publishing House, 1999.

Libicki, Martin, *Conquest in Cyberspace: National Security and Information Warfare*, New York: Cambridge University Press, 2007.

——— *Cyberdeterrence and Cyberwar*, Santa Monica, CA: RAND Corporation, 2009.

Liddell-Hart, Basil, *Paris, Or The Future of War*, London: Faber and Faber, 1925.

——— *The Ghost of Napoleon*, New Haven, CT: Yale University Press, 1934.

——— *Thoughts on War*, London: Faber and Faber, 1944.

——— (ed.) *The Rommel Papers*, New York: Harcourt, Brace, 1953.

Lieber, Robert, *The American Era: Power and Strategy for the Twenty-First Century*, Cambridge: Cambridge University Press, 2005.

Lieven, Anatol, *Chechnya: Tombstone of Russian Power*, New Haven, CT: Yale University Press, 1998.

Lippmann, Walter, *Public Opinion*, Minneapolis, MI: Filiquarian Publishing, 2007.

Livy, *The War with Hannibal: The History of Rome from Its Foundation*, London: Penguin Classics, 1965.

Loyn, David, *Butcher and Bolt: Two Hundred Years of Foreign Engagement in Afghanistan*, London: Windmill Books, 2008.

Lynch, Marc, *Voices of the New Arab Public: Iraq, Al-Jazeera, and Middle East Politics Today*, New York: Columbia University Press, 2006.

Lyotard, Jean-François, *The Postmodern Condition: A Report on Knowledge*, Manchester: Manchester University Press, 2001.

Maalouf, Amin, *In the Name of Identity: Violence and the Need to Belong*, New York: Penguin Books, 2000.

MacCulloch, Diarmaid, *Christianity: The First Three Thousand Years*, London: Penguin, 2009.

McInnes, Colin, *Spectator-Sport War: The West and Contemporary Conflict*, London: Lynne Reinner, 2002.

Mackay, Charles, *Memoirs of Extraordinary Popular Delusions and the Madness of Crowds*, 2nd. edn., London: Robson, Levey and Franklyn, 1852.

Mackinlay, John, *The Insurgent Archipelago: From Mao to Bin Laden*, London: Hurst, 2009.

McLuhan, Marshall, *Understanding Media: The Extensions of Man*, New York: McGraw-Hill, 1964.

Mahnken, Thomas, *United States Strategic Culture*, Washington, DC: Defense Threat Reduction Agency, Advanced Systems and Concepts Office, 2006.

Mann, James, *Rise of the Vulcans: A History of Bush's War Cabinet*, New York: Penguin, 2004.

Marx, Karl and Friedrich Engels, *Manifesto of the Communist Party*, New York: New York Labor News Co., 1908.

Masuda, Yoneji, *The Information Society as Post-Industrial Society*, Bethesda, MD: World Future Society, 1981.

Mazarr, Michael, Jeffrey Shaffer and Benjamin Ederington, *The Military Technical Revolution: A Structural Framework*, Washington, DC: Center for Strategic and International Studies, 1993.

Merom, Gil, *How Democracies Lose Small Wars: State, Society, and the Failures of France in Algeria, Israel in Lebanon, and the United States in Vietnam*, Cambridge: Cambridge University Press, 2003.

Metz, Steven, *Iraq and the Evolution of American Strategy*, Dulles, VA: Potomac Books, 2008.

Mitchell, Greg, *So Wrong for So Long: How the Press, the Pundits—and the President—Failed on Iraq*, London: Union Square Press, 2008.

Mockaitis, Thomas, *British Counterinsurgency, 1919–1960*, New York: St. Martin's Press, 1990.

Moisi, Dominique, *The Geopolitics of Emotion: How Cultures of Fear, Humiliation, and Hope are Reshaping the World*, New York: Random House, 2009.

Morrow, John, *The Great War in the Air: Military Aviation from 1909 to 1921*, Washington, DC: Smithsonian Institution Press, 1993.

Mouffe, Chantal, *The Return of the Political*, London: Verso, 1993.

Mueller, John, *Retreat from Doomsday: The Obsolescence of Major War*, New York: Basic Books, 1989.

Münkler, Herfried, *The New Wars*, Cambridge: Polity, 2005.

Murray, Williamson and Robert Scales, *The Iraq War: A Military History*, Cambridge, MA: Belknap Press of Harvard University Press, 2003.

Naisbitt, John, *Megatrends: Ten New Directions transforming our Lives*, New York: Warner Books, 1984.

Neumann, Peter, *Old and New Terrorism*, Cambridge: Polity, 2009.

Neumann, Ronald, *The Other War: Winning and Losing in Afghanistan*, Washington, DC: Potomac Books, 2009.

Nye, Joseph, *Soft Power: The Means to Success in World Politics*, New York: PublicAffairs, 2004.

O'Hanlon, Michael, *Technological Change and the Future of Warfare*, Washington, DC: Brookings Institution, 2000.

Orwell, George, *Nineteen Eighty-Four*, 1949, republished in *The Complete Novels of George Orwell*, London: Penguin, 2009.

O'Shaughnessy, Nicholas, *Politics and Propaganda: Weapons of Mass Seduction*, Manchester: Manchester University Press, 2004.

Owens, William, *Lifting the Fog of War*, London: Johns Hopkins University Press, 2000.

Pakenham, Thomas, *The Boer War*, illustrated edn., London: Weidenfeld and Nicolson, 1979.

Parker, Geoffrey, *The Thirty Years War*, London: Routledge, 1984.

Phillips, T.R., *Roots of Strategy*, Mechanicsburg, PA: Stackpole Books, 1985.

Pinker, Steven, *The Better Angels of Our Nature*, London: Penguin, 2011.

Pollack, Kenneth, *Arabs at War: Military Effectiveness, 1948–1991*, Lincoln, NE: Nebraska University Press, 2004.

Polybius, *The Rise of the Roman Empire*, London: Penguin Classics, 1979.

Porch, Douglas, *Counterinsurgency: Exposing the Myths of the New Way of War*, Cambridge: Cambridge University Press, 2013.

Porter, Patrick, *Military Orientalism: Eastern War through Western Eyes*, London: Hurst, 2009.

Potts, David (ed.), *The Big Issue: Command and Combat in the Information Age*, Washington, DC: Department of Defense, Command and Control Research Programme, 2006.

Powell, Colin, *My American Journey: An Autobiography*, New York: Random House, 2005.

Price, Alfred, *The History of US Electronic Warfare*, 1st. edn., Arlington, VA: Association of Old Crows, 1984.

Priest, Dana and William Arkin, *Top Secret America: The Rise of the New American Security State*, London: Little Brown, 2011.

Prochnau, William, *Once Upon a Distant War: David Halberstam, Neil Sheehan, Peter Arnett-Young—Correspondents and Their Early Vietnam Battles*, New York: Vintage Books, 1995.

Qutb, Sayyid, *Milestones*, New Delhi: Abdul Naeem for the Islamic Book Service, 2007 [1964].

Rankin, Nicholas, *Churchill's Wizards: The British Genius for Deception, 1914–1945*, London: Faber and Faber, 2008.

Record, Jeffrey, *Hollow Victory*, Washington, DC: Brassey's, 1993.

Reid, Brian Holden, *J.F.C. Fuller: Military Thinker*, New York: St. Martin's Press, 1987.

——— *Studies in British Military Thought: Debates with Fuller and Liddell-Hart*, Lincoln, NB: Nebraska University Press, 1998.

Ricks, Thomas, *Fiasco: The American Military Adventure in Iraq*, London: Allen Lane, 2006.

——— *The Gamble: General Petraeus and the Untold Story of the American Surge in Iraq, 2006–2008*, London: Allen Lane, 2008.

Rid, Thomas, *War and Media Operations: The US Military and the Press from Vietnam to Iraq*, Abingdon: Routledge, 2007.

——— *Cyber War Will Not Take Place*, London: Hurst, 2013.

Rid, Thomas and Marc Hecker, *War 2.0: Irregular Warfare in the Information Age*, London: Praeger, 2009.

Robb, John, *Brave New War: The Next Stage of Terrorism and the End of Globalization*, London: Wiley, 2007.

Rommel, Erwin, *Infantry Attacks*, Novato, CA: Presidio Press, 1990.

Ropp, Theodore, *War in the Modern World*, new revised edn., London: Collier Macmillan, 1962.

Sanger, David, *Confront and Conceal: Obama's Secret Wars and Surprising Use of American Power*, New York: Crown Publishers, 2012.

Scales, Robert, *Firepower in Limited War*, Novato, CA: Presidio Press, 1995.

Schelling, Thomas, *Arms and Influence*, New Haven, CT: Yale University Press, 1966.

Seib, Philip, *The Global Journalist: News and Conscience in a World of Conflict*, Oxford: Rowman and Littlefield, 2002.

Shamir, Eitan, *Transforming Command: The Pursuit of Mission Command in the US, British and Israeli Armies*, Stanford, CA: Stanford University Press, 2011.

Sherry, Michael, *The Rise of American Air Power*, New Haven, CT: Yale University Press, 1987.

Shirky, Clay, *Cognitive Surplus: Creativity and Generosity in a Connected Age*, New York: Penguin Press, 2010.

Simpkin, Richard, *Race to the Swift: Thoughts on Twenty-First Century Warfare*, London: Brassey's, 1985.

Singer, P.W., *Corporate Warriors: The Rise of Privatized Military Industry*, Ithaca, NY: Cornell University Press, 2003.

Sloan, Elinor, *The Revolution in Military Affairs: Implications for Canada and NATO*, Montreal: McGill and Queen's University Press, 2002.

Smith, Rupert, *The Utility of Force: The Art of War in the Modern World*, London: Allen Lane, 2005.

Smith, Sebastian, *Allah's Mountains: The Battle for Chechnya*, London: I.B. Tauris, 1998.

——— *Allah's Mountains: The Battle for Chechnya*, London: I.B. Tauris, 2001.

Sorel, Georges, *Reflections on Violence*, trans. T.E. Hulme, London: George Allen & Unwin, 1915.

Stein, Janice Gross and Eugene Lang, *The Unexpected War: Canada in Afghanistan*, Toronto: Viking, 2007.

Sterling, Bruce, *The Hacker Crackdown*, New York: Bantam, 1994.

Strachan, Hew, *Clausewitz's On War: A Biography*, New York: Grove Press, 2007.

Sullivan, Gordon and James Dubik, *Land Warfare in the 21st Century*, Carlisle, PA: US Army War College, Strategic Studies Institute, 1993.

Sumida, Jon Tetsuro, *Decoding Clausewitz: A New Approach to On War*, Lawrence, KS: Kansas University Press, 2008.

Sun Tzu, *The Art of War*, trans. S.B. Griffith, London: Oxford University Press, 1971.

——— *The Art of War*, in Thomas Cleary (trans.), *Classics of Strategy and Counsel*, Boston: Shambhala Publications, 2000.

Suskind, Ron, *The One Percent Doctrine: Deep Inside America's Pursuit of Its Enemies Since 9/11*, New York: Simon and Schuster, 2007.

——— *The Way of the World: A Story of Truth and Hope in an Age of Extremism*, New York: HarperCollins, 2008.

Taylor, Philip, *Munitions of the Mind: A History of Propaganda from the Ancient World to the Present Day*, 3rd. edn., Manchester: Manchester University Press, 2003.

Thompson, Robert, *Defeating Communist Insurgency*, St. Petersburg, FL: Hailer Publishing, 2005.

Thucydides, *History of the Peloponnesian War*, trans. Rex Warner, London: Penguin, 1954.

Tierney, Dominic and Dominic Johnson, *Failing to Win: Perceptions of Victory and Defeat in International Politics*, Cambridge, MA: Harvard University Press, 2006.

Till, Geoffrey, 'British Strategy After Afghanistan', in Michael Codner and Michael Clarke (eds), *A Question of Security: The British Defence Review in an Age of Austerity*, London: I.B. Tauris for the Royal United Services Institute, 2011.

Tocqueville, Alexis de, *Democracy in America*, vol. 2, trans. Henry Reeve, Pennsylvania, PA: Pennsylvania State University Electronic Classics, 2002 [1840].

Todorov, Tzvetan, *The Fear of Barbarians: Beyond the Clash of Civilizations*, Cambridge: Polity, 2010.

Toffler, Alvin and Heidi Toffler, *War and Anti-War: Making Sense of Today's Global Chaos*, New York: Warner Books, 1993.

Trobisch, David, *The First Edition of the New Testament*, Oxford: Oxford University Press, 2000.

Ucko, David, *The New Counterinsurgency Era: Transforming the US Military for Modern Wars*, Washington, DC: Georgetown University Press, 2009.

Ullman, Harlan and James Wade, *Shock and Awe: Achieving Rapid Dominance*, Washington, DC: National Defense University Press, 1996.

Urban, Mark, *Task Force Black: The Explosive True Story of the SAS and the Secret War in Iraq*, London: Little, Brown, 2010.

US News and World Report, *Triumph Without Victory*, New York: Random House, 1992.

Van Creveld, Martin, *The Transformation of War*, New York: The Free Press, 1991.

——— *The Sword and the Olive: A Critical History of the Israeli Defence Force*, New York: PublicAffairs, 1998.

——— *The Changing Face of War: Lessons of Combat from the Marne to Iraq*, New York: Ballantine Books, 2006.

Waldman, Thomas, *War, Clausewitz, and the Trinity*, Farnham: Ashgate, 2013.

Warburton, Robert, *Eighteen Years on the Khyber, 1879–1898*, London: John Murray, 1900.

Wells, H.G., *The Work, Wealth, and Happiness of Humankind*, Garden City, NY: Doubleday, Doran and Company, 1931.

West, Bing, *The Strongest Tribe: War, Politics, and the Endgame in Iraq*, New York: Random House, 2008.

West, Bing and Ray Smith, *The March Up: Taking Baghdad with the First Marine Division*, London: Pimlico, 2003.

Winsor, Philip, *Strategic Thinking: An Introduction and Farewell*, Mats Berdal and Spyros Economides (eds), London: Lynne Reinner, 2002.

Woodward, Bob, *Plan of Attack*, London: Pocket Books, 2004.

Wright, Evan, *Generation Kill: Living Dangerously on the Road to Baghdad with the Ultraviolent Marines of Bravo Company*, London: Bantam Press, 2004.

Book chapters

Antal, John, 'Battleshock XXI', in Robert Bateman (ed.), *Digital War: The Twenty-First Century Battlefield*, New York: iBooks, 1999.

Arendt, Hannah, 'Karl Jaspers: Citizen of the World' (1958) republished in *Men in Dark Times*, New York: Harcourt Brace and World, 1968.

Arquilla, John and David Ronfeldt, 'Cyberwar is Coming!', in John Arquilla and David Ronfeldt (eds), *In Athena's Camp: Preparing for Conflict in the Information Age*, Santa Monica, CA: RAND Corporation, 1997.

Arquilla, John, David Ronfeldt and Michele Zanini, 'Networks, Netwar, and Information Age Terrorism', in Zalmay Khalilzad and John White (eds), *Strategic Appraisal: The Changing Role of Information in Warfare*, Santa Monica, CA: RAND Corporation, 1999.

Barber, Benjamin, 'Democracy and Terror in the Age of Jihad vs. McWorld', in Ken Booth and Tim Dunne (eds), *Worlds in Collision: Terror and the Future of Global Conflict*, Houndmills, Basingstoke: Palgrave Macmillan, 2002.

Berdal, Mats, 'The New Wars Thesis Revisited', in Hew Strachan and Sibylle Scheipers (eds), *The Changing Character of War*, Oxford: Oxford University Press, 2011.

Bin Laden, Osama, 'Tactical Recommendations (Excerpts)', in Gilles Kepel and Jean-Pierre Milelli (eds), *Al Qaeda in Its Own Words*, Cambridge, MA: Harvard University Press, 2008.

Blumenson, Martin, 'Rommel', in Corelli Barnett (ed.), *Hitler's Generals*, London: Weidenfeld and Nicolson, 1989.

Carlyle, Thomas, 'The Signs of the Times', in *Critical and Miscellaneous Essays by Thomas Carlyle*, Boston, MA: Dana Estes and Charles F. Lauriat, 1884.

Chomsky, Noam, 'Who are the Global Terrorists?', in Ken Booth and Tim Dunne (eds), *Worlds in Collision: Terror and the Future of Global Conflict*, Houndmills, Basingstoke: Palgrave Macmillan, 2002.

Clarke, Michael, 'The United Kingdom's Strategic Moment', in Michael Codner and Michael Clarke (eds), *A Question of Security: The British Defence Review in an Age of Austerity*, London: I.B. Tauris for the Royal United Services Institute, 2011.

Coy, S.J., 'Depth Firepower: The Violent, Enabling Element', in Brian Holden Reid (ed.), *The Science of War: Back to First Principles*, London: Routledge, 1993.

Daase, Christopher, 'Clausewitz and Small Wars', in Hew Strachan and Andreas Herberg-Rothe (eds), *Clausewitz in the Twenty-First Century*, Oxford: Oxford University Press, 2007.

Dandeker, Christopher, 'The End of War? The Strategic Context of International Missions in the Twenty-First Century', in Magnus Christiansson (ed.), *Eight Essays in Contemporary War Studies*, Stockholm: Military Academy Karlberg, Acta Politica II, 2007.

Davis-Biddle, Tami, 'British and American Approaches to Strategic Bombing: Their

Origins and Implementation in the World War II Combined Bomber Offensive', in John Gooch (ed.), *Airpower: Theory and Practice*, London: Frank Cass, 1995.

Dunsmore, Barrie, 'Live from the Battlefield', in Pippa Norris (ed.), *Politics and the Press: The News Media and Their Influences*, London: Lynne Reinner, 1997.

Forbes, R.J., 'Power to 1850', in C. Singer (ed.), *A History of Technology, Vol. 4: The Industrial Revolution, 1750–1850*, Oxford: Oxford University Press, 1958.

Hazlett, 'Just-in-Time Warfare', in Martin Libicki and Stuart Johnson (eds), *Dominant Battlespace Knowledge*, Washington, DC: National Defense University Press, 1995.

Lawrence, T.E., 'The Science of Guerrilla Warfare', in *Encyclopaedia Britannica*, 14th. edn., New York: Encyclopaedia Britannica, 1929, reprinted in Thomas Mahnken and Joe Maiolo (eds), *Strategic Studies: A Reader*, Abingdon: Routledge, 2008.

Libicki, Martin, 'Sub Rosa Cyberwar', in Christian Czosseck and Kenneth Geers (eds), *The Virtual Battlefield: Perspectives on Cyber Warfare*, Amsterdam, IOS Press, 2009.

McMaster, H.R., 'Foreword', in G.J. David, Jr. and T.R. McKeldin III (eds), *Ideas as Weapons: Influence and Perception in Modern Warfare*, Dulles, VA: Potomac Books, 2009.

Mack, Andrew, 'Why Big Nations Lose Small Wars', in Klaus Knorr (ed.), *Power, Strategy, and Security: A World Politics Reader*, Princeton, NJ: Princeton University Press, 1975.

Marshall, Andrew, 'Foreword', in Zalmay Khalilzad and John White (eds), *The Changing Role of Information in Warfare*, Santa Monica, CA: RAND Corporation, 1999.

Moltke, Helmuth von, 'On Strategy', in Daniel Hughes (ed.), *Moltke on the Art of War: Selected Writings*, New York: Ballantine Books, 1993.

Owens, William, 'Introduction', in Martin Libicki and Stuart Johnson (eds), *Dominant Battlespace Knowledge*, Washington, DC: National Defense University Press, 1995.

Warden, John, 'Employing Air Power in the Twenty-First Century', in Richard Schultz, Jr. and Robert Pfaltzgraff (eds), *The Future of Air Power in the Aftermath of the Gulf War*, Maxwell Air Force Base, AL: Air University Press, 1992.

Weber, Max, 'Class, Status, Party', in Hans Gerth and C. Wright Mills (eds), *From Max Weber: Essays in Sociology*, London: Routledge and Kegan Paul, 1948.

Winter, Jay, 'Reflections on War and Barbarism', in George Kassimeris (ed.), *The Barbarisation of Warfare*, London: Hurst, 2006.

Zacher, Mark, 'The Decaying Pillars of the Westphalian Temple: Implications for International Order', in James Rosenau and Ernst-Otto Czempiel (eds), *Governance without Government: Order and Change in World Politics*, Cambridge: Cambridge University Press, 1992.

Articles

Aday, Sean, Sean Cluverius and Steven Livingston, 'As Goes the Statue, So Goes the War: The Emergence of the Victory Frame in Television Coverage of the Iraq War', *Journal of Broadcasting and Electronic Media* 49:3, 2005.

Ankersen, Christopher and Losel Tethong, 'Rapid Decisive Ops are Risky Business', *US Naval Institute Proceedings* 129:10, October 2003.

Aylwin-Foster, Nigel, 'Changing the Army for Counterinsurgency Operations', *Military Review* 85:6, November/December 2005.

Barzashka, Ivanka, 'Are Cyber-Weapons Effective?', *RUSI Journal* 158:2, April/May 2013.

Bellamy, Alex, 'The Great Beyond: Rethinking Military Responses to New Wars and Complex Emergencies', *Defence Studies* 2:1, Spring 2002.

Benson, Kevin. 'OIF Phase IV: A Planner's Reply to Brigadier Aylwin-Foster', *Military Review* 86:2, March/April 2006.

Betz, David, 'The Virtual Dimension of Contemporary Insurgency and Counterinsurgency', *Small Wars and Insurgencies* 19:4, December 2008.

——— 'Counterinsurgency, Victorian Style', *Survival* 54:4, August/September 2012.

Betz, David and Anthony Cormack, 'Iraq, Afghanistan and British Strategy', *Orbis* 53:2, Spring 2009.

Betz, David and Tim Stevens, 'Analogical Reasoning and Cyber Security', *Security Dialogue* 44:2, April 2013.

Beyerchen, Alan, 'Clausewitz, Nonlinearity and the Unpredictability of War', *International Security* 17:3, Winter 1992.

Biddle, Stephen, 'Victory Misunderstood: What the Gulf War Tells Us about the Future of Conflict', *International Security* 21:2, Fall 1997.

Bolt, Neville, 'The Leak Before the Storm: What Wikileaks Tells Us About Modern Communication', *RUSI Journal* 155:4, August/September 2010.

Boot, Max, 'The New American Way of War', *Foreign Affairs* 89:4, July/August 2003.

Byman, Daniel and Matthew Waxman, 'Kosovo and the Great Air Power Debate', *International Security* 24:4, Spring 2000.

Cassidy, Robert, 'The British Army and Counterinsurgency: The Salience of Military Culture', *Military Review* 85:3, May/June 2005.

Cebrowski, Arthur and John Garstka, 'Network-Centric Warfare: Its Origin and Future', *US Naval Institute Proceedings* 124:1, January 1998.

Cohen, Eliot, 'The Mystique of US Air Power', *Foreign Affairs* 73:1, January/February 1994.

Coker, Christopher, 'The Unhappy Warrior', *RUSI Journal* 150:6, December 2005.

——— 'A Low, Dishonest Decade', *RUSI Journal* 156:4, August/September 2011.

Deibert, Ronald, 'The Growing Dark Side of Cyberspace (… And What to Do About It)', *Penn State Journal of Law and International Affairs* 1:2, November 2012.

Dexter, Byron, 'Clausewitz and Soviet Strategy', *Foreign Affairs* 29:1, October 1950.

Dorn, Walter and Michael Varey, 'Fatally Flawed: The Rise and Demise of the "Three-Block War" Concept in Canada', *International Journal* 63:4, Autumn 2008.

Duffield, Mark, 'War as a Network Enterprise: The New Security Terrain and Its Implications', *Cultural Values: Journal for Cultural Research* 6:1–2, January/April 2002.

Elkus, Adam, 'Only the West Has Seen the End of War', *Infinity Journal*, August 2012.

Evans, Michael, 'From Kadesh to Kandahar: Military Theory and the Future of War', *Naval War College Review* LVI:3, Summer 2003.

Farrell, Theo, 'Sliding Into War: The Somalia Imbroglio and US Army Peace Operations Doctrine', *International Peacekeeping* 2:2, Summer 1995.

Finch, Raymond, 'A Face of Future Battle: Chechen Fighter Shamil Basayev', *Military Review* 77:3, May/June 1997.

Fletcher, Joseph, Heather Bastedo and Jennifer Hove, 'Losing Heart: Declining Support and the Political Marketing of the Afghanistan Mission', *Canadian Journal of Political Science* 142:4, December 2009.

Freedman, Lawrence, 'Prevention, Not Preemption', *Washington Quarterly* 26:2, Spring 2003.

——— 'War Evolves into the Fourth Generation: A Comment on Thomas X. Hammes', *Contemporary Security Policy* 26:2, August 2005.

——— 'The Special Relationship—Then and Now', *Foreign Policy* 85:3, May/June 2006.

Gallie, Walter, 'Essentially Contested Concepts', *Proceedings of the Aristotelian Society*, new series 56, 1956.

Gat, Azar, 'Clausewitz and the Marxists: Yet Another Look', *Journal of Contemporary History* 7:2, April 1992.

Gates, Robert, 'A Balanced Strategy: Reprogramming the Pentagon for a New Age', *Foreign Affairs* 88:1, January/February 2009.

Gentile, Gian, 'Let's Build an Army to Win All Wars', *Joint Force Quarterly* 52, January 2009.

Gibbs, Norman, 'Clausewitz and the Moral Forces in War', *Naval War College Review* 27:4, January/February 1975.

Hammes, T.X., 'War Evolves into the Fourth Generation', *Contemporary Security Policy* 26:2, August 2005.

Hayden, Dale, 'Air Mindedness', *Air and Space Power Journal* 22:4, Winter 2008.

Herbert, Paul, 'Deciding What Has to be Done: General William E. Dupuy and the 1976 Edition of FM 100–5, Operations', *Leavenworth Papers* 16, Fort Leavenworth, KS: Combat Studies Institute, July 1988.

Herring, George, 'America and Vietnam: The Unending War', *Foreign Affairs* 70:5, Winter 1991/1992.

Howard, Michael, 'The Use and Abuse of Military History', *RUSI Journal* 138:1, February 1993.

——— 'A Long War', *Survival* 48:4, Winter 2006.

Iron, Richard, 'The Charge of the Knights', *RUSI Journal* 158:1, February/March 2013.

Kinross, Stuart, 'Clausewitz and Low-Intensity Conflict', *Journal of Strategic Studies* 27:1, March 2004.

Kiszely, John, 'Learning About Counterinsurgency', *RUSI Journal* 151:6, December 2006.

Krepinevich, Andrew, 'Cavalry to Computer: The Pattern of Military Revolutions', *The National Interest* 37, Fall 1994.

Krulak, Charles, 'The Strategic Corporal: Leadership in the Three Block War', *Marines Magazine*, January 1999.

Klingert, Simon, 'Losing the War on Perception', *Foreign Policy*, 13 September 2011.

Kuperman, Alan, 'Rwanda in Retrospect', *Foreign Affairs* 79:1, January–February 2000.

Lambeth, Benjamin, 'Russia's Wounded Military', *Foreign Affairs* 74:2, March/April 1994.

——— 'Airpower, Spacepower, and Cyberpower', *Joint Force Quarterly* 60, January 2011.

Layne, Christopher, 'Kant or Cant: The Myth of the Democratic Peace', *International Security* 19:2, Autumn 1994.

Libicki, Martin, 'The Spectre of Non-Obvious Warfare', *Strategic Studies Quarterly* 6:3, Fall 2012.

Lind, William, Keith Nightengale, John Schmitt, Joseph Sutton and Gary Wilson, 'The Changing Face of War: Into the Fourth Generation', *Marine Corps Gazette* 73:10, October 1989.

Luttwak, Edward, 'Toward Postheroic Warfare', *Foreign Affairs* 74:3, May/June 1995.

——— 'Give War a Chance', *Foreign Affairs* 78:4, July/August 1999.

Mahnken, Thomas and Barry Watts, 'What the Gulf War Can (and Cannot) Tell Us About the Future of Warfare', *International Security* 22:2, Autumn 1997.

Mueller, John, 'The Perfect Enemy: Assessing the Gulf War', *Security Studies* 5:1, Autumn 1995.

Nagl, John, 'Let's Win the Wars We're In', *Joint Force Quarterly* 52, January 2009.

Nye, Joseph and William Owens, 'America's Information Edge', *Foreign Affairs* 75:2, March/April 1996.

Osiander, Andreas, 'Sovereignty, International Relations, and the Westphalian Myth', *International Organization* 55:2, Spring 2001.

Owen, William, 'Killing Your Way to Control', *British Army Review* 151, Spring 2011.

Pipes, Daniel, 'The Gulf War Did Not Take Place' [review], *Middle East Quarterly* 3:2, March 1996.

Powell, Colin, 'US Forces: Challenges Ahead', *Foreign Affairs* 71:5, Winter 1992/1993.

Reid, Julian, 'Foucault on Clausewitz: Conceptualising the Relationship Between War and Power', *Alternatives: Global, Local, Political* 28:1, January/February 2003.

Rice, Condoleeza, 'Promoting the National Interest', *Foreign Affairs* 79:1, January/February 2000.

Rid, Thomas and Peter McBurney, 'Cyber-Weapons', *RUSI Journal* 157:1, February/March 2012.

Roennfeldt, Carsten, 'Productive War: A Reconceptualisation of War', *Journal of Strategic Studies* 34:1, February 2011.

Rogers, Bernard, 'Follow-On Forces Attack: Myths and Realities', *NATO Review* 32:6, December 1984.

Smith, M.L.R., 'Guerrillas in the Mist: Reassessing Strategy and Low-Intensity Warfare', *Review of International Studies* 29:1, January 2003.

—— 'Politics and Passion: The Neglected Mainspring of War', *Infinity Journal* 4:2, Fall 2014.

Stern, Jessica, 'The Protean Enemy', *Foreign Affairs* 82:4, July/August 2003.

Stone, John, 'Cyberwar Will Take Place!', *Journal of Strategic Studies* 36:1, 2013.

Strachan, Hew, 'The Lost Meaning of Strategy', *Survival* 47:3, Autumn 2005.

Terriff, Terry, 'Of Romans and Dragons: Preparing the US Marine Corps for Future Warfare', *Contemporary Security Policy* 28:1, April 2007.

Van Creveld, Martin, 'It Will Continue to Conquer and Spread', *Contemporary Security Policy* 26:2, August 2005.

Vought, Donald, 'Preparing for the Wrong War?', *Military Review* 62:6, May 1977.

Documents

9/11 Commission Report, Washington, DC: National Commission on Terrorist Attacks on the United States, 2004.

Cabinet Office, *Cyber Security Strategy of the United Kingdom: Safety, Security and Resilience in Cyberspace*, Norwich: The Stationery Office, 2009.

—— *The UK Cyber Security Strategy: Protecting and Promoting the UK in a Digital World*, London, November 2011.

Collins, John, *Desert Shield and Desert Storm: Implications for US Force Requirements*, Washington, DC: Congressional Research Service, 1991.

Conduct of the Persian Gulf War, Final Report to Congress, Washington, DC: Department of Defense, 1992.

Developments, Concepts, and Doctrine Centre, *Strategic Trends Programme: Future Character of Conflict*, London: UK Ministry of Defence, 2010.

FM 3–24 Counterinsurgency, Washington, DC: Headquarters, Department of the Army, December 2006.

Independent Panel on Canada's Future Role in Afghanistan, 'The Manley Report', Ottawa: Her Majesty the Queen in Right of Canada, represented by the Minister of Public Works and Government Services, 2008.

International Commission on Intervention and State Sovereignty, *The Responsibility to Protect*, Ottawa: International Development Research Centre, 2001.

Joint Security Commission, *Redefining Security*, Washington, DC, 28 February 1994.

National Security Strategy: A Strong Britain in an Age of Uncertainty, London: The Stationery Office, 2010.

The National Security Strategy of the United States of America, Washington, DC: The White House, September 2002.

Stephen Lawrence Inquiry Report, London: The Stationery Office, 1999.

United Nations, *Arab Human Development Report: Creating Opportunities for Future Generations*, New York: United Nations Development Programme, Regional Bureau for Arab States, 2002.

United Nations Charter, San Francisco, CA, 26 June 1945, http://www.un.org/en/documents/charter/intro.shtml.

US Army Capstone Concept, *Operational Adaptation: Operating Under Conditions of Uncertainty and Complexity in an Era of Persistent Conflict*, TRADOC Pam 525–3–0, 21 December 2009.

US Army Center for Lessons Learned, 'Biometrics in Support of Information Dominance', Newsletter 09–35, May 2009.

US National Security Strategy, Washington, DC: The White House, 2010.

US Office of the Director of National Intelligence, letter from Ayman al-Zawahiri to Abu Musab al-Zarqawi, 2005.

White House, *Cyberspace Policy Review: Assuring a Trusted and Resilient Information and Communications Infrastructure*, Washington, DC: United States Government Printing Office, 2009.

Other

Bacevich, Andrew, 'The Petraeus Doctrine', *The Atlantic*, 1 October 2008, http://www.theatlantic.com/magazine/archive/2008/10/the-petraeus-doctrine/306964/

Bamford, James, 'The Secret War', *Wired*, 12 June 2013.

BBC, 'Outrage at "Old Europe" Remarks', 23 January 2003.

BBC, 'The Virtual Revolution', Episode 2, 'The Enemy of the State', 6 February 2010.

BBC News, 'London Bomber: Text in Full', 1 September 2005.

BBC Radio 4, 'In Our Time', 17 May 2012.

Bernanke, Ben, 'Remarks of the Chairman of the US Federal Reserve on "The Great Moderation"', Washington, DC: Eastern Economic Association, 20 February 2004.

Brzezinski, Zbigniew and John Mearsheimer, 'Clash of the Titans', *Foreign Policy*, 5 January 2005.

Bush, George W., 'Remarks at the Citadel', Charleston, SC, 11 December 2001.

——— 'State of the Union Address', Washington, DC: United States Congress, 29 January 2002.

——— graduation speech at the US Military Academy, West Point, NY, 1 June 2002.

——— Remarks at a rally in support of the Senate candidacy of Elizabeth Dole, Charlotte, NC, 24 October 2002.

——— 'The New Strategy in Iraq', Primetime Address to the Nation, 10 January 2007.

Canadian Broadcasting Corporation, 'Marshall McLuhan in Conversation with Norman Mailer', *The Way It Is*, 26 November 1967.

Carter, Ashton, 'Remarks by Deputy Secretary Carter at the Center for a New American Security on Defense Priorities in an Era of Constrained Budgets', Washington, DC, 12 June 2013.

Cheney, Dick, speech to the Veterans of Foreign Wars national convention, full text in *The Guardian*, 27 August 2002.

Chilcot, John, statement by the Chairman of the Iraq Inquiry, London, 30 July 2009.

Clark, Tom, 'Iraq War "Delivered Little But Bloodshed", Say Britons in Ten Year Anniversary Poll', *The Guardian*, 15 February 2013.

Corn, Tony, 'Clausewitz in Wonderland', *Policy Review*, Hoover Institution, 1 September 2006, http://www.hoover.org/publications/policy-review/article/6795

Daley-Nicholson, Jennifer, 'Do We Live in George Orwell's 1984, Aldous Huxley's Brave New World—or 2013?', *News Limited Network*, 12 June 2013.

Dannatt, Richard, speech to the Royal United Services Institute Land Warfare Conference, London, 12 June 2008.

Davis, Joshua, 'If We Run Out of Batteries, This War is Screwed', *Wired*, 11.06, June 2003.

Defence News, 'Interview with General James Mattis, Commander US Joint Forces Command', 23 May 2010.

Devenny, Patrick and Robert McLean, 'The Battle for Basra', *The American Spectator*, 11 January 2005.

The Economist, 'The Company that Spooked the World', 4 August 2012.

Fallows, James, 'Blind Into Baghdad', *Atlantic Monthly*, 293:1, January/February 2004.

Fleishman, Glenn, 'Cartoon Captures Spirit of the Internet', *New York Times*, 14 December 2000.

Fulghum, David, David Wall and Amy Butler, 'Cyber Combat's First Shot', *Aviation Week and Space Technology* 167:21, 2007.

Garamone, Jim, 'Lynn Calls for Collaboration in Establishing Cyber Security', *Armed Forces Press Service*, 1 October 2009.

Gates, Robert, speech, West Point, NY, 25 February 2011.

Grey, Stephen, 'Cracking On in Helmand', *Prospect*, 27 August 2009.

——— 'Retreat from Basra—Learning the Lessons', *Sunday Times*, 20 September 2009.

Grossman, Lev, 'Why the 9/11 Conspiracy Theories Won't Go Away', *Time*, 3 September 2006.

Habib, Randa, 'Saddam Fled Just Before Bombing', *Agence France—Presse*, 6 November 2003.

Hague, William, chair's statement, London Conference on Cyberspace, 2 November 2011.

Hanson, Victor Davis, 'Don Rumsfeld, A Radical for Our Time', *National Interest Review Online*, 5 May 2003, reprinted in Victor Davis Hanson, *Between War and Peace: Lessons from Afghanistan to Iraq*, New York: Random House, 2004.

——— 'Postbellum Thoughts', *National Interest Review Online*, reprinted in Victor Davis Hanson, *Between War and Peace: Lessons from Afghanistan to Iraq*, New York: Random House, 2004.

Katz, Yaakov, 'Stuxnet Virus Set Back Iran's Program by Two Years', *Jerusalem Post*, 15 December 2010.

King, Anthony, 'Why We're Getting It Wrong in Helmand', *Prospect*, 4 September 2009.

Kozaryn, Linda, '"Regime's Collapse Evident, But Hard Fighting Ahead", Cheney Says', *Armed Forces Press Service*, 9 April 2003.

Langewiesche, William, 'Letter from Baghdad: Life in the Wilds of a City Without Trust', *The Atlantic*, 1 January 2005.

Levin, Carl, opening remarks of the Senate Armed Services Committee hearing on 'Lessons Learned from Operation Iraqi Freedom', Washington, DC, 7 September 2003.

Maass, Peter, 'The Toppling: How the Media Inflated a Minor Moment in a Long War', *The New Yorker*, 10 January 2011.

MacAskill, Ewan, Richard Norton-Taylor and Julian Borger, 'US May Go It Alone as Blair is Caught in Diplomatic Deadlock', *The Guardian*, 12 March 2003.

Mahmoud, Mona, Maggie O'Kane and Ian Black, 'UK Has Left Behind Murder and Chaos, Says Basra Police Chief', *The Guardian*, 17 December 2007.

Makiya, Kanan, 'The Arab Spring Started in Iraq', *New York Times*, 6 April 2013.

Marr, Andrew, 'Digital Cameras Have Dispelled the Fog of War', *Daily Telegraph*, 12 May 2004.

Mulrine, Anna, 'CIA Chief Leon Panetta: The Next Pearl Harbor Could Be a Cyber-attack', *Christian Science Monitor*, 9 June 2011.

Obama, Barack, remarks to the Veterans of Foreign Wars annual conference, Phoenix, AZ, 17 August 2009.

Panetta, Francesca, Mona Mahmood, Chris McGreal, Martin Chulov, Peter Beaumont, Nina Perry, Chris Fenn and Alan Yuhas, 'Faces of War: Hear the Stories Behind Iconic Images of Iraq Conflict', *The Guardian*, 15 March 2013.

PBS Frontline, 'Kill/Capture', 'Interview: General David Petraeus', 14 June 2011.

PBS Newshour, 25 June 1999.

Peters, Ralph, 'Shock, Awe and Overconfidence', *Washington Post*, 25 March 2003.

——— 'The Counterrevolution in Military Affairs', *The Weekly Standard* 11:20, 6 February 2006.

Rayner, Gordon and Steven Swinford, 'Woolwich Attack: Terrorist Proclaimed "An Eye for an Eye" After Attack', *Daily Telegraph*, 22 May 2013.

Reuters, 'UK Troops Recount Burning Tank Escape', 22 September 2005.

Rice-Oxley, Mark, 'War and McPeace: Russia and the McDonalds Theory of War', *The Guardian*, 6 September 2008.

Richards, David, 'Future Conflict and Its Prevention: People and the Information

Age', speech at the International Institute for Strategic Studies, London, 18 January 2010.

Ricks, Thomas, 'Reading Lists: The West Point History Dept. Selects Its Top 10 Military Classics', *The Best Defense*, 19 September 2012.

Roberts, Adam, 'Theatre of Blood', *Independent*, 11 November 2005.

Ross, Tim, 'Osborne Promises No Further Cuts to Soldier Numbers—And More Funding for Cyber Warfare', *Daily Telegraph*, 23 June 2013.

Sanders, Richard, 'The Myth of Shock and Awe: Why the Iraqi Invasion was a Disaster', *Daily Telegraph*, 19 March 2013.

Sands, Sarah, 'Sir Richard Dannatt: A Very Honest General', *Daily Mail*, 12 October 2006.

'Statement of Major General Robert Scales, USA (ret.), "Army Transformation: Implications for the Future"', Testimony before the House Armed Services Committee, 15 July 2004.

Strachan, Hew, 'The Changing Character of War', Europaeum Lecture, Graduate Institute of International Relations, Geneva, 9 November 2006.

Ucko, David, 'Gates on COIN: What was Really Said', *Kings of War*, 27 February 2011, http://kingsofwar.org.uk/2011/02/gates-on-coin-what-was-really-said/

INDEX